MW01529129

The Lost Will and Testament
and The Problem of Perfection

Printed in the U.S.A.

Cover artwork by Shawna Wright

Quotation underlining and emphasis supplied by author.

Unless otherwise noted, Scripture quotations are taken from
THE HOLY BIBLE, KING JAMES VERSION.
(Nashville, Tennessee: Thomas Nelson Inc., 1972).

Scripture quotations marked NLT are taken from THE HOLY BIBLE: NEW
LIVING TRANSLATION, copyright © 1996, 2004, 2015
by Tyndale House Foundation

~The author wishes to thank all those who made
this book possible, God "knows" you, and will reward you for all
your kindness & loving service to Him.~

You can obtain additional copies of this book by visiting:

shawnawrightart.com/store or emailing us at:
lostwillandtestament@gmail.com

ISBN: 978-1-7344691-2-7

Contents

• **Part III The Problem of Perfection?**

Introduction
(Don't skip it this time...)

"For behold, the darkness shall cover the earth,
And deep darkness the people; But the LORD will arise over you,
And His glory will be seen upon you."
Isaiah 60:2

An agitation fills our world, it is seen in everything around us. Even among those who do not claim to know God, there is an awareness that something is coming on this world that is momentous. It is becoming increasingly hard for those of us who claim to know God to ignore the signs of His soon return. In many minds there is a realization that this world is about to end. There is an understanding that behind the invisible curtain the work of Christ is almost completed and that the last act in the drama of the ages is about to commence. The time is soon to arrive when all, both small and great, will see with actual sight the face of God. Then all will either run from that face or turn towards it with joy.

In the year 1844, the 2300 prophetic days spoken of in Daniel (Daniel 8:14) terminated. At that time the first angel's message of Revelation 14 went out, *"Saying with a loud voice, Fear God, and give glory to Him; for <u>the hour of His judgment is come</u>: and worship Him that made heaven, and earth, and the sea, and the fountains of waters"* (Rev. 14:7). Here was/is announced that judgment which we all must meet. It is a solemn declaration. Concerning the judgment, such things as these are written: *"But I say unto you, That every idle word that men shall speak, they shall give account thereof in the day of judgment"* (Matt. 12:36).

Today the judgment seems to have almost no practical impact on the lives of God's people. Can you recall the last sermon you heard on this momentous subject? It appears that we have relegated the judgment of God, to one of those things we trot out like a pet pony at Daniel and Revelation seminars to prove we are not mistaken in our doctrine, "See William Miller was correct..." 174 plus years ago. But on a personal level there seems to be a criminal indifference to this truth! The events transpiring around us should be changing that indifference. This doctrine of the investigative judgment has also been the source of much controversy within the church. Does it exist or doesn't it?

Why is the judgment such a controversial or ignored topic? I believe it is controversial because it ultimately forces us to confront the question of our standing before God. It forces us to examine a reality which we as sinners find very uncomfortable. It forces us to examine <u>absolute moral perfection</u> and our obvious lack and need of that perfection. If you are required to be perfect to be safe in the end; if the investigative judgment is to find out if you <u>make the cut</u>, then thinking seriously about the judgment will be an exercise which is, at the very least, disturbing! It will most likely be an exercise which is terrifying! Is this what the investigative judgment is all about? Yes? No?

There is coming a day when the atoning and sanctifying blood of Christ shall cease its pleading on the behalf of mankind. A day when we who are yet alive will stand without an intercessor in heaven. On that day we shall be before God what we actually are! That is a solemn thought! How are God's believing but still erring children, to find a way to survive the soon coming face to face encounter with a Holy God? The Bible states clearly that, *"we must all appear before the judgment seat of Christ; that every one may receive the things done in his body, according to that he hath done, whether it be good or bad* (2 Cor. 5:10). We must always remember that God is holy, and that when it comes to sin *"our God is a consuming fire"* (Heb. 12:29). Sin and sinners cannot survive in His presence! It is written, *"Thou art of purer eyes than to behold evil, and canst not look on iniquity"* (Hab. 1:13).

The answers to these questions are vital if we are to stand before God and look Him in the face! These questions need to be examined head on. In this book I will not be telling you that you have to achieve perfection, or that you must work/choose your way into heaven by your own efforts and willpower. Nor will I be telling you that Christ Jesus came to save His people **_in_** their sins.

What we as a church and as individuals need is a clear and <u>scriptural</u> resolutions to these problems "s*o we will not be afraid on the day of judgment, but we can face Him with confidence*" (1 John 4:17 NLT). This book is put forward in the hope that it will furnish you a plain, straightforward and Biblical explanation of these vital questions: An explanation that will bring you an assurance, a faith and a peace in Christ. A peace that will carry you through what is right before us. It is my aim, with the aid of the Spirit, to present the promises of God in such a way that when this book is finished, you will exclaim with Paul, *"O the depth of the riches both of the wisdom and knowledge of God!"* (Rom. 11:33)

For this blessing the author humbly entreats the "God of Peace."

Troy A Wright

PART I
The Problem of Perfection

"Perfection," If you ever want to explore a hot button topic within the church, well, this is your big red "Easy Button"[1] right here! I have done some informal polling among the brethren, and almost always, when I bring up the subject of perfection, I get a similar reaction. The response is something akin to the releasing of a skunk into a crowded room... all of a sudden everybody seems to have some place to go in a hurry!! No one wishes to confront it, discuss it, or address it. It is a kind of "La perfection Le Pew"! ☺

What is it that engenders such a response in God's people? I have had reactions to this subject that range from bursting into tears on the one hand, trying anything to change the subject on the other hand, or actually running away. (I assure you I left off the pursuit of that particular interview.☺) People suddenly want to talk about Aunt Margret's cat or their latest knitting project. Anything but that topic please. Why is this? We treat this subject of perfection like a diseased blanket. We don't want to touch it with a ten foot pole. No thank you very much indeed, now go away!

The problem is that everywhere in Scripture we find perfection being insisted upon. It is often paired with the other side of the same coin which we have already touched upon in the introduction, the judgment. This coin with its two sides will keep popping up! It will not go away at all.

Chapter 1
Perfection It's Personal

As with everything one learns in life, it seems the most profound lessons are learned by personal experience. When it comes to this problem of perfection I have had perilous encounters with most of the issues we will be looking at in in this book. If it were not for the long suffering grace of God I would have given up Christ as a hard task master, One who demanded the impossible from His fallen creatures. It has been a very painful process but along with the anguish and peril that these encounters have brought, there have also come the answers to this problem of perfection. Answers which are based on the simple declarations of the Word of God. I hope, by the Grace of God, to share them clearly with you.

A Gauntlet Thrown Down

The gift of God's grace in my life first manifested itself on a conscious level one autumn night in northern Alberta, Canada. I had been out carousing with friends that weekend and on this particular evening I was very restless for some unaccountable reason.

Before I go on, I would like to say to my shame that I was a very wicked young man, about nineteen years of age, when our story commences. I do not wish to go into the sordid details. They are to this day very painful when I recall them. What I will say, is that I was a willing sinner and slave to most of the vices I could find. I was also a very dangerous sinner and very calculating in my crimes. I was intelligent enough to stay away from those vices that might bring an early end to my selfish career of sin. I especially suffered from the sins of anger, violence, and licentiousness. I seemed so hardened in sin that neither my friends nor I would have forecast any change.

This particular night as I have said, I was strangely restless. This strange restlessness had been occurring a lot. There seemed to be a growing dissatisfaction with my life and a sense of meaninglessness and emptiness. These were alien feelings for this young man. I had been brought up in a loving Christian home. I had gone to Church, with its Sabbath schools, grade schools and Christian academies. In spite of all this I was virtually an atheist. I considered God to be a crutch for people who were weak. The witness of my parents didn't count either. They were good people not because of "God," but because they were, well, good people. This particular evening my agitation became so great that I got in my sports car and raced out into a star-draped prairie night.

That night, under those stars, God spoke to an angry young enemy. His disquieting questions came in the dark. Was I sure that all those stars were just an accident? Wasn't it possible that there really was a God? Probably not, but was it possible? Just maybe...? I replied to the night sky, that if there was a God, then He was welcome to take a "shot." Well since there is a God, predictably He did take a shot! Not long after that night strange things began to happen. There was no resolve on my part to "do better," just that challenge I had flung at the night sky. The things that followed weren't initiated by myself. They were a loving and Divine intervention by Christ through His Spirit. I found old motives receding and new motives mysteriously surfacing. This was seen in new appetites in my music and the surfacing of new emotions among other things. There was an ever growing, and slightly distressing, distaste for what I had once loved.

I recall one day about a week after that challenge, I was driving under an overpass and listening to some poisonous metal rock "music." All of a sudden I remember feeling, amid the cacophony of hate-filled screaming and obscenities, a disgust and weariness come over me. I did not realize that this was God's Spirit at the time, but it was. I wondered out loud if there was something less jagged and jarring that I could listen to. Maybe a classical music station? I remember doing a startled double take and feeling very relieved that none of my friends were there to hear me say a crazy thing like that!

The faith that Jesus gives is a powerful, restless and living thing! It wasn't long after this experience that I was to find myself happily flinging that same music along with thousands of dollars worth of its fellow imps into a jolly great bonfire. The motivations for that bonfire were not based on a fear of displeasing God, or from a desire to win His favor. I burned that "music" because He had created a change in me. A new and outside power was now in control. My heart no longer harmonized with that hate, despair and rebellion.

Suddenly my friends didn't know who I was, but then how could they? I didn't recognize myself either. I remember marveling at the change that had come over me. As a spectator, almost as a third person, I watched as the old life of sin was stripped away. A filthy lying mouth was replaced with purity and sincerity. Hate was replaced with love and remorse. One night I found myself driving down to the home of someone whom I had hated with a passion. Someone whom I would have gladly seen dead if I could have gotten away with murder. (Sadly I mean that literally.) That night I found myself going up to their door and asking forgiveness for that hatred. I remember walking away almost giddy with disbelief, asking myself, "did that just happen?" This incredible transformation was not self initiated. It was not brought into being by my will or choosing. It came from the will and power of another. I found the Scripture to be true which says, *"...it is God which worketh in you both to will and to do of His good pleasure"* (Phil. 2:13). Another miracle which I experienced, was a deep and profound peace. This was a new and a merciful relief for me. A beautiful rest from the turbulent, hate-driven character that I had been. Love for God, the One whom I had formerly despised, eclipsed all other things! I had a new sense of freedom! Like a bird rescued by a loving God from a deadly net! It was a miraculous liberation of heart and mind! It was all too amazing and wonderful! And then I bought a book!

Self Help!

I say I bought a book, but that is so I may relate a story that happened to me just before my apprehension by Deity. As so often happens this story involves a girl... Now this young lady and I fell passionately, madly in love. It was unbelievable!! (Apologies here to my dear long-suffering wife. She could never hold a candle to you, darling 😊) So deep was our love, so rare and precious...Too much? Sorry, I don't mean to induce literary nausea, so I'll stop. I think you get the idea. We both thought our new found "love," was amazing and wonderful. We wanted to keep a good thing going so we decided to buy a self help book and follow the instructions in said book. We thought that this would ensure that our twitterpated romance would continue unabated. Well the methods, the means, and the injunctions in that book made short work of our "love." It hardly lasted the two hour ride home (sounds of wife cheering in the background). In a similar way I found my relationship with Christ imperiled, not this time by a self help book for "lovers," but I found it imperiled because I embraced a doctrine which is far more dangerous. This doctrine was of essentially the same ilk though. It taught me that I should base my spiritual life upon myself! This idea was all very logical from the standpoint of human reasoning. This doctrine however turned out to be that *"...way that seems right unto a man"* (Prov. 14:12), but which ends in death!

A Darkening of the Son

This new way did lead to spiritual death. In an attempt to enhance my relationship with Jesus, I decided to attend a series of meetings. Looking back, I can see that the basic motivator I found at those meetings was predominantly one of fear. The searching questions were asked; "What does your life look like?" "How good are you?" "Were you ready for Jesus to come"? "What about the coming time of trouble"? "Are you good enough to be counted worthy of eternal life"? "Where were you on the road to perfection? Would you be able to stand perfect through the time of Jacob's trouble"? (see Jer. 30:7) They also made many assertions like these:

"There is a record also of the sins of men. *'For God shall bring every work into judgment, with every secret thing, whether it be good, or whether it be evil.' 'Every idle word that men shall speak, they shall give account thereof in the day of judgment.'* Says the Saviour: *'By thy words thou shalt be justified, and by thy words thou shalt be condemned.'* (Eccles. 12:14; Matt. 12:36, 37). The secret purposes and motives appear in the unerring register; for God *'will bring to light the hidden things of darkness, and will make manifest the counsels of the hearts'* (1 Cor. 4:5). *'Behold, it is written before Me,...your iniquities, and the iniquities of your fathers together, saith the Lord'* (Isa. 65:6, 7)."[2]

Other, still more crushing arguments, were put forward, like these; "Every man's work passes in review before God and is registered for faithfulness or unfaithfulness. Opposite each name in the books of heaven is entered with terrible exactness every wrong word, every selfish act, every unfulfilled duty, and every secret sin, with every artful dissembling. Heaven-sent warnings or reproofs neglected, wasted moments, unimproved opportunities, the influence exerted for good or for evil, with its far-reaching results, all are chronicled by the recording angel."[3]

Those were/are some heavy Scriptures and statements if you take them seriously! I did. Many of us do not take them seriously. We view them with fear, and to cut the knot of difficulty we often dismiss and ignore them. This fear and apprehension has caused many of these writings with their Scripture references to be marginalized. They are explained away, (I have been guilty of this) or worse yet rejected as either entirely false, or misguided. For those of us who take these things seriously they almost always bring on a feeling of dread and terror.

---

2 Christ in His Sanctuary pg.117.3
3 Christ in His Sanctuary pg. 118.1

New Motivations

The thought that went through my mind when attending those meetings was, "I'm in BIG trouble here!" "How will I face the judgment of God? I don't want to be lost. I'm full of sin! How was this perfection to be achieved?? What must **I do** to be saved"? Or more accurately the question was, "what must I do to save myself"? The last sentiment sums up the whole theology I found at those meetings. We had a work to do to become perfect!! We had within ourselves a self-determination that could choose to "walk in the light" or not. The final idea that came through was that by walking in revealed light we could "qualify" for more light. If we were "faithful" in that light, more would be given. Like stair steps, we could climb to holiness. If we walked in more and more light, we would eventually see all the light there was to see, walk in all the light there was to walk in, and so come to perfection. Then, the attainment of perfection by the saints would enable Jesus to come again! This teaching, which is still being taught, seemed logical. It seemed "right." It's ends however, as I was about to discover, were the ways of death! The problems of the judgment and actual personal moral perfection, had suddenly reared their formidable heads in my brand new Christian life!

There are different ways which people employ to deal with this perfection/judgment issue which I had run headlong into. I hope you will bear with me now as I break away from my experience to examine four divisive positions that arise within the church from this problem of perfection. After we examine them I will return to my personal experience regarding perfection.

Chapter 2
Four Divisions

When it comes to dealing with the problem of perfection there seem to be four main groups, divisions, or camps in the church. These camps are at war with each other. Sometimes this is a hot war, most of the time it is an unspoken, cold stalemate! The First World War with its prickly barbed wire, snipers, shelling, and trenches comes to mind as an appropriate illustration of the entrenched positions, feelings, and tactics that have arisen from this "problem of perfection."

In describing these different camps, I am speaking from painful, frustrated experience. I have no intention of supporting one group at the expense of another or condemning one group more than another. Polished sinners, full of self-confidence, spiritual pride and self righteousness, are in big trouble, though they may not know it. Also in dire straights are those who think Christ's righteousness is a cloak for sinning and so walk hand in hand with this sinful world. In just as much, or even more trouble are those of us (maybe the majority of us) who synthesize an idol of our own spiritual "achievements" by blending those achievements with the righteousness of Christ. All of the above mentioned, church going, "believing" Christians, are just as poor and miserable, blind and naked, as those who have turned their backs on the church. All are in desperate need of a living Saviour.

Division #1
The "Conservderate Army"
(Con-serve-der-ate)

"I fast twice in the week,
I give tithes of all that I possess"
Luke 18:12

In the first division are those of us who, reading the preceding Scriptures and quotations and being predictably freaked out, decide to go at it and achieve perfection. The sad result is that we do not find what we are seeking. The only result we realize from our efforts is negative. We inevitably become legalistic. The forces that drive this quest are the troubled awareness that *"Without holiness no man shall see God"*(Heb. 12:14), and the flawed human reason and selfish pride native to the human heart. It seems to some of us from reading the Bible and the writings of the Spirit of Prophecy, that <u>we</u> must overcome and <u>achieve</u> perfection or be lost. The same idea drove the Jews of Paul's time to a similar conclusion and to their man-dependent solution; *"For they being ignorant of God's righteousness, and going about to establish their own righteousness, have not submitted themselves unto the righteousness of God"* (Rom. 10:3).

And yet there is an argument that can be made for this position, as we shall see. It is however, an argument, surrounded by confused ideas and a lack of knowledge. There is a requirement of being actually perfect, not just accounted perfect or perfect at any stage of spiritual development or growth. God's people must be absolutely, morally, spotless in the final analysis. The vastly important question is how and by whom is this perfection realized? Many of us sincerely think that it is achieved through our own efforts and set out like the Jews, with great zeal, to "keep the law" and to "overcome." The tragic and spiritually fatal result to us is that we trust in our "overcoming" to secure a place in God's kingdom. The actual fruit of such an experience is not what is desired. It is quite the opposite. This theology almost always makes for cruel, proud, and exacting people! We eventually lose almost all compassion for the spiritually weak and if love is exhibited at all, it is a "love" that is driven by duty and ultimately tends towards the superficial. One disastrous result which those of us who inhabit this camp find, is that real love for Christ is almost totally eclipsed in the soul. This view of God makes Him a harsh, exacting task master who demands the impossible. It ends up casting a cold, sad, and deadly shadow across our lives. I should know, and I will share my experience with this sincere, but sadly misguided theology in chapter three.

Division #2
The "Non-Combatants"

"And he came to the second, [son] and said likewise.
And he answered and said, I go, sir: and went not."
Matthew 21:30

In the 2nd division, entrenched directly opposite to the "Conservderate Army," are those of us who see, either by painful personal experience or by the experience of others, that we cannot achieve actual moral perfection. As a solution to the problem, we settle for a cheap, "Free Grace" message in which the Law of God is done away with because we are "saved." Just "believe in Jesus" we say, "all you need is love," just love Jesus and no further progress in heart holiness is sought for or anticipated. Saying we go, we go not! We forget or ignore the fact that if we love Him, He said it would be shown in keeping His commandments. (Please note that He was talking of true heart obedience here, not a checklist obedience!) The living, vigorous faith and life of Christ, with its very personal results, or fruit, if you like, is beyond the practical experience of those of us who believe this way. We look to the cross, to the lamb of God who takes away the sins of the world and are fooled into a fatal lethargy. "The Cross, the Cross" is the cry. We are content with the justification that is in Christ's blood and are unaware that there is coming an end to that mercy. We have no understanding that soon the throne of mercy will be empty and like the Ark in Noah's day, the door of mercy will be forever closed. We think that the existence of the cross is enough. We forget what the angel said to Joseph, *"You shall call His name Jesus for He shall save His people from their sins"* (Matt. 1:21), not *in* their sins! We listen to the Scripture-quoting devil and cast ourselves from the pinnacle of the temple, so to speak. (see Matt. 4:6, Luke 4:9) We presumptuously "trust" that Christ will catch us when He comes. We say things like "God will make it okay somehow, so why should I bother with the details? I'm just going to trust and have faith that He will save me. He will make up the difference." We forget that we are saved by grace, through faith alone, and that faith comes by hearing, and hearing by the Word of God (Eph. 2:8 / Rom. 10:17). We ignore the command that "... *ye should earnestly <u>contend</u> for the faith which was once delivered unto the saints"* (Jude 1:3). We are content to be non-combatants in this war between good and evil.

Many of us do not wish to tackle the painful question of our sins. Like Ignatius of Loyola, the founder of the Jesuit order, we decide "never to think of them ever again."[4] There is a substitution of the true, heart-searching, and often painful convicting work of the Spirit of God, for a counterfeit. An experience of spiritual ecstasy, meditations, feelings, and impressions is sought. When those of us in this camp come up against the problem of perfection, you will hear things like, "We'll be sinners till Jesus comes." "We can never be perfect so why fret about it..." Well, if we are sinners when Jesus comes, we're in BIG trouble: *"...then shall that Wicked be revealed, whom the Lord shall consume with the spirit of His mouth, and shall destroy with the brightness of His coming"* (2 Thess. 2:8). One look into that holy face, surrounded by the glory of the Father and all the holy angels (Luke 9:26), will send anyone who is imperfect in any way, running in terror. They will beg to be hidden from the face of Him who sits on the throne (Rev. 6:16). That idea can be so scary that occasionally, it is enough to cause some, through fear of punishment, to desert the camp of the "Non-Combatants" for enlistment in the "Conservderate army" (By the way, I made that word up, so put down your dictionary. ☺) However, as has been previously stated, in that camp they will find themselves just as lost while "overcoming," as they were here.

---

4 History of the Reformation of the Sixteenth Century, Volume three, book ten, page 354

Division #3
The "Deserters"

"My people hath been lost sheep: their shepherds have caused them to go astray, they have turned them away on the mountains:"
Jeremiah 50:6

Another group of us just do not see how perfection can ever be a realistic expectation, and we desert the church for the world. I had the story related to me of one poor sister who just got fed up with the whole thing. She said that she couldn't see how it all worked. How was it that she was accepted by God because of Jesus, but still had to get busy making good choices so she would become good enough to be allowed to live in the end? At the same time, her Bible told her that she offended in many things and that she fell (present tense) short of the glory of God! It was clearly stated in her Bible that, *"... if we say that we have no sin* [are perfect!], *we deceive ourselves, and the truth is not in us"* (1 John 1:8). If that was so, then how was she supposed to come to a place where she could say that she had no sin? She felt that there were insurmountable contradictions here. She left the church, as many of us have for similar reasons. Many of the lost sheep secretly long to come back if they could just see how it works. Most of us in this division are too honest to accept a cheap grace theology. Many of us also know the limitations of our own efforts and have become discouraged. We see a vast crowd of our children in this group. They recoil from that harsh, exacting, and unreasonable portrait of God which many of us have painted by our words or actions. They also see no point in a neutered God who says He loves you and will save and rescue you, but who isn't a real and present reality in their own personal lives. Many have been exposed to the recruiting messages of the previous two camps. The mixed and confused message comes across that God expects you to do most of the saving yourself, or that He only means to save you by proclamation and rhetoric, but not in reality. By these conflicting ideas, many of us are brought to the point where we consider God to be a social myth. He is considered as nothing but perhaps a philosophy, or a false bogeyman, and we have walked away into the dark night of this world.

Division #4
The "No Man's Landers"

*"Because thou sayest, I am rich,
and increased with goods, and have need of nothing."*
Revelation 3:17

You may have been saying, "I thank you Lord I'm not like those folks! Whew!" But now it gets scary! On the battlefields of WWI the most dangerous place to be was in "No Man's Land," wandering around somewhere between the two sides. This division is the most pitiable group of us all. Most of us are caught out on this ground. This is also the most deceptive position when it comes to perfection. The lies found here take so many of us in because they are almost true. The Devil's most dangerous deceptions are always those lies that are laid most closely beside the track of truth.

This zigzagging division is by far the most prominent group in our ranks. Most of us in this camp, are sincerely preaching out of both sides of our mouth. Or if you prefer, have one foot in the liberal camp and one foot in the conservative camp. We are not usually aware of this condition however. We're not one of those "hot head" legalists, nor one of those, "cold," lifeless worldly ones. We pride ourselves on being "balanced," middle of the road" Christians. I also used to take great pride in my own centrist, and neutral position. In case you are tempted to think this is a safe position to occupy, I would like to point out to you that the middle of hot and cold is... lukewarm! Of the last days church the True Witness says: *"I know thy works, that thou art neither cold nor hot: I would thou wert cold or hot. So then because thou art lukewarm, and neither cold nor hot, I will spue thee out of My mouth. Because thou sayest, I am rich, and increased with goods, and have need of nothing; and knowest not that thou art wretched, and miserable, and poor, and blind, and naked"* (Rev. 3:16,17). It seems that those of us who hold this position are in big trouble!

When it comes to actual moral perfection, those of us in this group have an indistinct and hazy understanding somewhere in the back of our minds. We know that in heaven there will be no sin. There is an acknowledgment, that in heaven people will be perfect. However, when it comes to how this sinlessness is to be realized, we have very vague ideas indeed! As a solution to the problem, we find ourselves blending, or synthesizing, two spiritual positions. To find a solution to this problem we have mixed some of the beliefs from each of the "Conservderate Army" and the "The Non-Combatants." In "no man's land" we generally call perfection "righteousness," a nice neutral, mildly warm term. A sermon which I heard recently started out so beautifully! Christ and the Holy Spirit alone can be in control of our motives, actions, thoughts and feelings etc.... My heart was rejoicing as I listened! But to my horror the sermon rapidly degraded from there into..."You must change yourself and your thinking patterns. It's all in your mind, so... this is the formula by which YOU can effect (should I say "perfect") real change in your lives"! "Then [when you're good enough or in other words perfect or righteous] Jesus can come. So get busy"! ...Ugh, the poor people were left with the impression that only Christ through the Holy Spirit could save them, so they had better get busy saving themselves! This could be done (something they were just told they couldn't do) by them changing their mind sets, their thoughts and feelings etc. This, the message said, must be done so that they could be saved by Christ and Jesus could come again! Oookay suuuure... Is it any wonder that with this kind of pasture to graze upon we find that the sheep are bewildered, feeble and sick?

The Roots of Our Confusion

"And make straight paths for your feet,
lest that which is lame be turned out of the way."
Hebrews 12:13

Why do we find this zigzagging, this limping between two opinions? The instinctual knowledge that perfection is required if one is to dwell in the presence of God, however dimly understood, drives this confusion and double talk. We are tricked into thinking that we can go about the attainment of this perfection from a human point of view. Human philosophy and reason are brought to bear on our thinking. We hear it from the cradle to the grave; things like; "Only 'good' little boys and girls will go to heaven…" Martin Luther called this "the sophistry of the school men." We have been taught, (not from the Word of God, mind you) that we possess independently, the ability for self determination or the power of personal choice. The Bible says the exact opposite: *"For the flesh lusteth against the Spirit, and the Spirit against the flesh: and these are contrary the one to the other: so that ye cannot do the things that ye would."* (Gal. 5:17).[5] It is true that we can choose this or that in the natural world. For example, we can choose what we want to eat, where we want to go, or what color we prefer our car to be etc... The flesh and the devil use this ability to choose this or that in our physical world as a snare for our reason. The idea is propagated that this power of choice works the same way in the spiritual world. All we need is some help from God, a divine boost or a spiritual energy drink, and we can get this mess cleaned right up. We are beguiled into making flesh our arm and as a result receive a curse. It is written, *"Cursed be the man that trusts in man, and makes flesh his arm, and whose heart departs from the LORD"* (Jer. 17:5). We look to our human capacities and abilities and forget that"... *the wisdom of this world is foolishness with God. For it is written, He takes the wise in their own craftiness"* (1 Cor. 3:19 -20).

Our human nature and fallen reasoning preaches that our will, aided by God's power, can hopefully bring us to perfection some day in the far distant future. The devil, the world, and our flesh, insist that when the Scriptures declare that *"of mine own self I can do nothing"* (John 5:30), it really means, not "nothing," but "something," even if it is just a small little something! Then, once we have been brought to believe this pleasing fable, it is an easy step to reason that if we can do something, however small, then surely we can strengthen that little something. The next thing you know, we're off in a deluded attempt to choose/perform our way into heaven! All the while, this is going on, it is under a banner of a pseudo-Protestantism that professes to believe in righteousness by faith in Christ alone. Do you

---

5   Also see Rom 7:14-18

see the echoes of both the trenches here? The Devil uses this double mindedness to derail the indispensable truth of righteousness by faith alone. We go back and forth, *"run to and fro,"* trusting partly in God's grace and trusting partly in the works of our own hands. This dualism is idolatry and a curse to God's people. The vital question needs to be asked again, *"How long halt* [limp/zigzag] *ye between two opinions"*? (1 Kings 18:21) In Revelation there is a woman dressed in scarlet who rides a beast. She mixes drinks that cloud the reason and cause men to stagger back and forth. That wine seems to have been bootlegged into our understanding of salvation too. This wine/doctrine that says that faith and works saves us. The truth is that grace saves us by faith alone! Don't worry though, the results of the faith of Jesus will always be seen in the life. A true connection to Christ the living vine always produces righteousness in those lives where He lives and which are under His control.

As you read the previous descriptions of these four camps, you may have seen yourself pictured there. I urge you not to despair! We have a loving Saviour who knows that we are made of dust and that we are easily duped! He has defeated the deceiver who is our adversary. He has promised to, *"...give unto you the Spirit of wisdom and revelation in the knowledge of Him: The eyes of your understanding being enlightened; that ye may know what is the hope of His calling, and what the riches of the glory of His inheritance in the saints"* (Eph. 1:17, 18). In His word is the cure for what sickens all of us stagnating in these positions. A proper understanding of perfection can and will break down these differences and bring a blessed harmony and peace to the children of God.

Chapter 3

Personal Experience Continued...

"There is a way that seemeth right unto a man,
but the end thereof are the ways of death."
Proverbs 16:25

Let us now go back to the story of that young man, who just "bought" a book. Now where was he..? Oh yes, he/I had just attended a series of "evangelistic" meetings.

After that weekend, things started to change. Just as that book I had bought on relationships had scuttled the "Love Boat,"[6] just so the doctrine of perfection by "light walking," law righteousness really, started to sicken and corrupt the faith I had been given. The new light of life which God had shone into my heart and mind was immediately darkened and I found anxiety growing. Was I doing all I knew and could to be "perfect"? Was I walking in all the light I had? Jesus was coming... Jesus was coming...was I ready?! "Oh I sure hope I'll be ready"... Panic rose to a high pitch, and I thought it was the convicting Spirit of God. I tried harder and therefore, dug my grave even deeper! The real author of all this distress was Satan and his false doctrine. I daily resolved to never do anything I knew to be outside of God's will. This was a good resolve to have, but my primary motive for doing so had now changed. I was no longer motivated by the love and life of Him Who had died for me. Now I was motivated by a growing fear that I would not be "perfect" when Jesus came. Time was limited and I'd better brush things up toot sweet before probation closed! If you feel, or have felt this way, you have my deepest sympathies and if I could I would give you a reassuring hug! I sure could have used one.

Another ugly thing now surfaced in my life. My previous love and acceptance for others quickly changed. That love was now replaced

---

6   Registered trade mark of ABC TV

with a Gestapo type watchfulness! (Always for the "saving of the lost," mind you.) To this day, I feel the keenest remorse for this "fruit" of my new-found "righteousness." I can still vividly remember bringing my dear mother to tears by telling her she would be lost because she ate the wrong things. The more I bought into this "way that seemed right," the worse this spiritual pride became.

It was not long before the doctrine of the "Super Saints" was discovered in the camp that I had enlisted in. This doctrine of the super saints usually goes by another name, the "144,000." I might as well begin to deal with it here and now. This was a rare club to aspire to. These folks are the ones, so the teaching goes, who will be able to somehow reach a level of righteousness and perfection that will "enable" Jesus to come. They will have a special place in heaven above everyone else and will be God's favorites. This was very attractive to my new found "spiritual" motivation. I will admit to some spiritual pride here, and a desire to be among these supermen/women. But mostly, I thought that membership in the 144,000 club was more of a necessary condition for salvation, as much as it was a goal. I believed that it was either do or die here. It was understood that if you were alive when Jesus came and you didn't stack up in your "sanctification"...if you weren't good enough to be translated because you were imperfect, well, then sizzle on you! To some this may seem to be ridiculous, but it is actually a serious problem for many of us. I have had numerous brothers and sisters tell me in all sincerity that they will have to die, and that they hope to die, before Jesus comes back. The exalted perfection of the 144,000 is just too much for them, and they prefer death instead. This is so incredibly sad that it is hard to adequately express. Why should the return of our loving Lord and Saviour be of such a nature that it causes His children to prefer death? The problem of perfection has been at the bottom of this death wish every single time I have come across it. Sadly, I come across it all the time.

Night Falls

"Having the understanding darkened,
being alienated from the life of God through the ignorance that is in
them, because of the blindness of their heart"
Ephesians 4:18

With all sincerity I took upon my shoulders a yoke of bondage. Supported by all sorts of quotes and texts, a great deal of self sufficiency and self reliance, I entered the *"way that seemeth right"*. I can still remember the very spot where it dawned on me that all the love, joy and peace had departed from me and that it had been replaced by anxiety, sadness, and fear! Seeing no way out but forward I soldiered on. It never occurred to me that the fruits of the Spirit are love, joy, and peace. I had left my Father's house and had been "cut off from Christ!" (the true life-giving vine) As it is written, I had *"fallen away from God's grace"* (Gal. 5:4).   How do I describe the following months? It is hard even now to think back on them. They are painful in the extreme. The sadness and loneliness, the feeling of separation from the One Whom I had loved so much and the fear and panic that had replaced that love is hard to express in words. I remember coming to the place where, I too, thought death preferable to life. I remember thinking that God was cruel to have given me life at all if He was just looking for a fault or imperfection so that He could take it away.

Externally my lifestyle was very rigorous. My twenty-year-old face became very solemn and sad. I went around with lowered eyes and the air of a beaten dog. My diet became severe. Following the "Light" I had cut out of my diet every food that was even remotely pleasant and had adopted the most austere dietary regimen. I was finally reduced to eating small (no sin of gluttony please) amounts of plain boiled potatoes, and boiled frozen vegetables, two times a day. My weight plummeted until, under my clothing I bore the appearance of a concentration camp survivor.

Just to inject a touch of humor into this very tragic story, I'll relate that in one of their meetings it was stated that the use of deodorant was very likely a sin, as it introduced chemicals into the "temple of God" which might "defile" it. True to their doctrine, I "walked in the light," and they soon had cause to regret the sentiments they had expressed. Undeodorized young men can be very pungent, even with frequent washing!

Things now, rapidly progressed from bad to worse. I became very sick both in body and spirit. I did not, like Martin Luther, beat myself raw with a whip, but there is a beating of the heart and mind which is in many ways more painful. I would take to the hills on long walks when not running myself into the ground working for the "Master." On these "death marches" I tried to find relief from the torment of my thoughts and feelings. I found none. The darkness and despair only increased. I was not alone in my sufferings. I remember one friend there who confessed to me one day that he was very wicked and in no small doubt regarding his salvation. Why? Because of a terrible besetting sin. The Sin? He would occasionally eat a small amount of french fries! For this he was probably to be consigned to the horrors of the lake of fire. You had to be there to appreciate the look of panic, fear, and despair in his eyes. It was heartbreaking!

Breaking Point

The human mind is only capable of so much distress before something in the will snaps. I still remember vividly the day that my will broke. I was returning to the "barracks" from one of my "death marches" when the loving Spirit of Jesus spoke to me. I didn't realize it as Him at the time, but the thought flashed through my mind that I had become a Pharisee of the Pharisees! I was walking in all the "light" I could find and had even manufactured some of my own to walk in as well, but at that moment I was made to realize that it was all external. I was, *"touching the righteousness which is in the law, blameless"* (Phil. 3:6). In my heart it was a different story. There I found no real holiness, just the frantic beating off of a dreadful, lurking monster that would immediately attack me if I relaxed my vigilance at all! My pursuit of perfection had brought me that day to the brink of ruin. If it were not for the unseen Spirit of God, I would have gone over that edge. I would have left Him, either from rebellion or insanity!

I still remember that evening vividly. This part of the story is hard on my pride to relate, but if it will encourage just one, I'm willing to bare it publicly and I will rely on your kindness and understanding. The evening was sunny and bright, ironic, considering the darkness of my heart and mind. In despair, I made my way back to my room, and as I did so the pressure increased to a level that I still cannot believe. When the mind is in that much distress one will try to relieve the mental and emotional suffering by a physical act. I did just that. I sought out the darkest corner I could find, the nearest thing to a hole in the ground, where I could escape. I crawled under my bed and like a frightened and abused child I curled up weeping and hid.

That evening under that bed, I reached a crisis. I came face to face with this problem of perfection. "Was this how perfection was reached?" It had become as plain as day that I was lost. I had no hope of standing before God in the Judgment. God had shown me, that I was an *"unclean thing"* and that all my righteousnesses were *"filthy rags"* (Isa. 64:6). I told God that I'd had it. I could not, no matter how hard I tried, become sinless. I told Him that even if I could attain perfection, I had no interest in looking over my shoulder in heaven for all eternity, trying to remain perfect. I told Him that I was finished attempting to do it here on earth too. I said that I was done for, lost. I informed Him that I would go back into the world. I didn't want to be the person I had been before, but I knew I couldn't be perfect. Looking back now I see evidence that even in my confusion and hypocrisy God was at work. (We should bear this in mind when dealing with each other). I told Him that when He came again He could just kill me and I that wouldn't blame Him because I knew what I was. With an unbelievable wrenching of emotion I told Him that if this was the way of salvation then I was unable to perform it and would have to die. Just then, at that moment, it was as though Christ stepped in between Satan and his cowering victim and said "Enough"! A quiet, calming voice seemed to gently say to me: "It's not like this, hold on. I will get you out of here." A great peace seemed to embrace me and I fell into an exhausted sleep there on that hard floor under my bed. It was a deep and peaceful sleep. A sleep that I had not known for many, many months.

It is wonderful how God works when He moves! Within three days I was out of that situation. Looking back now I find this small crumb of comfort. Upon my leaving that group of "righteous people," I was informed that I was altogether too extreme and legalistic for the saints there assembled. I may have mentioned to them that I was only carrying out to its logical and ultimate conclusion the method for the "perfecting of the saints" which they were advocating. The crumb of comfort comes in knowing that, having been a Pharisee of the Pharisees, I had thoroughly exhausted the limits of the theology of works righteousness. I had found it to be a cheat, a lie, and the ways of death.

Now What?

As I was driving back to my parent's home, I asked myself again and again the same question: "Now what?" If God wasn't in the perfection by choice/exertion business, then what was the truth? Was there such a thing as "perfection"? My exhausted nature just could not face the question. I decided to leave it alone and to focus only on Jesus and His Love. This was how He had first drawn me to Himself. This seemed like a good idea, but by adopting this course, I sailed dangerously deep into the shallow and schoaling waters of cheap grace. I decided that I would leave the "little red books," little read books, if you know what I mean? I did not know what to do with the hard passages, Scriptures and statements that I had found there. If I did read the books, I would always have flashbacks, a kind of spiritual PTSD. I would still occasionally read the commentaries on the life of Jesus and a few others, but that was the limit. By the grace of God, I did not drive my ship straight onto the reef. I did not say that those Scriptures and writings were rubbish. I came close though. I let these questions alone and took up the motto, *Sola Scriptura*!, the Bible and the Bible alone, and *Sola Gratia,* by Grace alone!! I again found the grace of God in the sacred pages of God's Word. Alongside that grace I still found a requirement for obedience, but this obedience, I discovered, was not something I had to produce. It was something which had its origins in God. Ezekiel 36:26, 27 became my lifeline... *"A new heart also will I give you, and a new spirit will I put within you: and I will take away the stony heart out of your flesh, and I will give you a heart of flesh. And I will put my Spirit within you, and cause you to walk in my statutes, and you shall keep my judgments, and do them."* But the text that gave me the most comfort concerning the whole "problem of perfection," was Hebrews 10:14, I'm looking at it now as I write this. It is engraved on the cover of my Bible: *"For by that one offering He perfected forever all those whom He is making holy"*!

For a long time this text was enough. Christ had somehow provided perfection. Somehow, Jesus would make it all right!

This conflict over perfection seemed to lay dormant in my heart for many, many years. When it reappeared, it did so with a vengeance. The catalyst for its reappearance was the death of a dearly beloved father. The bearing that occurrence has on the subject, I will relate when we deal with the subject of "the cheating dead..."

For now, let's examine in more detail, the real problems of perfection doctrine, starting by defining perfection as it appears in the Bible.

Chapter 4

Four Perfections

If we don't understand that there are different types of perfection taught in the Bible, the subject can be very confusing. To help break things down, we will look at the four basic types of perfection found in the Scriptures. We will look at them in the order that one does/will experience them when in a healthy walk with Christ.

Perfection #1
The Perfection of Justification

*"Being justified freely by His grace
through the redemption that is in Christ Jesus"*
Romans 3:24

"For God in all His fullness was pleased to live in Christ, and through Him God reconciled everything to Himself. He made peace with everything in heaven and on earth by means of Christ's blood on the cross. This includes you who were once far away from God. You were His enemies, separated from Him by your evil thoughts and actions. Yet now He has reconciled you to Himself through the death of Christ in His physical body. As a result, He has brought you into His own presence, and you are holy and blameless as you stand before Him without a single fault" (Col. 1:19-22 NLT).

Without fault! This is the majestic doctrine of justification by grace. God made peace with everything, by means of Christ's blood on the cross. He has brought you, me, and the whole world back as His friends by the means of His own death on the cross in His own human body! This is a work that is completely and utterly outside of, and apart from ourselves. It is like creation. Just as we had nothing to do with the creation of this world or our first parents, so justification is the work of God. On the cross God reconciled man to Himself, as it is written, *"God was in Christ, reconciling the world unto Himself"*

(2 Cor. 5:19). He made peace with everything the Bible says, both in heaven and earth. He did it for the entire human race. "*...He was wounded for our transgressions, He was bruised for our iniquities: the chastisement of our peace was upon Him; and with His stripes we are healed. All we like sheep have gone astray; we have turned every one to his own way; and the LORD hath laid on Him the iniquity of us all*" (Isa. 53:5).

Through the death of Christ on the cross, the justice of God was satisfied, and the guilt barrier which had kept the human race separated from God was removed. This was and is the glad tidings of the gospel. It was sin that had cut Adam and Eve and all their children to the nth degree off from Him who is life. Because Christ would, and has tasted death for everyone, the entire human race, though many of us choose to reject Him, is restored to that communion of life. Since all our sins were laid on Him, the world can truly stand "*holy and blameless*" before God. The Lamb of God has taken away the sins of the world. All the faults mankind has, or will commit, and the guilt for the good and righteous things we fail to do, were laid to the account of the blessed Lord Jesus.

Question: Now that we stand perfect in Him, are we ready to go? Some like to say, "Ya, Jesus paid it all," and He did, but if you stop there you end up with a grace that leaves us in the clutches of an enemy. Something more is needed. There is a law in the world against suicide, but it is no good to tell a person that is bleeding to death from a self-inflicted, mortal wound, that they have broken the law. It isn't even very helpful to tell them that you have paid the penalty imposed by the law on anyone who harmed themselves that way. Even if you informed them that you had gotten them a full pardon from the magistrate, would there be any point to finish by saying, "Oh and by the way, could you see your way clear to come to dinner next Saturday?" The invitation would be completely pointless. Why pointless? Well, because he/she won't be alive by then! Unless there is a saving, healing action, on the part of a "Great Physician," the invitation to communion is useless! What the poor dying one needs is help. Lying by the road bleeding out, they need a life-saving, life-giving transfusion. They need their wound healed.

This idea that salvation by grace is simply and <u>only</u> a legal declaration, that has no practical life-saving or life-giving substance denies the name of Jesus. The angel told Joseph that, *"You shall call His name Jesus for He shall save His people,* [not <u>in</u>, but] *from their sins"* (Matt. 1:21.

Perfection #2
Relative Perfection

"Let us therefore, as many as be perfect, be thus minded."
Philippians 3:15

So now that God has given us peace solely through His work on the cross and the whole world has been brought into His arms by Christ, are we actually Holy? Are we actually blameless in our thoughts, feelings, and innermost desires? Some new converts have thought that now that they were justified they would never ever transgress again! Yaaay... (Cue the sounds of screeching tires, breaking glass and crumpling metal in the back ground.) It quickly becomes apparent to anyone who thinks this way that there is some actual saving still to be done after all.

When someone is converted there is a new creature. They are, spiritually speaking, like a little baby that has just been created by God. Because of the justifying merits of Christ Jesus, this new child is just perfect in God's eyes. A dead branch has just been grafted onto the life-giving Vine (Christ). The life blood of the Vine has begun to flow into and give nourishment to a heretofore dead branch.

Question: Are we actually perfect now? We are accounted perfect by God because of the blood of Christ. We have the life and presence of Christ in us subduing our sinful natures. His life in us is supplying new thoughts and feelings. As it is written, "... *you are not controlled by your sinful nature. You are controlled by the Spirit if you have the Spirit of God living in you. (And remember that those who do not have the Spirit of Christ living in them do not belong to Him at all)* (Rom. 8:9 NLT). (See also Phil. 2:5 KJV)

Question: Is our salvation complete now? In other words, are we completely perfect in reality? Christ, by the Spirit, is in the midst of the hearts and minds which the Father has drawn to Himself (John 6:44). God is working in those hearts to will and to do of His good pleasure (Phil. 2:13), but.... the Scriptures plainly declare in Romans 3:23 that *"all have sinned and fall* [present tense] *short of the glory of God.* So you see, we are not actually perfect, far from it. James says candidly that *"in many things we offend all"* (James 3:2). And John says that *"If we say that we have no sin, we deceive ourselves, and the truth is not in us"* (1 John 1:8). That "truth," which is not in us if we say we are sinless, is Christ Jesus, the way, the truth, and the life. Through faith and by virtue of the righteousness of Jesus we are accounted of God as perfect at every point in our Christian walk, though the reality is that we still fall short and still offend in many things.

Some will say, "Well that's it then, job done! We have righteousness by faith in Christ alone, He is at work in us both to will and to do of His good pleasure and as we grow, we are perfect at every stage! I'm not sure how, but when we die, God will wink or some such thing and, hey presto, we'll be in the kingdom!" That conclusion, leaves me wanting... I have known God-fearing men and women who at times could behave like devils. (Myself not excepted!) Will heaven have in it some church board meetings or planning committees such as I have seen? Committees where the proceedings very closely resemble a blood bath? Will the saints still be slitting throats and stabbing backs over the color of the carpet that is to go under the new benches by the tree of life? I think not. Something more permanent is needed.

Eternal Struggle?

Have you noticed that even though we are in a saving relationship with Christ, the sinful nature will exhibit itself occasionally? Thank God that by the controlling power of His Spirit the "old man" can be put to death again, but our sinful nature is still warring against God in a struggle for control. (see Rom. 7:14-25, and Gal 5:17) Will this terrible struggle go on for all eternity? Some speculate that maybe sanctification will end in the <u>achievement</u> of perfection. If the goal of sanctification is to achieve perfection, what of those whose probation has been closed by death? What of the thief on the cross? He certainly had not attained perfection through sanctification before his death. Will he have a time-out room when Christ comes? Somewhere he can attain perfection through sanctification after his resurrection? Will Paul or anyone else have more time upon their resurrection to achieve the perfection all must have to live in the presence of a Holy God? Preposterous! If you follow this idea to its logical conclusion, where does it get you? Do you see that here our thinking can quickly run into a pseudo-purgatory doctrine similar to that of the Roman church! Is this the case? Well, Paul had not attained perfection before his death when he wrote *"Not as though I had already attained, either were already perfect: but I follow after, if that I may apprehend that for which also I am apprehended of Christ Jesus. Brethren, I count not myself to have apprehended"* (Phil. 3:12).[7]

Paul candidly admits he had not gotten his hands on perfection. He says that his being perfect in the future is what Jesus Christ has gotten a hold of him for, but he candidly admits that he is not yet in possession of that perfection. In this passage he clearly shows two perfections, one that is absolute (which he does not yet have) and one that is relative to experience. He says in verse fifteen; *"Let us therefore, as many as <u>be perfect</u>, be thus minded: and if in any thing ye be otherwise minded, God shall reveal even this unto you"*(Phil. 3:15). The fact that he includes himself in this group by using the word *"us"* shows that he is not speaking to others who may have reached perfection, but to us that are accounted perfect through the faith of Jesus.

Here we see presented a relative perfection, a perfection that is perfect at every stage of its progression. This is not the actual attainment of absolute sinlessness of character. This is a perfection in

---

7   Please note that the word "apprehend" is not the same word as "attained." An important point.

Christ, as we walk trusting in Him. This is what is meant where the Spirit says; *"... if we walk in the light, as He is in the light, we have fellowship one with another, and the blood of Jesus Christ His Son cleanses us from all sin"* (1 John 1:7). Here is echoed the prayer of Jesus for us who believe on His name, *"I in them, and thou in me, that they may be made perfect in one"* (John 17:23). We are considered perfect in Christ as He walks in us, His children. We are accounted perfect by God as we walk in dependence upon Him.

So that's great!! All done, we're good to go right? Where is Jesus, by the way, why hasn't He returned, since we are so ready to go and look that God, who is a *"consuming fire,"* in the face? Justification and sanctification are all we need to see His face in its unveiled glory, right? Yes? We are complete now and wholly righteous by faith, right?

Uh... I will now throw a fly into the ointment by pointing out this seeming contradiction from Paul. Under inspiration he writes, *"For we through the Spirit wait for the hope of righteousness by faith"* (Gal. 5:5). This word "hope" means to have a confident expectation. So righteousness by faith is a present reality (again see Col. 1:22-23), but it's also something that we eagerly look forward to? Paul says: *"For we are saved by hope: but hope that is seen is not hope: for what a man seeth, why doth he yet hope for?"* (Rom. 8:24) Here we are told about a righteousness by faith that is hoped for... it is something future, something we do not yet possess. Though we by faith alone stand faultless in Christ, we are promised something more. Something we eagerly look forward to. Of Noah it is written, *"By faith Noah, being warned of God of things not seen as yet, moved with fear, prepared an ark to the saving of his house; by the which he condemned the world, and became heir of the righteousness which is by faith"* (Heb. 11:7). Please note and file away this phrase for future reference... It hints at something wonderful that has been promised by God to His children.

Perfection #3
Absolute Actual Moral Perfection

"Follow peace with all men, and holiness,
without which no man shall see the Lord"
Hebrews 12:14

It is a God-given desire to make one's life a success. God's picture of a successful life is not what the world thinks it should be. Worldly success is supposed to look something like this: A high degree of education which men will look on with awe and respect. They will listen to and admire a person for the letters after their name or the position they hold. One should be wealthy, have a secure, well-paying, not-to-strenuous career which everyone would follow closely and praise, beautiful wife or handsome husband, big house, model kids, expensive cars.... you get the picture. You see this ideal of what makes a successful life everywhere in the world and, sadly, in the church. This benchmark is held up as venerable, even though one of the most pernicious sins in our midst, is the respecting of the persons, titles, and possessions of men.

I'm not despising these attainments, well not all of them. Most of them, when sanctified by the grace of God, are great blessings. They are, however, temporary. Some day all of it, including its pride, will be burned up. What really lasts in this world? What does Heaven say a successful life looks like? God has given me a new benchmark for a successful life, and it puts very little emphasis on gathering laurels for kindling and possessions for firewood. When God got His hands on me, He created one overwhelming desire in my heart. To look on His face with undimmed joy and peace! The accomplishment of this God-given desire is no mean thing! Its realization, as we shall see, is impossible unless there is a Divine intervention and work.

Four Perfections • 37

Ensamples

The Scriptures declare of the history of the Children of Israel, that, *"Now all these things happened unto them for ensamples: and they are written for our admonition, upon whom the ends of the world are come"* (1 Cor. 10:11).

Let me interject a short author blurb here; This word translated "ensamples" is the Greek word "tupos" which means "type" or "prefigure," so one can say that these experiences and the history of what happened to Israel prefigured future events. When the events that were prefigured become a reality, they are then called "anti-types." This word "anti" does not often mean "against" as we commonly use it today. "Most of the time it means "in the place of a figure, type or shadow."[8] As an example, we see John the Baptist saying of Christ, *"Behold the Lamb of God that takes away the sins of the world"* (John 1:29). The Lamb, slain at the door of the tabernacle, is the type; Christ, hanging upon the cross, is the "anti type." So in the experiences of the people in the Old Testament we see parables or examples, which if studied, will help us to understand the greater realities of the plan of salvation. Armed with that very basic explanation of a "type," let's go on.

Peculiar Treasure

*"For the LORD hath chosen Jacob unto Himself,
and Israel for His peculiar treasure."*
Psalms 135:4

When the Children of Israel came to the foot of mount Sinai, they had seen a lot of God's miraculous power. The signs and wonders God had done for them while bringing them out of the slavery of Egypt were unmistakable signs of His love and regard for them. Not only had they seen the control He had over the elements of the natural world, but also on display had been His power over human

8   Strong's Exhaustive Concordance

nature. *"The king's* [in this case Pharaoh's] *heart is in the hand of the LORD, as the rivers of water: He turns it wherever He will"* (Prov. 21:1). In addition they had in front of them the testimony of the life of Moses. He had fled Egypt a rash hot-head who had made flesh his arm (with it's predictable results) and he had returned humble, subdued, and dependent on his God. The Israelites knew of the promise of inheritance that God had given to Abraham and his Seed. They had sacrificed the lamb, been baptized, eaten the manna, and drank from the rock; those mighty symbols of justification, death, re-birth and sanctification. They *"...were all baptized unto Moses in the cloud and in the sea; And did all eat the same spiritual meat; And did all drink the same spiritual drink: for they drank of that spiritual Rock that followed them: and that Rock was Christ"* (1 Cor. 10:2). They were justified and sanctified by faith in the Redeemer to come. They stood in a peculiar relationship to the omnipotent God and yet, when they came to Mount Sinai, they found a fence!

Veiled and at Arms Length!

"King of kings, and Lord of lords;
...dwelling in the light which no man can approach unto"
1 Timothy 6:15, 16

That fence. The boundary around Mount Sinai and the prohibitions regarding touching the mountain were very explicit; *"Mark off a boundary all around the mountain. Warn the people, 'Be careful! Do not go up on the mountain or even touch its boundaries. Anyone who touches the mountain will certainly be put to death"* (Exod. 19:12, 13 NLT).

Was that fence put up because Jehovah was a stern, unloving, stand-offish God? No, for in his blessing of the people before his death Moses said; *"The LORD came from Sinai, and rose up from Seir unto them; He shined forth from mount Paran, and He came with ten thousands of saints: from His right hand went a fiery law for them. Yea, He loved the people"* (Deut. 33:2, 3). It was not a disgust for His people, an "Eww, get away you dirty things..."

that commanded the building of that fence around the mountain. It was built because of God's protecting love and care. God was trying to get a point across to them and to us. The point? It was just this, that Israel, though justified, born again, and enjoying the sanctifying presence of Christ in the pillar of cloud and the pillar of fire; was still unable to come into the unveiled presence of a Holy God. This point was brought home to Moses when he begged to see the Glory of God. The LORD said plainly to His faithful servant, *"Thou canst not see My face: for there shall no man see Me, and live... I will put thee in a clift of the rock, and will cover thee with My hand while I pass by: And I will take away Mine hand, and thou shalt see My back parts: but My face shall not be seen"* (Exod. 33:20-23).

A little later when Moses, having seen God's back only, came down the mountain to the waiting people, they begged him in awe and fear to veil his face. The last lingering flickers of God's reflected glory were still too much for them to bear! This restriction imposed between God and His people is also seen in the handling of the earthly tabernacle. This is what the command was, even for the Kohathites, who were in charge of the holy things: *"But thus do unto them, that they may live, and not die, when they approach unto the most holy things: Aaron and his sons shall go in, and appoint them every one to his service and to his burden: But they shall not go in to see when the holy things are covered, lest they die"* (Num. 4:19, 20).

All throughout the typical history of Israel, we see this prohibition. When the LORD was fulfilling His promise to His people and bringing them across Jordan, He told them, *"Since you have never traveled this way before, they* [the priest carrying the Ark] *will guide you. Stay about a half mile behind them, keeping a clear distance between you and the Ark.* [That symbol of the throne of Deity] *Make sure you don't come any closer"* (Josh. 3:4). We see this idea of distance being needed again and again. The men who looked in the Ark, when the Philistines sent it back on a cart, were struck dead. Uzzah, when he came in contact with the Ark, died. There were also special instructions given to the priests for the safety of the people who were worshiping in the temple. The priests were to remove even the holy garments they ministered in before leaving the Temple: "*When they* [the priests] *return to the outer courtyard where the people are, they must take off the clothes they wear while ministering to Me. They must leave them in the sacred rooms and put on other clothes so they do* <u>*not endanger anyone by transmitting holiness to them*</u> *through this clothing*" (Ezek. 44:19 NLT). Why would the people be endangered by having holiness transmitted to them? The answer is, that, "*to sin wherever found*" "*Our God is a consuming fire*" (Heb. 12:29).[9] Nothing that is unholy in any way can survive an encounter with that "fire," including God's people.

How About Us?

Only the High Priest could enter the most holy place once a year, and then, only with blood could he appear before the visible presence of God, the Shekinah Glory. **Question:** Can you or I live in the unveiled presence of God? At this very moment, even though we have been justified and are being sanctified, are we fit to appear in the midst of that all consuming fire? Ellen White recorded a vision about this very thing; she wrote, "I saw the beauty and loveliness of Jesus, and it seemed as though I could never bear to be parted from His lovely presence. Then I saw a light coming from the excellent glory that encircled the Father. It approached nearer and nearer unto me. I began to tremble, my body shook like a leaf; <u>it seemed to me if that light came close to me, I should be dissolved or struck out of existence</u>, but the light passed me. Then could I realize what a terrible God we have to do with, and that we must be so holy that we can live in His sight."[10] Do you feel confident enough in yourself and your sanctification to stroll up to that glory right now? Any takers? This sister was in a saving relationship with God, through Christ and yet we... "*all fall short of the glory of God.*"

It says in the Scriptures that "*the Son of man shall come in the glory of His Father with His angels; and then He shall reward every*

---

9 Desire of Ages pg.107
10   Manuscripts 5 1851.1

man according to his works" (Matt. 16:27). It says that because of the glory of God, no man can approach Him. We read "H*e shall shew, who is the blessed and only Potentate, the King of kings, and LORD of lords; Who only hath immortality, <u>dwelling in the light which no man can approach unto</u>; whom no man hath seen, nor can see"* (1 Tim. 6:14-16). We are told that the second coming of Christ will be a catastrophic event for <u>any</u> who are not actually, morally perfect at His appearing. The Glory of God will consume them. "*And then shall that Wicked be revealed, whom the Lord shall consume with the spirit of His mouth, and shall destroy with the brightness of His coming"* (2 Thess. 2:8). It is also written: "*…the kings of the earth, and the great men, and the rich men, and the chief captains, and the mighty men, and every bondman, and every free man, hid themselves in the dens and in the rocks of the mountains; And said to the mountains and rocks, fall on us, and hide us from <u>the face of Him</u> that sitteth on the throne, and from the wrath of the Lamb: For the great day of His wrath is come; and who shall be able to stand"?* (Rev. 6:15-17)

It is clear from the Scriptures that sin, and by extension sinful man, cannot abide the presence of a Holy God. In order to live in His presence, we must be without "spot *or wrinkle or any such thing"* (Eph. 5:27). The Word of God declares that we are not yet, actually, morally perfect! We are still not on the mark, we still offend in many things (see James 3:2). Yet we have this beautiful promise from the midst of that same consuming fire, *"They shall see His face…"* (Rev. 22:4). How can these things be? The Scriptures say this will become a reality. The ways and means which God has provided to accomplish this seeming impossibility have yet to be seen. The Scriptures yet to be studied in part II of this book will reveal how God will bring this about.

Perfection #4
Physical Perfection

Now for the last of our four perfections. The physical, immortal body, promised us by God through the same power that raised Jesus from the dead; *"But if the Spirit of Him that raised up Jesus from the dead dwell in you, He that raised up Christ from the dead shall also quicken your mortal bodies by His Spirit that dwelleth in you"* (Rom. 8:11). We know the texts: *"For if we believe that Jesus died and rose again, even so them also which sleep in Jesus will God bring with Him. For this we say unto you by the word of the Lord, that we which are alive and remain unto the coming of the Lord shall not prevent them which are asleep. For the Lord Himself shall descend from heaven with a shout, with the voice of the archangel, and with the trump of God: and the dead in Christ shall rise first: Then we which are alive and remain shall be caught up together with them in the clouds, to meet the Lord in the air: and so shall we ever be with the Lord"* (1 Thess. 4:14-17). That there will be a change of our physical person at the second coming of Christ is evident where the Scriptures says: *"Now this I say, brethren, that flesh and blood cannot inherit the kingdom of God; neither doth corruption inherit incorruption"*(1 Cor. 15:50). Please don't misinterpret that text though and think it says we won't have a physical body. Christ, after His resurrection, when He appeared to His disciples said: *"... spirit hath not flesh and bones, as ye see me have"* and the promise is that Christ *"... shall change our vile body, that it may be fashioned like unto His glorious body, according to the working whereby He is able even to subdue all things unto Himself"* (Luke 24:39, Phil. 3:21).

Paul also wrote: *"Behold, I shew you a mystery; We shall not all sleep, but we shall all be changed In a moment, in the twinkling of an eye, at the last trump: for the trumpet shall sound, and the dead shall be raised incorruptible, and we shall be changed. For this corruptible must put on incorruption, and this mortal must put on immortality. So when this corruptible shall have put on incorruption, and this mortal shall have put on immortality, then shall be brought to pass the saying that is written, Death is swallowed up in victory"*

(1 Cor. 15:50-54). Please notice that this is a <u>physical</u> transformation, for the living and the dead.

Question: Is this <u>a moral change</u> for the living and the dead? I don't believe the Scriptures say that it is a moral transformation, but only a physical one. "Why," you ask? Well, the Bible says that before the coming of our Lord Jesus the pronouncement has gone out: "*He that is unjust, let him be unjust still: and he which is filthy, let him be filthy still: and he that is righteous, let him be righteous still: and he that is holy, let him be holy still*" (Rev. 22:11). The spiritual condition of all will then be fixed for eternity. Those who are justified will remain in that state and those who are holy will remain that way. On the other hand those who are not justified and holy will be forever lost. It says in Scripture that when Christ returns His reward will be with Him. "When the work of the investigative judgment closes, the destiny of all will have been decided for life or death. Probation is ended a short time before the appearing of the Lord in the clouds of heaven."[11] If the moral perfection of all the saints was not complete before the return of Jesus, how could their cases be closed and their reward calculated? The new bodies we will receive must only be the final cherry on the top of our salvation.

So there we have the four perfections that are listed in the Scriptures. Whenever we are dealing with this topic of perfection, whether in Scripture or other writings, a proper understanding of which perfection is being talked about, will help to safeguard our thinking.

Caution!
Obstructions Ahead!

"Many therefore of His disciples, when they had heard this, said, This is an hard saying; who can hear it?"
John 6:60

Before we go on, I would like to give you a heads up. A fair warning. In this next section it could get a bit rough! What we have

---

11 Christ in His Sanctuary pg. 127

to deal with will be done candidly and on purpose. I have no desire to scare you. If a person only obeys and toes the line because they are scared, we don't have a righteous person, just a poor, scared hypocrite! That is not what God wants. There is, however, a need for us to look at some hard things. There are problems that need to be faced head on! Most times it is better to look under the bed and confront the monsters lurking there than to cower in the dark under the blankets. It may appear that the contradictions we will be looking at are just too much to resolve and that they threaten our very faith, but please hang in there. There is light in God's Word that will dispel the shadows. Please, as you read what follows and if you discuss it with others, don't try to wish or spiritualize these hard things away. Face them bravely with prayer. Allow them to exist for a little while without trying to rationalize them into oblivion.

Please realize as we examine these subjects, that I'm not expressing my own beliefs. In these subjects we find many incompatible ideas. Something seems off when we examine our understanding of these issues. When looking at some of these incongruent ideas, I will only be pointing out inconsistencies and contradictions which cripple our understanding of God. If we don't have a correct understanding of them they can warp our picture of Him and His plan for our salvation. We need to confront these issues, and as John Bunyan wrote in his "Pilgrim's Progress," attack and slay these paper giants! So please hang in there with me as we go storm this castle, and don't recycle this book just yet. There is something, some truth that we may have missed in the Scriptures which can harmonize all these problems that we will be looking at. A truth that will bring peace, faith, and relief to those who understand it.

Chapter 5
A Dog's Breakfast

Anyone who has ever planned a formal dinner knows that a lot of preparation and planning goes into the endeavor. To have a successful banquet, there must be a progression that is harmonious. Not so with the dog's breakfast. As those of us from Canada will know, "a dog's breakfast" is comprised of any and all the leftovers. These leftovers are jumbled up together and served all at once. These are the things that no one wants to deal with. Poor dogs! If people were to eat like that, it would have a very sickening and debilitating effect on us. Well the same is true in spiritual things. There is a logical and beautiful harmony in the truth of salvation. When it is presented in it's entirety it is a wonderful feast for the hungry soul. That being said, I see evidence all around me that we are looking peaked and sick. It seems we may have tucked into a kind of dog's breakfast spiritually speaking. If we have jumbled and mixed up ideas regarding the plan of salvation, it should be no wonder that we are spiritually ill. There are some confused ideas in our beliefs, that are not compatible. Let's examine six of these and see if you agree with me that what we have on our hands is a kind of "Dog's Breakfast," and it is making us spiritually sick!

Dog's Breakfast, Ingredient 1
"The Judgment"

"Fear God and give glory to
Him for the hour of His Judgment is come!"
Revelation 14:7

The Advent movement arose from the judgment and sanctuary message. As the year 1844 approached, God began to reveal these truths to His people. We realized that there was a heavenly sanctuary. We discovered that Christ, "... *has entered that greater, more perfect Tabernacle in heaven, which was not made by human hands and is not part of this created world*" (Heb. 9:11 NLT). We saw that we had a Great High Priest who had ascended into heaven to minister for us, and then what happened to us? What happened to our passion and our desire to comprehend God's word? It seems that these two great inseparable truths were lost sight of; not perhaps in a doctrinal way, but it seems clear that in our everyday practical experience they have either ceased to be a reality or have at best stagnated and been relegated to our history. Yet these truths are vital to our faith and salvation. "The subject of the sanctuary and the investigative judgment should be <u>clearly understood</u> by the people of God. All need a knowledge <u>for themselves</u> of the position and work of their great High Priest. Otherwise it will be <u>impossible</u> for them to exercise the faith which <u>is essential</u> at this time or to occupy the position which God designs them to fill. Every individual has a soul to save or to lose. Each has a case pending at the bar of God. Each must meet the great Judge face to face. How important, then, that every mind contemplate often the solemn scene when the judgment shall sit and the books shall be opened, when, with Daniel, every individual must stand in his lot, at the end of the days."[12]

As a church and as individuals we have had some problems coming to grips with the judgment. The judgment brings us face to face with our own sinfulness and obvious deficiencies. As stated earlier, *"all fall short of the glory of God"* and offend in many things. Many find it is almost impossible to see how the judgment can be a survivable process when their names are called and their deeds are examined. This has led many to claim that the message of the 2300 days, the cleansing of the sanctuary, and also the investigative judgment are downright false teachings. Many, when faced with the prospect of this very personal examination, abandon sound prophetic interpretations in an attempt to "fix" the problem. Because the sayings of God's word seem hard, many turn back. They wish, like ancient Israel did, to return to the easy living in Egypt. Many have left God's revealed truth, sailing back to Egypt, down "De Nile" as it were. Others decide to ignore the sanctuary and the judgment and just hope for the best. While I do not share these sentiments, I can certainly see how people can come to these conclusions, and I sympathize with the fear and confusion which has

---

12 The Great Controversy. Pg. 488

prompted many of us to go down these various roads. The question is, did/do we need to? First, let us look at the evidence in Scripture that shows plainly that there is a judgment. For many of us this will be rhetorical and obvious, for some of us it will not be the simple restatement of some well worn facts.

The Judgment in Scripture

The earliest reference I can find to the judgment in Scripture is that mentioned in the book of Jude: *"And Enoch also, the seventh from Adam, prophesied of these, saying, Behold, the LORD cometh with ten thousands of His saints, to execute judgment upon all, and to convince all that are ungodly among them of all their ungodly deeds which they have ungodly committed, and of all their hard speeches which ungodly sinners have spoken against Him"* (Jude 1:14,15). There was, from as early as Enoch's time, an understanding that justice would be satisfied. In a vision given to Ezekiel God prefigured the judgment of His own people: *"And the LORD said unto him, Go through the midst of the city, through the midst of Jerusalem, and set a mark upon the foreheads of the men that sigh and that cry for all the abominations that be done in the midst thereof. And to the others He said in mine hearing, Go ye after him through the city, and smite: let not your eye spare, neither have ye pity: Slay utterly old and young, both maids, and little children, and women: but come not near any man upon whom is the mark; and begin at my sanctuary. Then they began at the ancient men which were before the house"* (Ezek. 9:4-6). The "house" here mentioned is the temple and it is with the leaders of His people that God begins. Not that anyone should find comfort in that, everyone was judged in the end. It is also written, *"it is appointed unto men once to die, but after this the judgment"* (Heb. 9:27). Another fascinating statement says that, *"...the time is come that judgment must begin at the house of God: and if it first begin at us, what shall the end be of them that obey not the gospel of God? And if the righteous scarcely be saved, where shall the ungodly and the sinner appear?"* (1 Peter 4:17,18)

Here, I'll introduce you to something we will be doing throughout this study of the Scriptures. We must sometimes look at what we read in the Scriptures in its original language...I know, I know... shudders all around, but I'll try to take the sting out of it, and the experience will be well worth the trouble, I promise! So, as an example of what is to come please take a second look at the underlined portion of that Scripture. The words "*is come,*" are italicized in the KJV. This means that these words were not in the original text. The word "time" in this verse is the Greek word "**kairos,**" which translates as "*an occasion or time which is set*"[13] So this text should read, "The time of the judgment to begin at the house of God has been set" This translation of the text harmonizes with the Advent understanding of a definite time for the judgment of God's people spoken of in Daniel.

This time began in 1844 and Scripture specifically says that it begins with the professed people, or church of God. The Bible plainly states; "*For we know Him that hath said, Vengeance belongeth unto Me, I will recompense, saith the Lord. And again, The Lord shall judge His people*" (Heb. 10:30). We could go on and on with verse after verse showing the judgment in Holy Scripture, but that would swell this book and tire you, the reader. Suffice it to say that the Bible clearly states, as much as some of us might wish it didn't, that there is a judgment and not just for the wicked.

Now that we have established what some may consider obvious, lets look at some of the confusing and seemingly contradictory texts we find when it comes to the judgment.

Weights and Balances

Question: Is the judgment a matter of weights and balances as many believe? We know the story of Belshazzar's feast and the hand writing on the wall, with it's interpretation, - "*TEKEL; Thou art weighed in the balances, and art found wanting*" (Dan. 5:27). Is that the sum total of the Judgment? All my bad acts and sins on one side

---

13 See Strong's Exhaustive Concordance #G2540

and all my good acts on the other? God then opens up my page and takes a cold hard look at it; if my good deeds outweigh my bad deeds I get a big thumbs up from God, and if they don't then, "SIZZLE," I burn! This has been the view, to a greater or lesser extent, that many of us have had of the judgment. We seem either consciously or subconsciously to hold this idea. There are Scripture texts that seem to support this view, and there are some that seem completely at odds with this concept. Let's examine these Scriptures with a "Pros & Cons" list, and see what we find.

Balance Scale Theory:
Pros and Cons Scripture List

1st Argument
in favor of a balance scale theory

"*For God shall bring every work into judgment, with every secret thing, whether it be good, or whether it be evil*" (Eccles. 12:14). Here we seem to have a balance scale idea, good things and bad things submitted as evidence. Everything will have its due weight in determining our fate.

Contrary Statement

"*Knowing that a man is <u>not</u> justified by the works of the law, but by the faith of Jesus Christ, even we have believed in Jesus Christ, that we might be justified by the faith of Christ, and not by the works of the law: <u>for by the works of the law shall no flesh be justified</u>*" (Gal. 2:16). Here is a contrary statement. We can never be justified by the works of the Law. It states plainly that our justification comes solely by the Faith of Jesus. So our right standing before God and our salvation is not based on law righteousness, even though every work will be brought into the judgment either good or bad? A tad confusing, right?

2nd Argument
in favor of a balance scale theory

"For we must all appear before the judgment seat of Christ; that every one may receive the things done in his body, according to that he hath done, whether it be good or bad" (2 Cor. 5:10). So we will get what's coming to us then...? What is it we deserve? If you read Romans chapters 1-3, our just desserts become painfully obvious and the fact that all, both Jew and Gentile, are under sin is very plainly stated.

Contrary Statement

"If thou, LORD, should <u>mark</u> iniquities, O Lord, who shall stand? But there is forgiveness with Thee, that Thou may be feared" (Ps. 130:3, 4). That word "mark" means to make a note of or to look closely at and preserve. Maybe to write them in a book? It also says that with God there is forgiveness. So if we are forgiven, why drag up our past sins in a judgment? Can't we just let forgiven sins, like sleeping dogs, lie? Many have said that God will wink until His people get their act together and become perfect... then those sins that were forgiven, can stay forgiven and we can stand in the judgment perfect by sanctified achievement. Many of us, possibly unbeknownst to ourselves, hold this idea as well. We hear it expressed in sentiments like, "Jesus can't come till we finish the work," or "He is waiting for us to 'do our job," as if we were a member of a great football team that could win the Superbowl if we just did things right with the help of our great coach!

3rd Argument
in favor of a balance scale theory

"A fiery stream issued and came forth from before Him: thousand thousands ministered unto Him, and ten thousand times ten thousand stood before Him: the judgment was set, and the books were opened" (Dan. 7:10). I thought we just read that if God marked iniquities we would be in big trouble? Here there seems to be a

record, or account book, kept of every life, right down to the last detail, (again, see Eccles. 12:14).

Contrary Statement

I thought I'd better throw this one in here, so no one goes and jumps off a spiritual bridge! *"For God so loved the world, that He gave His only begotten Son, that whosoever believeth in Him should not perish, but have everlasting life. For God sent not His Son into the world to condemn the world; but that the world through Him might be saved. He that believeth on Him is not condemned: but he that believeth not is condemned already, because he hath not believed in the name of the only begotten Son of God" (John 3:16-18).* So again the question arises, why a judgment? It is clear that a judgment is going on, but to what purpose?

4th Argument
in favor of a balance scale theory

We have two contradicting passages in Romans only a few verses apart. In these verses Paul seems to totally contradict himself where he says, *"For not the hearers of the law are just before God, but the doers of the law shall be justified"* (Rom. 2:13).

Contrary statement

Immediately in the next chapter we read, *"Therefore by the deeds of the law there shall no flesh be justified in His sight"* (Rom. 3:20). So on one hand you read, that those who obey, or do the law, will be justified, but then Paul states that you will not be justified in God's sight by obedience to the law? This can be very puzzling and confusing!

5th Argument
in favor of a balance scale theory

Here's a scary Scripture! In Matthew 12: 36, 37 it says, *"But I say unto you, That every idle word that men shall speak, they shall give account thereof in the day of judgment. For by thy words thou*

shalt be justified, and by thy words thou shalt be condemned."
These words were spoken by our Saviour Himself. Every idle word
will come up in judgment, not just bad words which did harm, but
also words that did nothing at all. It also says we will be "justified"
by our words? I thought we just read that by the works of the law we
could not be justified? (see Gal. 2:16) Good words and bad words are
"works," so what gives here? Do you see how we may come to a
place where we are confused? Is there any way this confusion can be
cleared up? Read on…

Augmentation Anyone?

When confronted with the judgment, some people reason that
maybe we can do a little extra good works. The idea is put forward,
one way or another, that we can do something to top up the scale on
the plus side of things in the judgment. This was indeed the position
of the church which ruled in the dark ages, and a position it still
holds. **Question:** Can we do extra good things to top up our lack of
good works? Can we pad our stats as it were? I would ask you to
reflect on the fact that God's law requires perfect love from a person
all the time and if you were to do all things perfectly, all the time,
you would still only be doing the bare minimum required by God's
Law. So where can a person or church get some "extra"
righteousness to offset the continual sinning we see in all of us?
Think about it. Augmentation is an impossibility. We cannot help to
"make up" for our offenses.

Problems With Choreography

Another problem that rears its head with the judgment arises
when you consider the judgment of the living. Have you ever
wondered how it will work with the living? "The judgment is
now passing in the sanctuary above… Soon—none know how
soon—it will pass to the cases of the living. In the awful
presence of God our lives are to come up in review… While the
man of business is absorbed in the pursuit of gain, while the
pleasure-lover is seeking indulgence, while the daughter of
fashion is arranging her adornments,—it may be in that hour the

Judge of all the earth will pronounce the sentence, *"Thou art weighed in the balances, and art found wanting"*[14]

Okay, how will this work? Is it alphabetical with the living? Will God start with the people with a last name starting with "A" and finish with those that start with "Z"? If so will the poor folks who go first have to maintain perfect righteous longer than those of the "Z" clans? Maybe it will go something like this: Brother A's name has come up and he is now judged whereas brother Wright's name is not due for a bit and he still has time to amend his ways? (I know I'm being a little bit facetious.) What if those whose names begin with "A" fall short of the glory of God and offend in anything, let alone many things, before God gets to "Z"? Will their cases have to be re-visited and their names struck out of the book of life? Is there a kind of double jeopardy, based on the alphabet or some such thing where some might have to stand trial twice? Will it be white knuckles and cliff hanging by their fingernails for those who go first? Would that be fair? I don't think so. Then if you throw the people who have died into the equation, which we will do shortly, it gets really murky and even more unfair yet.

This still leaves the question: Why a judgment of investigation? Many of us have denied the doctrine of the investigative judgment from the sheer bewilderment brought on by all the seeming contradictions we just looked at. When some of us couple this with the reality we see in the mirror every day, the reality of our own faults and failings, well, this rejection is hardly to be wondered at is it? However it does not mean we should reject the judgment. The problem may be our understanding of God's word, not God's Word itself.

If there was a simple explanation to these apparent contradictions would that help the children of God? I think it would, I think it will. These problems must be resolved if we are to be freed from the idolatrous ideas that we are saved by Grace through faith and by our sanctification/works as well. There is a way to reconcile these problems indeed; but before we look at that explanation we might as well get all the dog scraps together.

---

14 The Great Controversy 490,491

Dog's Breakfast, Ingredient 2
"A Perfect Remnant"

If we say that we have no sin, we deceive ourselves,
and the truth is not in us.
1 John 1:8

Now we have to look candidly at the idea of the personal perfection of the last remnant before Christ's return. Many believe, and have good-looking material to back it up, that the last remnant will attain perfection and be without moral stain before the return of our Lord. Here we are again confronted with the 144,000. These are represented as the elite, the best of the best or the "Super Saints." The Bible leaves no doubt that they will exist. Who they are, and what achievements they must have...well, here is where the confusion of the saints comes "marching in." Here we have the opportunity for self-dependency, self-seeking, and pride to parade through the front door of the church arrayed in robes of self righteousness. Many have desired to be among this group so that they might have a privileged place in heaven. It was no different in Christ's days on earth. The disciples weren't looking to be in the 144,000, but first place in the kingdom was set firmly in each of their sights. Some even tried to have their mom influence Christ to secure them first prize. (A bit of a low blow if you ask me!)

Christ laid out a principle which will come into this discussion a little later on. Christ said to His self-seeking disciples (past and present), *"You know that those who are regarded as rulers of the Gentiles lord it over them, and their high officials exercise authority over them. Not so with you. Instead, whoever wants to become great among you must be your servant, and whoever wants to be first must be slave of all. For even the Son of Man did not come to be served, but to serve, and to give His life as a ransom for man"* (Mark 10:42-45). "What constitutes true greatness in God's kingdom? *"Whosoever will be great among you, let him be your minister!"* (Matt. 20:26) In My [God's] kingdom the principle of preference and supremacy has no place. The only greatness is the greatness of humility. The only distinction is found in devotion to the service of others."[15]

---

15 Desire of Ages pg. 650

It is the inspiring Spirit of Jesus that shows itself to a greater or lesser degree in His children. The greater the display of genuine loving service, the greater in the eyes of heaven is the individual in whom it is seen. Some people, sadly missing the whole point, rush out and serve as much as possible so they can be the greatest. I don't think that was what our Lord meant. The more Christ lives in and controls His children, the more evidence of His presence there will be. The point being, that in God's kingdom, the least are greatest. This principle runs clean contrary to the idea some of us have of a super-saint elite.

Every time I have met this problem of a perfect last remnant, I have observed a certain disposition toward pride, self-righteousness, and self-exultation. **Question:** Will the truth suddenly change right at the end? Will self-reliance and achievement, replace self-abasement and God-dependent humility? It will not. Yet many of us have this idea that God's children, during the last great trouble, will be relying on their own strength of character and achieved righteousness for their standing before God. This idea has propagated the fearful idea that once Christ steps down from His mediatorial role we will be on our own!

The fact that there will be a last remnant should be obvious, someone has to be last. Soon probation will close and the last pronouncement will be made: "*He that is unjust, let him be unjust still: and he which is filthy, let him be filthy still: and he that is righteous, let him be righteous still: and he that is holy, let him be holy still*" (Rev. 22:11). These people will be alive and remain when Christ returns. We have already talked about what we must be to see His face and survive. We have a few more insights from the author Ellen White to consider concerning what the remnant's spiritual condition must be:

"I also saw <u>many do not realize what they must be</u> in order to live in the sight of the Lord without a high priest in the sanctuary through the time of trouble. Those who receive the seal of the living God and are protected in the time of trouble <u>must reflect the image of Jesus fully</u>."[16]

16 Manuscript releases 41.2

Now that's heavy if you take it seriously! What must it be to "reflect the image of Jesus fully?!" It is certainly not talking about His physical image here; so it must be speaking of His moral image or likeness of character. This likeness is not what we see in ourselves. Mankind, even those who are in a saving relationship with God, have imperfections in their thoughts and feelings. The combined thoughts and feelings of an individual when considered together make up his or her moral character. The Scriptures declare; "*O generation of vipers, how can ye, being evil, speak good things? for out of the abundance of the heart the mouth speaketh*" (Matt. 12:34). The real problem is not with the outward actions, they are simply a manifestation of what is in the heart. It should be apparent that the hearts of men, even the hearts of God's real children, do not reflect the image of Jesus fully. Is this a call to get busy and become perfect?

Corrupt, Godly, Prophet!

Some will say, "Well maybe these people will be better than others, the "Best of the best!" Do you remember the prophet Daniel in the Bible? There is not one mention made of egregious sins in his life. No Bathsheba like David, no striking The Rock instead of speaking to it, like Moses. Not even showing off to the Babylonian ambassadors, as King Hezekiah did. Daniel was "*a man greatly beloved*" (Dan. 10:11). Yet when he saw in vision the glory of the messenger from heaven, he said that "*there remained no strength in me: for my comeliness was turned in me into corruption, and I retained no strength*" (Dan. 10:8). He also related that "*I Daniel alone saw the vision: for the men that were with me saw not the vision; but a great quaking fell upon them, so that they fled to hide themselves*" (Dan. 10:7). The men that were with him, the Bible says, didn't even see the vision, but the mere sense of the invisible glory, sent them running to hide. As for Daniel, who remained, he said that all his "comeliness or grandeur, imposing form, and honor or majesty,"[17] was instantly turned into "corruption." In modern speech, he would have said that anything in himself that he had thought

---

17Strong's #H1935

excellent or righteous, now resembled a stinking and rotting corpse in comparison with the glory he then beheld! That was this holy prophet's reaction to the <u>outward</u> vision of Godliness. What will the effect be on the conscience when it is confronted, face to face, on a <u>spiritual</u> level? What would our thoughts be if we were to come into the actual presence of the Word of God; that Word which cuts through to our innermost thoughts and desires and exposes us for what we really are? (See Heb. 4:12, 13 and John 1:1)

In the book "Maranatha" we read, "Let all remember that God is holy and that <u>none but holy beings can ever dwell in His presence</u>."[18] The above statement of facts sends many scrambling for the checklist. They completely forget that righteousness is not a checklist of actions, but a condition of the heart. They get busy in a cold sweat trying to do "good"! To every one of us who attempts this, God raises the question along with its answer; *"Who can bring a clean thing out of an unclean? not one"* (Job 14:4). This conundrum is getting more than uncomfortable, right?

The scriptural correctness of the assertions above, have already been shown in the section on "Absolute Actual Moral Perfection" We must be holy, and that means *"without spot or wrinkle or any such thing"* (Eph. 5:27). We must be sinless in order to live in Jehovah's presence. Is this a moral perfection that is ours by attainment? In other words will the last people of God, the 144,000, be expected to attain greater righteousness than any of the people that have gone before? Will they have to be "super-saints" who stand atop Mt. Sinai with their attained righteousness flowing behind them in the wind like a cape? Will they be required to reach, in actuality, a standard which others have not had to reach? But of us and our righteousness the Scriptures declare "...*we are all* as an unclean thing, and *all our righteousnesses are as filthy rags; and we all do fade as a leaf; and our iniquities, like the wind, have taken us away"* (Isa. 64:6). Note it says "ALL" of us...not all of us except the 144,000. Also, will the dead who died believing in Christ be held to a lower standard? We'll get to that seeming contradiction shortly.

---

18 Maranatha 41.4

According to the Scriptures and the quotations just cited, <u>absolutely perfect</u> is what the remnant must be to live in the sight of God through the time of trouble spoken of by Daniel (see Dan. 12:1). I hope I'm not belaboring this too much, but just let that sink in! The remnant must fully reflect the character (moral thoughts and feelings) of Jesus. They will offend in no way, either in word, action, or even in thought. They must be holy beings. The challenge is immediately screamed at you where you may now be hiding under your bed as I was: **"How about it?! Are you ready for that?! Well, are you?!"** The honest among us echo the same question the disciples did when they were confronted by Christ regarding how hard it was to enter the kingdom of heaven. *"They were astonished out of measure, saying among themselves, Who then can be saved?"* (Mark 10:26) Thank God for Christ's answer which gives us hope in God: *"And Jesus looking upon them saith, With men it is <u>impossible</u>, but not with God: for with God all things are possible"* (Mark 10:27).

Terrible Evangelistic Result?

Another serious problem regarding the "super saints," arises when we look at the last message of warning that is sent out into the world. In Revelation it says; *"after these things I saw another angel come down from heaven, having great power; and the earth was lightened with His glory"* (Rev. 18:1). **Question:** Will there be no last minute conversions under the outpouring of the Holy Spirit? No thief on the cross experiences from this great and powerful message? Or is the last call to repent just a "na-na na-na boo-boo" taunt? Will there be no burning brands snatched from the flames in the last minutes? (See Zec. 3:2) I don't think so. If there are some newly converted people, will they be as righteous as, say, a Christian of long experience in the sanctification of Christ? I doubt it would be reasonable to expect that. Of that great outpouring of God's power we read in the book The Great Controversy, "Now the rays of light penetrate everywhere, the truth is seen in its clearness, and the honest children of God sever the bands which have held them. Family connections, church relations, are powerless to stay them now. Truth is more precious than all besides. Notwithstanding the agencies combined against the truth, a large number take their stand upon the Lord's side."[19]

These people who take their stand on the Lords side, may not have known that they should have been honing their perfection, right? Will they be in big trouble? Do you see any inconstancy here? If our membership into this perfect "remnant club" is based on how much we have done in the fields of our master, these "newbies" should not be admitted. If you recall, Jesus told a parable about this very thing. I will relate it here, as it has a direct bearing on the idea that membership in the 144,000 is purchased by overcoming, longstanding service and/or heavy labor.

Jesus spake a parable to them saying: *"For the Kingdom of Heaven is like the landowner who went out early one morning to hire workers for His vineyard. He agreed to pay the normal daily wage and sent them out to work. At nine o'clock in the morning He was passing through the marketplace and saw some people standing around doing nothing. So He hired them, telling them He would pay them whatever was right at the end of the day. So they went to work in the vineyard. At noon and again at three o'clock He did the same thing. At five o'clock that afternoon...* [The King James says it was the 11th hour, we would say "at quitting time," just at the closing bell so to speak.]...*He was in town again and saw some more people standing around. He asked them, 'Why haven't you been working today?'" "They replied, 'Because no one hired us.'" "The landowner told them, 'Then go out and join the others in My vineyard.'" "That evening He told the foreman to call the workers in and pay them, beginning with the last workers first. When those hired at five o'clock were paid, each received a full day's wage. When those hired first came to get their pay, they assumed they would receive more. But they, too, were paid a day's wage. When they received their pay, they protested to the owner, 'Those people worked only one hour, and yet you've paid them just as much as you paid us who worked all day in the scorching heat.' He answered one of them, 'Friend, I haven't been unfair! Didn't you agree to work all day for the usual wage? Take your money and go. I wanted to pay this last worker the*

_____
19 The Great Controversy pg.612.2

same as you. Is it against the law for Me to do what I want with my money? Should you be jealous because I am kind to others?'"So those who are last now will be first then, and those who are first will be last" (Matt. 20:1-16 NLT).

Please notice in the parable, the landowner's question to the 11th hour or five o' clock workers. *"Why haven't you been working today?"* They had not been working! Yet they were sent to the fields, and because of the generosity of the Master, they received the same wages as those who had worked all through the heat of the day.

This misunderstanding has given birth to another baby of speculation that maybe you have heard expressed. Some say, "Well, of course there will be conversions at the last minute, but those who are converted in the last moments before probation closes will all have to be laid to rest because they aren't perfect." I will ask you to consider the conversion of the thief on the cross. He at the last minute saw Christ, the *"Lamb of God, which taketh away the sin of the world"* (John 1:29). He didn't even ask for forgiveness, just remembrance (See Luke 23:42). He was given the assurance that he would be with Christ in paradise. This was just a few short hours before probationary time closed for him. That he died shortly after makes no difference to the equation. Will there have to be entire equality of attainment among the saints before the close of probation? Will the Gospel suddenly flop from the good news that we have peace with God through the blood of our Lord Jesus Christ and an assurance of eternal life by that blood, to a message of righteousness and eternal life by attainment? Can you see some of the contradictions and difficulties here? How are these to be resolved? Again, I would encourage you to stay tuned. There is a clear, scriptural way to explain and reconcile these difficulties.

Dog's Breakfast, Ingredient 4
"The Cheating Dead?"

*"For the Lord Himself shall descend from heaven with a shout,
with the voice of the archangel, and with the trump of God:
and the dead in Christ shall rise first"*
1 Thessalonians 4:16

A Personal Tragedy

I will now pick up one of the last remaining threads of my personal experience recorded in this book. As I have said, I had laid aside all these problems of perfection which had nearly caused me to make a shipwreck of the faith of Jesus. I was not going to tackle the monsters under my bed, they were ugly, scary things! I walked down the years eating and drinking of Him who is the life of the world, and these thoughts and questions slumbered.

Then came that terrible morning when I found myself in a hospital in Portland, Oregon. Almost as if in a nightmare I heard the doctor say that my dear father was not going to live after his heart surgery. Shortly thereafter his words were confirmed and my life was left with a gaping hole in it. One can see a part of God's unsearchable wisdom displayed in His ability to make good come from tragedy. It didn't seem like it as we said good bye to George Clarence Wright, father of four and one of the most selfless men I have ever known. God, however, is not wasteful and He can use even our grief as a catalyst to disclose truth to us.

Not long after my father's death questions started to arise in my mind. Uncomfortable, irritating questions. I knew that my father had loved Jesus. I knew that my father trusted Christ to save him. BUT, I could not pretend that my dad had died perfect. I knew that even as loving as he was, and as giving as he was, he could still be grumpy and bullheaded at times. I knew he loved and trusted Christ, but was he saved? I tried to brush these concerns away, but the questions persisted: "Where would my father find perfection now?" "Had he dodged the bullet of perfection by dying?" "Was the grave a perfecting agent?" "Would the grave make not only my father's deficiencies, but also the deficiencies of every dead believer in Christ go away?" "Was death a kind of Saviour? Was the grave a perfecter?" I didn't like these questions at all! They brought the problem of perfection squarely back into the light and into my life again!

Two Ways of Salvation?

If you look through the Bible, you will find many people who have died with less than perfect characters. In spite of their failings we are told that they were accounted by God as righteous, as having received a good report. In Hebrews chapter 11 we have a long list of Bible heroes. Of these people the Bible says, *"All these people we have mentioned received God's approval because of their faith"* (Heb. 11:39 NLT). We see people like Gideon, who, *"made an ephod... and put it in his city...: and all Israel went thither a whoring after it: which thing became a snare unto Gideon"* (Judges 8:27). We see the flawed and failing David, and many others... Scripture says that, *"... all, having obtained a good report through faith, received not the promise: God having provided some better thing for us, that they without us should not be made perfect"* (Heb. 11:39, 40). That is an encouraging and comforting statement for those of us who are able to look candidly at the lives of our loved ones who have fallen asleep in Jesus. I say encouraging and comforting because any honest reflection on the lives of even the saints mentioned in Hebrews is bound to show deficiencies, failings, and sins or imperfections in them. Yet these people are spoken of as secure in Christ. Have you ever stopped to ask the question, "How?" How will the imperfect dead rise from their graves perfect and able to look God square in the face?

Question: Are there two ways to be saved? Let me elaborate. All who have died believing in Jesus have not reached a state of actual moral perfection before their death. The Bible, in Hebrews and other places, declares the salvation of these people. Remember the thief on the cross? He had the promise that he would be with Christ in paradise. And Sampson? He committed suicide! Yet he is in the faith chapter (Heb. 11:22). They died flawed and imperfect! Now contrast this seeming leniency regarding perfection with the requirements of perfection which it seems those who are *"alive and remain..."* (1 Thess. 4:17) must deal with.

On the one hand we have those who have gone into their graves trusting Christ. They *"fell short"* and still offended in many things, yet they will rise up to meet God face to face in peace. They fell asleep imperfect and yet, because they died do they get to cheat? Do they somehow get to "Pass Go, and collect $200" while the living are stuck in a hotel on "Park Place"[20] paying through the nose? Is it because of death that they can rise perfectly capable of looking the great and terrible God in the face with undimmed joy? Is death their perfecter? Is death now not the author maybe, but the "finisher," of their faith? How can that be, since in Scripture the grave is always spoken of as an enemy? Maybe there is some sort of "purgatory" for the dead as the Roman church claims? This cannot be, for the Bible knows of no such doctrine as purgatory. That being said, the dead must somehow be cleansed from the sin that still plagued them when their probation closed at death. Again I have to ask, do they get a free pass? Would that be just and fair?

Now on the other hand we have the poor folks who will not die and have to live through the *"time of trouble"* (Dan. 12:1), they have to deal with an experience which does not involve death. Some have said, "Well, they had better pull it together because they have to be perfect!" "If they are even a tad off, if they offend in action or even in thought either consciously or subconsciously, well then, sizzle on them!" I've already shown what the Word says about sinners seeing the face of God. If we have sin within us that meeting is not a

---

20 These two references are from the game of Monopoly published by Hasbro.

survivable experience. We also read things like the following from the book The Great Controversy: "Now, while our great High Priest is making the atonement for us, we should seek to become perfect in Christ. **Not even by a thought could our Saviour be brought to yield to the power of temptation...** <u>This is the condition in which those must be found who shall stand in the time of trouble.</u>"[21]

With those kinds of assertions, is it any wonder that some people's hearts *"fail them for fear?"* (Luke 21:26). It is stated that the living must be completely empty of all sinful desire, with no hint of rebellion or any sympathy with the *"enemy of God and man."*[22] Since that's how the living must be found. I'll ask you a question: Is that how you find yourself? I can tell you I don't. Even with all that Christ Jesus has done for me and in me, I still fall woefully short of true holiness.

So the question persists, are there two Saviors? Two ways to be saved? Is there one Saviour and one way for those who die? Do they get a free pass by the justifying blood of Christ and absolute moral perfection "<u>somehow</u>" by way of the grave? Is there another Saviour and another way for the living? This other way would be blatantly unfair compared to the righteous dead's requirements. It requires the living to obtain actual moral perfection here and now. Oh, and what's more, they must maintain this perfection in the face of mental, emotional, and physical conditions whose extreme severity will have been unparalleled in this world's history. (See Dan.12:1) We are told that there will be no restraint placed on the devil's tempting of the righteous during the time of trouble. "As Satan accuses the people of God on account of their sins, the Lord permits him to try them to the uttermost."[23] To the uttermost!! WOW!! If they crack, then what?

It sure seems that there is a huge and unfair difference here! If you aren't careful you run the risk of thinking that all are saved by faith in Christ alone, except the last poor "les miserables.'[24] They must somehow pull it together and keep it together. Is this idea

---

21 The Great Controversy pg. 623
22 Desire of Ages pg. 209
23 The Great Controversy pg.618
24 les miserables Victor Hugo Published 1862

consistent with a just God who is no respecter of persons? Will it be a "survival of the fittest" in the end? Are those who can't "cut it," cut? There must be a way to reconcile these contradictions. They seem so mixed up, so dead wrong... (Sorry, I couldn't resist the pun.) There is a way to reconcile them however! *"Thy way, O God, is in the sanctuary: who is so great a God as our God?"* (Ps. 77:13)

Dog's Breakfast, Ingredient 4 "The Empty Throne"

"And at that time shall Michael stand up,
the Great Prince which standeth for the children of thy people:
and there shall be a time of trouble, such as never was since
there was a nation even to that same time"
Daniel 12:1

Now some will strenuously object to all this perfection talk and say, "Hold your horses, bub! I'm relying on the justification that is in the blood of Jesus! I'll be okay! I'm good to go, safe as houses!" "The death of Christ for my sins is all I need during the time of trouble! I'll be fine!! I'll be relying on that sacrifice for the covering of my sins and shortcomings!"

I will reply that your confidence in the blood of Jesus to justify you is wonderfully commendable. But you need to ask yourself one thing. Will that blood still be available in the time of trouble to cover your sins and shortcomings? Will the ministry of Christ still be going on during the great time of trouble? Is that ministry to go on for all time?

An End to the Atoning, and Justifying Blood

"Now where remission of these is, there is no more offering for sin."
Hebrews 10:18

You will remember that when Jesus instituted the Lord's supper He told His disciples, *"This is My blood of the New Testament, which is shed for many. Verily I say unto you, I will drink no more of the fruit of the vine, until that day that I drink it new in the kingdom of God"* (Mark 14:24, 25). Have you ever stopped to ask yourself why Jesus would not drink of the fruit of the vine until He drank it new in the kingdom? I remember being sad as a child when I heard this. "Poor Jesus," I thought, "why can't He have grape juice for so long?" To understand why Christ will not drink the juice of the grape until He drinks it new in the kingdom, we must ask the following question: What did/does the blood in the symbol of the Lord's supper signify?

God told the children of Israel, *"... the life of the flesh is in <u>the blood</u>: and I have given it to you upon the altar to <u>make an atonement for your souls</u>: for it is the blood that maketh an atonement for the soul"* (Lev. 17:11). It is the blood that justifies the sinner before God. At the institution of the Lord's Supper Christ established the symbol of the wine representing His blood. His blood brings atonement to the sinner. If you will reflect a moment, it will become apparent that Christ is not in need of an atonement. He is the sinless, spotless Lamb of God. If He were to afterward drink of the fruit of the vine, the symbol of the atonement, some might say that He was also in need of atonement. This is not the case. If Jesus is not sinless He cannot be our perfect sacrifice. He could not be our Saviour if he had any blemish of sin. For our sake, Christ would not leave us in the slightest doubt as to the validity of His sacrifice for us. Therefore He declared that He would not drink of the fruit of the vine.

Question: Why then did He go on to say that He would some day drink it new with us? He was leaving us a powerful declaration that the day was coming when the atonement would be completed. Then the symbol would no longer be needed. Remember the Lord's supper was only to be observed *"till He come"* (1 Cor. 11:26). After His coming He can drink of the vine because the atonement will have been finished. The ministry of Christ for sin will have ceased. This same truth is also shown in the Sanctuary service of the Old Testament.

A Parable of Salvation

The whole sanctuary service is an illustration of the plan of salvation. This plan has been prefigured by the services that took place in the earthly sanctuary. The substance or reality of the prefigured salvation began for real with the death of Christ, the Lamb of God. As Paul says: *"This* [the sanctuary service] *is an illustration pointing to the present time. For the gifts and sacrifices that the priests offer are not able to cleanse the consciences of the people who bring them"* (Heb. 9:9 NLT). In the sanctuary of the Old Testament we have an <u>illustration</u> of how God is now working in <u>reality</u> for our salvation. Since that is the case we should be able to use the illustrations in the sanctuary services on earth to understand what is going on in heaven.

This book is not going to go into all the types we see in the earthly sanctuary services in great detail. That is not the purpose of this book. It was not Paul's purpose in writing Hebrews either, as he said, *"Above the Ark were the cherubim of divine glory, whose wings stretched out over the Ark's cover, the place of atonement. But we cannot explain these things in detail now"* (Heb. 9:5 NLT).

We do need to take a broad overview of those services however. The service in the earthly sanctuary as a whole was called the "yearly service," and it had two parts. The "daily" service culminated in the service called "The Day of Atonement." After this last service was performed, the people were blessed by the high priest and were considered to be perfect before God. Of course, the symbolic daily service was repeated every year. This repetition was to instruct, through types, figures, and symbols all future generations. The point we want to especially note, is that at the end of the day of atonement, the sacrifice for sin ceased! This was to illustrate that there is going to come an end to Christ's work in heaven as well. There is coming a time when the justification that is in the blood of Jesus will no longer be available. It is by virtue of that atoning blood that the whole world now stands justified before God. (see Col. 1:20, 22 NLT)

If the sacrifice of Christ is to end then it will no longer be available to cover the sinner. It can no longer be something which can be relied on or offered to God for our sins or our sinful condition. When the ministry of Christ ceases in heaven <u>we will be before God what we are</u>! Anyone who is in any way sinful will then be exposed! The dreadful thing is that we are all sinful, and none of us are perfect! How can we live before God when the throne of mercy is vacated? Again the question must be asked, *"How can these things be?"*

Have a Seat!

The Bible says that the work of Christ in the heavenly sanctuary began with Him taking a seat: *"Who being the brightness of His glory, and the express image of His person, and upholding all things by the word of His power, when He had by Himself purged our sins, <u>sat down</u> on the right hand of the Majesty on high"* (Heb. 1:3). We read also, *"... this man, after He had offered one sacrifice for sins for ever, sat down on the right hand of God"* (Heb. 10:12).

It may surprise you to learn that He hasn't moved since, for *"...there He waits until His enemies are humbled and made a footstool under His feet"* (Heb 10:13 NLT). Christ Jesus doesn't have to move around the heavenly sanctuary, performing all the various sacrifices as the earthly priests did, in order to cover all the aspects of salvation. (See Heb. 9:24-26) Those different sacrifices, all prefigured the one all-sufficient sacrifice that Jesus made on the cross, *"For by <u>that one offering</u> He perfected forever all those whom*

He is making holy" (Heb. 10:14 NLT). He then sat down there at the right hand of God in honor and power.

Waiting...Waiting...

So Christ is sitting on the throne of God, mediating for His people and waiting. This is what Daniel prophesied about. Christ will sit at the right hand of God until His work there is done, and then *"shall Michael stand up,...and there shall be a time of trouble,...and at that time Thy people shall be delivered, every one that shall be found written in the book"* (Dan. 12:1). Christ will wait until His work on behalf of sinners is completed. Then John the revelator declares, "... *the seventh angel poured out his vial into the air; and there came a great voice out of the temple of heaven, from the throne, saying, It is done*" (Rev. 16:17). There is coming an end to the plan of salvation! Very soon the work will be complete. The final atonement will be made. Noah's Ark was a long time in the making and then one day it was done. The animals entered it, the last invitation to mercy was given by Noah, and unexpectedly the door of mercy was shut. It was suddenly all over. It was a week later that the wicked knew it, mind you, but when that door closed there was no more provision for salvation! When the work on the ark was complete, the offer of salvation expired!

In Hebrews we read, *"Now where remission of these is, <u>there is no more offering for sin</u>"* (Heb. 10:17, 18). The sense of the original language in this passage says in essence that when the plan of salvation is finished, there will be no more need to offer up sacrifice. If the final offering for sin is made and you are found outside the results of that grace, is there now any other sacrifice that you can use to be saved? The door will be closed! The justifying blood of Christ will cease its pleading in the sinners behalf. God has illustrated this truth in other ways as well. Do you remember what Paul said in Hebrews? That the cover of the ark in the sanctuary was the place of atonement? It also had another name, "the Mercy Seat!" (see Exod. 25:20) It was on that seat of mercy that Christ sat when He took His place at the right hand of God. When He stands up that seat will be vacant, symbolizing that God's mercy will have come to an end. Then, as stated previously, we will be before God what we truly are! The declaration will go out: *"He that is unjust, let him be unjust still: and he which is filthy, let him be filthy still: and he that is righteous, let him be righteous still: and he that is holy, let him be holy still"* (Rev. 22:11). Absolute, actual, moral perfection will again be the only acceptable condition before God. It will be a very solemn moment.

I can hear some of us wailing, "How is such a thing to be?" "If we are not able to achieve this condition of perfection, how is this perfection to be realized"? Do you remember the four divisions we talked about? The "Conservderate Army," The "Non-Combatants," the "Deserters" and the "No Man's Landers"? When you understand the reality of the "Empty Throne" and realize that God's offer of mercy has an expiration date, well, it is then that we see the various reactions that we discussed. It is then that they exhibit themselves and their destructive influence in our church family.

There are only two last problems to tackle before we start to examine some reassuring and beautiful things in Scripture. Beautiful things that will reconcile all of these seeming contradictions and problems. I know, that's a lot to promise, but this is God's truth we are talking about, and His word produces results that are incredible.

Dog's Breakfast, Ingredient 5
"The Delayed Coming of Christ!"

"And as it was in the days of Noe,
so shall it be also in the days of the Son of man."
Luke 17:26

The fifth ingredient of our dog's breakfast has to do with the seemingly long delay in the return of Jesus. Many of us say, by our actions if not by our words, that Christ's second coming is a long way off. We live as though this delay means that the time for His return may never come in our lifetime. Many of us say that it has been a long, long time since 1844 and the midnight cry *"Behold the bridegroom cometh"* (Matt. 25:6). No need to get excited. *"My lord delayeth His coming"* (Matt. 24:48). One Sabbath I mentioned the soon return of Jesus in a chapel session I was conducting. A young man in the congregation piped up. He stated with great emphasis and confidence that nothing has ever really changed. People had always killed other people, there had always been natural disasters. We had been saying Christ was going to come "forever!" All of this skepticism was expressed with the most provokingly smug sneer you can imagine. I was tempted to be irritated with this guy, but the Spirit of God kept control of my sinful nature and I heard myself thanking this lad for helping me make my point. He looked puzzled and didn't seem to regard my gratitude with much appreciation. I then quoted the Scripture that he had, doubtless, been referring to: *"Knowing this first, that there shall come in the last days scoffers, walking after their own lusts, and saying, Where is the promise of His coming? for since the fathers fell asleep, all things continue as they were from the beginning of the creation"* (2 Peter 3:3,4). Funny thing, his helpful comments seemed to dry up after that, but before we are too hard on that young man it must be acknowledged that these are sentiments which many people, even Seventh-day "Adventists" share.

Why So Long?

Why so long? It is a question that has been asked by the homesick children of God and scoffers down through time; *"And they cried with a loud voice, saying, How long, O Lord, holy and true, dost thou not judge and avenge our blood on them that dwell on the earth?"* (Rev. 6:10) This was the cry of the souls of them that were *"slain for the word of God, and for the testimony which they held"* (Rev. 6:9). It is a valid question. When Christ cried out on the cross *"It is finished!"* (John. 19:30), why wasn't it "finished?" Was it actually finished? What was finished? I always wondered that as a kid. Why did this horrible nightmare of sin not come to an end then and there at the cross? "Well" some will say, "the world had to be told about Jesus!" Fair enough, but doesn't the Bible say that the

Gospel went everywhere? Some Jews in Thessalonica when, (unintentionally) testifying to the power of God in the disciples stated that, *"these that <u>have turned the world upside down</u> are come hither also"* (Acts 17:6). The Gospel under the power of the Holy Spirit had spread everywhere, even into Caesar's Palace. (see Phil 4:22). Couldn't things have ended then and there? The population at that time is estimated to have been around 150-330 million people. That's a lot less people to reach with the Gospel than there are now. Now there are more than 7.5 billion!

I have heard it said that "God is waiting for one more." There is certainly some truth to this for we read, *"The Lord is not slack concerning His promise, as some men count slackness; but is longsuffering to us-ward, not willing that any should perish, but that all should come to repentance"* (2 Peter 3:9). However, it says right after, that *"...the day of the Lord will come as a thief in the night."* (2 Pet. 3:10). The day is coming like a thief! It appears that the suddenness of Christ's return will be like the closing of a trap to the unready. If so, it will catch many off guard. Christ warned about this over and over again. If some are caught unready, doesn't that fact conflict with the idea of just waiting for one more? Peter's words indicate that if some are caught sleeping, they could have been that "one more."

Christ warned that, *"... as the days of Noe were, so shall also the coming of the Son of man be. For as in the days that were before the flood they were eating and drinking, marrying and giving in marriage, until the day that Noe entered into the ark, And knew not until the flood came, and took them all away; so shall also the coming of the Son of man be"* (Matt. 24:37- 39). Life was going along, just as it had since the beginning and then, one day, the work on the ark was finished and the door to the ark which had stood open all those years was abruptly closed! All of a sudden it was forever too late. Many who fought for their lives in the waters of the flood soon after, must have vainly wished for a do over. They must have longed for one last chance to enter into the sanctuary provided by God.

God is not trying to trick people is He? Is He blamable for lulling everyone into a false sense of security so He can catch them napping? That is not in line with the character of One who does not want even one to perish! There is a promise given for us who live in this time. *"A noise shall come even to the ends of the earth; for the LORD hath a controversy with the nations, He will plead with <u>all flesh</u>"* (Jer. 25:31). Notice it says it will be noisy. The Lord says that no one will be left "un-pled" with. No one in the world will be left out. All will have an opportunity to enter into the safety of the Sanctuary that God has provided, but the end will come, and very suddenly.

Tick Tick

There is a warning needed here before we head to the last of our dog's breakfast ingredients. It is a warning against complacent, spiritual hammock surfing. When it comes to the return of Jesus, many of us have grown tired and seemingly bored. We say, "the clock has been ticking a long time now." We are tempted to turn away from our watching for Christ's return to see if there is something fun going on out there in the world. I'd like to make an observation and give a warning to those of us buying into this temptation.

Have you ever watched a movie about a ticking time bomb? I saw a movie like that in my teens. This was during the cold war era (I know, I just dated myself). I can't remember the title now, but that movie really stressed me out! If I remember correctly there was a nuclear bomb in the harbor of a big city. It had a timer on a detonator counting down to "Dooms Day." The suspense I felt watching that movie was intense and grew more intense as the story unfolded. Imagine yourself, if you will, in that scenario. A nuclear bomb is set to detonate and there is nowhere to go to get away! Now imagine, unlike the movie, that the timer on this bomb has no display on it to tell you when it is going to go off. You only know that the bomb is on a timer wired to a thermonuclear warhead with a big red hammer and sickle on it (it was the 80s). You can hear the clock ticking and know that it will go off without warning.

Would it be reasonable to expect you, and the people working to diffuse the bomb, to become more and more complacent the longer the ticking went on? Maybe you would order in a pizza and a couple of hammocks, right? Maybe head off down the street and catch a movie to pass the time? Of course you wouldn't! No one in their right mind would relax because someone said "hey, don't sweat it. It's been ticking a long time now, no need to worry, it could go on for years!" That would be crazy, right? If they <u>truly believed</u> a catastrophic explosion was coming, the tension would rise with every second that went by!

Well, the clock has been ticking, brothers and sisters. It has been counting down to the actual, real life return of Christ. It has been ticking for more than 174 years....ticktock, ticktock... soon it will stop ticking! Is now any time for God's professed people to become complacent? Is this the time to turn from your working and watching? There is an explanation for why the time has been so long. This explanation is found in a legal process which takes a certain amount of time. Like the work on the ark, that process is almost finished. Soon this process of "probation" will be over!

Dog's Breakfast, Ingredient 6
"Probationary Time"
Our Very Own Adventist Hell Fire?

*"For yourselves know perfectly that the day of the Lord
so cometh as a thief in the night. "*
1 Thessalonians 5:2

When I was growing up, I encountered an evangelistic tactic used by some preachers to get the attention of young people. They had an ace up their sleeves called "The Close of Probation!" To this day the hair on the back of some people's necks stands up when they hear that phrase! They get cold sweats and a resentment towards those preachers is often still felt. People don't like to be threatened and coerced by fear. I can sympathize with the preachers from my youth to an extent. Getting the young people to think about eternal things while they are so full of the newness of life, their future, and the world all around them, is no easy task. But many preachers have forgotten that Jesus said, *"...Suffer little children, and forbid them not to come to Me"* (Matt. 19:14). He did not say, "Scare the stuffing out of the little children so that they will come to Me." Using the threat of being lost to gather souls is a proposition of diminishing returns! People may come from fear, but the sad result is that once the fear has died out, they drift away. Like the villagers in the story of the shepherd boy that cried "WOLF," they become hardened against warning.

Also, there is another more deadly idea that comes from this "Adventist hell fire/close of probation" message. It seems that many of us look on the close of probation as a last chance proposition. You'd better get ready, smarten up, and toe the line before time runs out! Some of us either think or say we are on "probation" like a person released from prison. We seem to think, that God is looking to see if we can keep our nose clean in the spiritual world. If we can't, and violate our probation, well...sizzle on us! Many of us view the close of probation as a threat! "Am I ready?" Those stressed out and tearful words have been uttered in my hearing by many a saint. Many of us have no certain hope to base our salvation on. We view the "close of probation" as a hard deadline. We had better have arranged all our filthy-rag-righteousness in just such a way that if God squints just so at a distance of a hundred paces, we will pass our final "parole" hearing and "squeak in." Is this the basis of a healthy relationship between God and His children? Will this view result in true love to God? Is this what the Bible means when it says, *"I led Israel along with My ropes of kindness and love. I lifted the yoke from his neck, and I Myself stooped to feed him"* (Hosea. 11:4 NLT)? I don't think so.

Question: Is uncertainty in regards to our eternal life what God wants? If that were the case, why did the Spirit say, *"These things have I written unto you that believe on the name of the Son of God; that ye may know that ye have eternal life, and that ye may believe* on the name of the Son of God" (1 John. 5:13)? This phrase "Close of Probation" has been used a lot. It has been used to frighten many people into a cowering, fearful and unhealthy, association with God. Is it a phrase that should never be used at all? I don't believe so. If it is used, it should be used after explaining what it is referring to and that may not be what most people think! This term is used for a legal process which we will explore later, and not as a threat, so stay tuned.

"Les Restes"
(french for "leftovers")

So there we have our leftovers for the dogs. We have some serious conundrums here. There are some grave problems among them! Problems that derail and sicken peoples' lives. It's time for a recap of our "Dog's Breakfast":

1) The Judgment
2) The Perfect Remnant
3) The Cheating Dead
4) The Empty Throne
5) The Delayed Return
6) Probationary Time

That's our mess. For years, I just couldn't see any scriptural doctrine that could resolve and reconcile these seeming contradictions of Scripture with Scripture, and spirit of prophecy quote with spirit of prophecy quote. No matter how many platitudes and trite spiritual "Band Aids"[25] I was offered, there always seemed to be another contradiction in this dilemma of a justified but imperfect people and a soon visible, Holy, God. I could not square these things with the reality of the human frailties and weaknesses, that we are all confronted with every day. It had all been to me a "Dog's Breakfast," until now...

---

25 *BAND-AID*®

PART II
The "Lost" Will and Testament

"...It was needful for me to write unto you,
and exhort you that ye should earnestly contend
for the faith which was once delivered unto the saints."
Jude 1:3

Now we come to the second part of this book. I am so glad to leave for a while the previous section with its difficulties, paradoxes, and confusing contradictions. This next section will require some reflection. Too often we are content to be spoon fed instead of trying to comprehend the truth for ourselves. Please take the time for prayerful reflection and really try to understand what you are reading. This is not a race. The Scripture above calls us to earnest effort when it comes to securing a true faith. We must have the original and correct faith, the faith which is from Jesus and that will give us access to His grace. The fact that this faith was *"once delivered.. unto the saints,"* and that we *"should earnestly contend"* for it, hints at the probability that it has been misplaced, if not lost.

Let's look at something in the Scriptures that has been hiding in plain sight from me and apparently everyone else I know. I had seen hints of this marvelous truth here and there in the Scriptures. Those hints had been fragmented in my mind until the day I confessed to God that I didn't understand things at all. Then I experienced the truth of the Scripture that says: *"When you bow down before the Lord and admit your dependence on Him, He will lift you up"* (James 4:10 NLT). True to that promise He has answered me in His own good time and way. I would like to share with you what He has revealed to me in His word. It has brought me peace as I work and wait for that great day and *"the appearing of our LORD Jesus Christ"* (1 Tim. 6:14).

As we go through the next section we will have to do a bit of rubble clearing. There have been many man-based theories put forward when it comes to the perfecting of the saints. They have come in and destroyed the Christ-centered simplicity and symmetry of the Gospel. These theories have undermined and pulled down the truth until it seems like there is nothing left but a jumbled up pile of rubble. The devil has been hard at work warring against the truth and God's people. It has been a long and protracted siege. As when Nehemiah repaired the walls of Jerusalem; that which Babylon has fragmented and broken down must be removed. The foundation of truth must be laid bare for us to build our hope and assurance on. That foundation is Christ Jesus alone. *"For other foundation can no man lay than that is laid, which is Jesus Christ"* (1 Cor. 3:11). It may take some time to dig down to that "Rock," but this is better than building our faith on sand (see Luke 6:47-49).

A Road Map

I don't know about you, but when I'm on a journey I really like to know where I'm going. I have noticed that I do much better if I have a general idea of the route I'll be taking. It gives me reassurance if I know what way marks I should be seeing. For the sake of book reading felicity, here is an outline of where we will be heading in the coming chapters:

1) The Lost Will and Testament
   a) There exists a Will.
   b) Why was this Will made?
   c) By whom was it executed?
   d) Who is this Will for? Is it for me?
   e) When are the riches in this Will to be dispersed to the heirs named in this Will.
   f) What does this Will means to you, me, and our loved ones; with the burning question, "What is in the Will for us / me?"

2) Revisit the "Dog's Breakfast" (which we have just finished) and plug those issues into this framework of understanding, and see if their seeming contradictions still remain.

3) Examine how an understanding of this important truth, should impact the various attitudes and reactions, we saw exhibited in the four divisions in the church; discussed at the beginning of this book.

Chapter 6
The Sanctuary

*"Thy way, O God, is in the sanctuary:
who is so great a God as our God?"*
Psalm 77:13

As a church we came out from the remnants of the Millerite movement, a movement in 1844 based on the prophetic 2300 day/year prophecy in Daniel (Dan. 8:14). It was confidently declared that Christ would return on October 22, 1844 to cleanse the sanctuary with fire and take His faithful and waiting children home to be where He is. This calculation of the 2300 day prophecy, though not shown by any of its opponents to be faulty, ended in disappointment. The discouragement of those who believed the Scriptures was severe!

That disappointment drove some of those believers to their Bibles. It was soon seen in the Scriptures that the sanctuary was not the earth, which was the opinion of most Christians at that time. That assumption was shown to be false. The Scriptures plainly declared in Hebrews and in other places, that God had built a sanctuary in heaven. *Now of the things which we have spoken this is the sum: We have such an high priest, who is set on the right hand of the throne of the Majesty in the heavens; A minister of the sanctuary, and of the true tabernacle, which the Lord pitched, and not man.... as Moses was admonished of God when he was about to make the tabernacle: for, See, saith He, that thou* <u>*make all things according to the pattern*</u> *shewed to thee in the mount"* (Heb. 8:1-5).

It was seen by those disappointed ones that the sanctuary on earth was a model, type, or illustration of a real sanctuary in Heaven. It was this heavenly sanctuary that was to be cleansed beginning on Oct. 22, 1844. The anti-typical day of atonement had then begun: *"It was therefore necessary that the patterns of things in the heavens should be purified with these* [earthly sacrifices]*; but the heavenly* *things themselves with better sacrifices than these. For Christ is not entered into the holy places made with hands, which are the figures of the true; but into heaven itself, now to appear in the presence of God for us"* (Heb. 9:23, 24). What a great and wonderful truth to discover! What a comfort this discovery must have been to those sad and disappointed ones. No matter what the scoffing church and world said, their faith in the Scriptures was seen to be validated.

Chotskies

"Chotskie" is a modern slang word for the little bobbles and trinkets that people buy to put on a shelf and clutter up their homes. The church was shown the truth about the sanctuary, its cleansing, and the judgment message associated with it. We also saw *"that we have a great high priest, that is passed into the heavens, Jesus the Son of God"* (Heb 4:14). A great spiritual awakening ensued, and then what happened? Did this great truth just become a Chotskie? It seems we settled down after wiping the sweat from our worried brows and felt in our hearts that we were *"rich, and increased with goods"* (Rev. 3:17). How is it with us today? How relevant is this great and vital truth to us as a church? How relevant is it to you and me in our everyday lives? Jesus has gone to heaven and will come again we say, and yes He will. But do you know <u>what</u> Jesus has been doing in heaven for almost two thousand years? I've heard many say, "well, He's building mansions" (quoting John 14). I would like to point something out to you about that text. It says, *"In my Father's house <u>are</u> many mansions: if it were not so, I would have told you. I go to prepare a place for you. And if I go and prepare a place for you, I will come again"* (John 14:2, 3). Please note the underlined. It says there "are" many mansions. It does not say "I'm going to <u>build</u> many mansions."

I've been involved with the building trades for a lot of years and believe me, I've seen how far behind and delayed building projects can get! Is that what we're looking at here? Is it logical to say that a God, who can speak this vast and intricate world, to say nothing of our solar system, into existence in six days would need over 700,000 days to build some mansions? Please note that Jesus said that He went to "*prepare a place*" for us. What does that mean? What does that work entail? "By His death He [Christ] began that work which after His resurrection He ascended to complete in heaven."[26] If the foundation of that work was the cross, then the work He is performing must be something of a spiritual nature. It must have something to do with the plan of salvation and the work of preparing a place for us spiritually. It cannot just be mansion building.

"What has He been doing then?" That was a question that was thrust on me one day by the Holy Spirit. I candidly had to admit to Him that I had no clear answer. When I've asked others the same question, I've gotten some of the same replies I gave myself back then. "He is pleading for us..." "He is interceding for us..." "He is our advocate in court..." Okay... but that told me very little on a practical level. What was He really doing?

I decided to ask God this question. A question which I didn't have any good, practical answers to. I asked Him, "Lord, does it really matter if I know?" Yes, it does! "The subject of the sanctuary and the investigative judgment should be clearly understood by the people of God. All need a knowledge for themselves of the position and work of their great High Priest. Otherwise it will be impossible for them to exercise the faith which is essential at this time or to occupy the position which God designs them to fill.[27] The more I looked into it, the clearer it became that a personal understanding of Christ's work in heaven right now is VERY important!

So how about you? Do you have a clear understanding of what is going on in the sanctuary in heaven? Is the mediation of Christ crystal clear to you? Do you know what it is all about? Do you have a knowledge for yourself, or is your understanding just based on vague platitudes and catch phrases? I had to be honest with God when I answered these questions. It was not clear to me at all. I didn't really know what Jesus has and will be doing, and that was a big problem!

---

26 The Great Controversy pg.489
27 The Great Controversy pg.488

The Scriptures say that it is Jesus that mediates the new covenant between God and Man in the sanctuary (See Heb. 12:24). Since that is the case, then the work that it is so vital for us to understand, the work that if not understood clearly will make it impossible for us to exercise a faith that we _must_ have, that work is found in the mediation of the New Covenant. Mediating the new covenant? What does that mean?

This is something which we must not just shrug our shoulders and relegate to the Chotskie shelf. I'll tell you now that a clear understanding of the mediation of the New Covenant by Jesus, and what its results are will resolve the problems that we have been looking at in this book regarding perfection and the judgment, etc... Shall we go on?

The Book of Hebrews

The book of Hebrews is a key in the New Testament. This key unlocks to our understanding the mysteries of the earthly sanctuary service of the Old Testament. It is similar to the book of Daniel which unlocks the mysteries of the book of Revelation. In Hebrews we find explained the important and vital themes that were prefigured by the earthly sanctuary and its services. Most importantly it tells us what Christ's work in the heavenly sanctuary will finally accomplish.

In the tabernacle which Moses built as a pattern of the real one in heaven (see Heb. 8:5), we see two services. The first service was known as the "Daily" service. It went on day by day throughout the year. The other service was called the "Day of Atonement." These two services were two parts of one whole.

Shadows Within Shadows

The Daily service in the earthly sanctuary built by Moses, was/is a representation of God's plan for the salvation of Man through the ministry of Jesus. In symbol we find the blood of the sacrifice, making the believer right with God. We see the sins of the individual transferred from themselves to the lamb, and by the lamb's blood, the sins of the believer were removed to the Sanctuary. We have the symbol of baptism in the washing laver. There is depicted the fiery consuming of the sin offering, representing the fierce indignation against sin that the Father poured out on His dearest Son for sinful man. Also we have the sanctuary building itself. In this tent, there were two compartments or rooms called the "Holy" and the "Most Holy" places.

Have you ever stopped to compare the inside of the Tabernacle? Have you looked at the similarities, between the "Holy Place" and the "Most Holy Place?" Remember, the symbols in these two rooms, were shadowy representations. They illustrated what Christ was to accomplish in Heaven after His death. But here in this foreshadowing we also find shadows within shadows. Lets take a look at a list of the symbols we see in each room:

"Holy Place"

1. The daily renewed bread of the presence in covered bowls.
2. An altar of incense.
3. Angels embroidered on the veil.
4. The light of the golden candlestick.
5. The blood of the sacrifice sprinkled.

"Most Holy Place"

1) The pot of manna in the Ark of the Covenant. This bread was never replaced, or ever spoiled!
2) An incense burner between the two Cherubim.
3) The two three-dimensional Cherubim on each side of the Ark.
4) The Shekinah Glory, God's visible presence.
5) The Blood of the final atonement sprinkled.

Do you see the similarities? The Most Holy Place has all the same representations as the Holy Place, but to a much greater degree. The daily services that were carried on in the first room and the furniture in that room were a lesser representation of what is hidden from sight just behind the veil in the Most Holy Place; which was off limits under pain of death.

Something More

This imagery was presented to show us that the Most Holy Place had something much more complete and real in it than the Holy Place. In the inner apartment, the Cherubim were in three-dimensional shape, unlike the two-dimensional images woven into the separating veil. In the Most Holy Place, was the unspoiled manna, contrasting with the Holy place's bread, that had to be continually renewed. Here, above all else, was seen, not seven dim oil burning candle sticks, but the actual, eternal, and visible glory of God! It's as if God was saying to them, and is saying to us, that in spite of the daily service and its ceremonies, "There is something more, behind the veil," something that is more complete and real, something yet to come on the anti-typical day of atonement.

We see this same intimation everywhere in the New Testament. There we find justification by Christ's blood through faith in God's promise. We have righteousness by faith, and yet it says,*"For we through the Spirit <u>wait</u> for the <u>hope</u> of <u>righteousness by faith</u>"*

(Gal. 5:5). As stated before, when Paul says "hope" he is speaking of something that is eagerly awaited. As he says, *"For we are saved by hope: but hope that is seen is not hope: for what a man seeth, why doth he yet hope for? But if we hope for that we see not, then do we with patience wait for it"* (Rom. 8:24, 25).   We are told in no uncertain terms that there is a righteousness by faith that is yet future! There is something more promised than the justification and sanctification which we now possess.

Paul states that *"...we believers also groan, even though we have the Holy Spirit within us as a foretaste of future glory"* (Rom. 8:23 NLT); and Peter says that *"...Now we live with great expectation, and we have a priceless inheritance—an inheritance that is kept in heaven for you, pure and undefiled, beyond the reach of change and decay. And through your faith, God is protecting you by His power until you receive this salvation, which is ready to be revealed on the last day for all to see"* (1 Peter 1:3-5 NLT). Just as there were shadows within shadows in the sanctuary, so it is with the work of salvation. We do not see or possess all that has been promised to us. There is a salvation yet to be reveled. There is something more yet to come, something better, something to be given in the future and it is found and revealed in an inheritance!

Chapter 7

Inheritance

There are seen throughout the Scriptures themes, fragments, and imagery which on the surface may seem to be random. One of these themes is that of an inheritance. From the earliest Scripture we find the promise of a Saviour. Hand in glove with that promise is also the promise of an inheritance. One of the first promises of this inheritance was the one given to Abraham by God. *"And He said unto him, I Am the LORD that brought thee out of Ur of the Chaldees, to give thee this land to inherit it. And he* [Abraham] *said, Lord GOD, whereby shall I know that I shall inherit it? And He said unto him, Take Me an heifer* [for a sacrifice] *of three years old"* (Gen. 15:7, 8, 9). This promise of an inheritance was confirmed and made binding by God through the death of a sacrifice. What was this covenant all about? What did Abraham receive from this covenant? Did he receive only a binding promise? When we look closely at this story we find something very interesting. Though Abraham received a confirmed promise from a God who can never lie, the question must be asked: Did Abraham receive the land as an inheritance?

The answer to that question is no. The Scriptures say, *"And He* [God] *gave him* [Abraham] *none inheritance in it, no, not so much as to set his foot on: yet He promised that He would give it to him for a possession, and to his Seed after him"* (Acts 7:5). So the Scriptures says that even though God had promised that Abraham would receive the land as an inheritance, Abraham did not receive it! Not even a square foot of it. Did God fail in keeping His promise then? How did Abraham understand this covenant promise? Did he consider it simply a gift of land, or was there something more to it? We might think that he took the promise to mean that it was his children which would inherit the land. But we must read the promise carefully. God told him that he and his seed would inherit the land. Yet, as we have just read, Abraham didn't receive a single solitary square foot!

How then did Abraham understand the inheritance God had promised him? We read the following: *"By faith Abraham, when he was called to go out into a place which he should after receive for an inheritance, obeyed; and he went out, not knowing whither he went. By faith he sojourned in the land of promise, as in a strange country, dwelling in tabernacles with Isaac and Jacob, the heirs with him of the same promise: For he looked for a city which hath foundations, whose builder and maker is God"* (Heb. 11:8-10). Please note the absence of earthly foundations in Abraham's life. Tents have no fixed foundations. His expectation was not to inherit the land of Canaan, as it was then constituted. His expectation of an inheritance was in an earth made new; in a city made by God, a city whose foundations are eternal. The New Jerusalem.

So the promise was seen by Abraham as a promise of heaven, not a promise of a dwelling place on this sin-filled planet. Was permanence of possession all that was implied? Was it just a temporal promise of prime heavenly real estate? No, this promise contained much more. Revelation tells us what kind of people will dwell in the city of God. It does this by giving us a clear picture of those who will and will not live there; *"And there shall in no wise enter into it* [the Holy city] *any thing that defileth, neither whatsoever worketh abomination, or maketh a lie"* (Rev. 21:27). We also read this concerning those who will live there: *"Blessed are they that do His commandments, that they may have right to the tree of life, and may enter in through the gates into the city. For without are dogs, and sorcerers, and whoremongers, and murderers, and idolaters, and whosoever loveth and maketh a lie"* (Rev. 22:14, 15).

It is plain from these Scriptures that those who live in that God-built city will be perfectly holy and righteous. Thus we see that along with the promise to Abraham and his seed of an inheritance in the city of God also comes the promise of actual holiness and purity of heart. This is the inescapable conclusion we must draw, for the Scriptures plainly state that no one enters into that city without perfect holiness. This promise was not just for Abraham, it is also for us: *"...For in Christ Jesus neither circumcision availeth any thing, nor uncircumcision, but a new creature. And as many as walk according to this rule, peace be on them, and mercy, and upon the Israel of God"* (Gal. 6:14-16). That this promise is for us, is also stated clearly here as well: *"And if ye be Christ's, then are ye Abraham's seed, and <u>heirs</u> according to the promise"* (Gal. 3:29). So with Abraham we, too, may be heirs of the city of God. By extension, we also have an inheritance which carries with it not just heavenly real estate, but more importantly, perfect righteousness as well.

Birthright

This promise of an inheritance is spoken of in many other places as well. The promise God made to Abraham was passed on to Isaac and from Isaac to Jacob!

Now Jacob is an interesting name. It means "heal snatcher" or "supplanter." We read: "*... Esau, who for one morsel of meat sold his birthright.* [to Jacob] *For ye know how that afterward, when he would have <u>inherited</u> the blessing, he was rejected: for he found no place of repentance, though he sought it carefully with tears"* (Heb. 12:16,17). It is interesting that the birthright and the inheritance of the blessing are here joined together.

Websters dictionary defines a birthright as: "Any right or privilege, to which a person is entitled by birth, such as an estate descendible by law to an heir." In other words Esau, sold his inheritance to Jacob for a worldly consideration! He sold his eternal inheritance in the city of God, and its accompanying righteousness, for pottage! Satan is constantly trying to sell us this world in exchange for our birthright. There is so much more I'm itching to say about this, but I'll refrain for the sake of simplicity. The main point is that Jacob supplanted Esau as heir to an inheritance. Are you at all curious about what that inheritance was? For now I will only quote the Scripture which says, *"Moses commanded us a law, even the inheritance of the congregation of Jacob* (Deut. 33:4). Here Moses says that the inheritance of Jacob, which was passed down to him from his Grandfather Abraham and then passed by him to his descendants, was the Law. The original Hebrew text in this passage, specifies this law as the Decalogue, the Ten Commandments. So it says that the Law of God was promised as an inheritance to the people of God!

Some may now be muttering under their breath something like, "...Nice inheritance! A list of rules..." It remains to be seen what this inheritance of "The Law" is; what it looks like when the Scriptures flesh it out. The Scriptures say "...*judge nothing before the time...*" (1 Cor. 4:5). Some of us may go from muttering to praising God...

New Testament Examples

We find this same inheritance theme in the New Testament as well. Peter writes. "*Whereby are given unto us exceeding great and precious promises*" (2 Peter 1:4). Paul says,"H*e has identified us as His own by placing the Holy Spirit in our hearts as the first installment that guarantees everything He has promised us*" (2 Cor. 1:22 NLT). God has made wonderful promises to His children. He hints that even though we have received a first down payment or installment of salvation, that there is much more yet to come. Speaking of the people in the Old Testament, Paul wrote, "*All these people earned a good reputation because of their faith, yet none of them received all that God had promised*" (Heb. 11:39 NLT). This "much more" comes to us by His promises. These are the same promises that were given to all the patriarchs and Israel. They are the promise of an inheritance, both temporal and spiritual: "*All praise to God, the Father of our Lord Jesus Christ. It is by His great mercy that we have been born again, because God raised Jesus Christ from the dead. Now we live with great expectation, and we have a priceless inheritance*" (1 Peter 1:3, 4 NLT).

The above examples are just a few of the many references to the promised inheritance of the children of God. Now I don't know anyone who objects to an inheritance. Most people are thrilled to be told they have an inheritance. The obvious implication is that if there is an inheritance there must also be a testator – one who has left a bequest. It also follows logically that the way this is done is by the legal execution of a Will! In this case a "Lost Will and Testament." "Why lost?" You ask? Well, I needed, and most of us need to have our eyes opened to recognize that there even is a Will and an inheritance. Christ told Paul when He sent him as an apostle, that his mission was, *"To open their eyes... that they may receive forgiveness of sins, and* <u>inheritance</u> *among them which are sanctified by faith that is in Me"* (Acts 26:18). This opening of our eyes is my prayer as well as we now take a look at what Christ sent Paul to reveal. This is a message concerning His "Will and Testament" and our inheritance therein!

Misapprehension

The word "misapprehension" means to have a mistaken belief about something you think you understand. This happens when we hear something that <u>we think</u> we know all about. In reality, we don't actually understand as we think we do. We slot in our mistaken "knowledge" and proceed in our quest for understanding on a flawed basis.

We as fallen people have motives which are vastly different from God's thoughts and motives, as it is written: "... *My thoughts are not your thoughts, neither are your ways My ways, saith the LORD"* (Isa. 55:8). Our ways are crooked. We received from our first fallen parents their wicked thoughts and desires. When it comes to the relationship we should have with God, this "misapprehension" comes built into us from birth. *"I knew that thou wouldest deal very treacherously, and wast called a transgressor from the womb"* (Isa. 48:8).

It is a hard-wired part of our fallen nature to always try to usurp the place of God. We see this expressed openly in all false religious systems and teachings which put man where God belongs. Mankind has been doing this ever since our first parents believed the lie, *"Ye shall be like Gods"* (Gen. 3:5). Most times this desire to be "God" is hidden subtly from our conscious minds. Whatever the case though, this desire to have a religion and salvation which is centered on man is the natural, humanly unbreakable, tendency of our hearts. This sinful idolatry has been mankind's undoing throughout history.

This man-centric or man-centered religion is seen in all the forms of idolatry which have existed or do exist. A figurehead is set up; this can be a physical statue, or a human leader, but in many cases, especially today, we find ideological idols. These have "God" as the figurehead for the religion, but man looks to himself for salvation. Men trust in their own efforts to please God and win His favor/salvation. This is the same system of deity appeasement that was the basis for the religion of ancient Egypt. If you were good enough, and if you had not done too many bad things, you went to a good place. If on the other hand you had displeased the gods through disobedience, well... you get the picture.

Contamination

For four hundred years, the Children of Israel had been exposed to this false Egyptian misapprehension about how to worship God! They knew of the promise given by God to their fathers to bring them out of Egypt and give them the inheritance of the promised land. Their religion however had become a religion of appeasement. This religion of <u>obedience for blessing</u> had been modeled for them all their lives in Egypt, and this false worship had rubbed off on them! It seems they had this misapprehension so deeply ingrained into their hearts and minds that even later, when they were worshiping God in the wilderness and performing the ceremonial rites He had established, they were essentially pagan at heart. God asked Israel through the prophet Amos, *"Was it to me you were bringing sacrifices and offerings during those forty years in the wilderness, Israel? No, you carried your pagan gods the shrine of Molech, the star of your god Rephan, and the images you made to worship them"* (Acts 7:42, 43 NLT). They were carrying around the tabernacle of God but the worship of their hearts was pagan in its essence. God said of them,*"like all these pagan nations, the people of Israel also have uncircumcised hearts"* (Jer. 9:26). Was it any wonder then, that when God spoke of a "covenant" with them, that they automatically misapprehended it as a, "<u>contract of blessings for services rendered</u>"? Is it strange that they automatically misapprehended His meaning and viewed this covenant as a reward to be given to them for their spiritual attainments?

Hebrews says that the children of Israel couldn't enter God's rest because of unbelief (see Heb. 3:19). They would not believe God would give them the rest He had promised them. Their hearts, being infected by paganism, turned them away from the living God. They misunderstood God's desires for them. They thought He wanted them to earn their covenant blessings by their obedience. They viewed their relationship with Jehovah in fundamentally the same way the Egyptians viewed their relationship with Ra, Horas, or Osiris, the pagan gods of Egypt.

We as Christians also struggle with this misapprehension of the "New Covenant" that has been provided for us. We are warned, *"Be careful then, dear brothers and sisters. Make sure that your own hearts are not evil and unbelieving, turning you away from the living God..."* [to yourselves, and your attainments as Israel was turned away to their idols, the works of their own wills/ hands]. *"You must warn each other every day, while it is still 'today,' so that none of you will be deceived by sin and hardened against God. For if we are faithful to the end, trusting God just as firmly as when we first believed, <u>we will share in all that belongs to Christ</u>"* (Heb. 3:12 NLT).

Human nature is fallen, and our reliance on ourselves for salvation is just as alive today as it was in ancient Israel. The religion of Egypt is still predominant in spiritual Israel today. In fact paganism has been re-branded as Christianity. Satan has just jacked up the hood ornament of the cross and parked a different car under it. Is it possible that we, like the children of Israel, may have misapprehended God's promises? Is our understanding of the covenant made for us also flawed? If it is, we only have to look at the history of Israel in the Old Testament to see that it will end badly for us!

Chapter 8

Diathēkē
What's in a word?

If there is an inheritance, a Lost Will and Testament, why do we not see it plainly presented in Scripture? You may be tempted to say to yourself: "This guy is crazy, where is this Will? I haven't seen it." It is there I can assure you, and it is hiding in plain sight! It is hidden behind a word, and that word is "diathēkē" pronounced "*dee-ath-ay'-kay.*" You may be thinking, "I have no idea what you are talking about, that stuff is all Greek to me." And you are exactly right! It is all Greek! Now I can already hear some of the groans. "Oh no, not a Greek lesson..." Well yes, yes it will be; but I promise to make it as painless as possible, and I can assure you it will be well worth your time, so hang in here!

This word "diathēkē" has been translated as "covenant" many times. "Aha!" you say, slipping on your scholastic cap and gown, "now you are talking! I know what that word covenant means..." Do you? I thought I knew what it meant too!

Okay, so right here and now, before you read on and without consulting your concordance, or dictionary, I'd like you to write out a definition for this word "covenant" (no reading ahead and cheating either).

A covenant is:

_____

_____

_____

Whenever I read this word "covenant," a preconceived definition would snap into place. For years I could instantly give you a definition for "covenant." It would be as follows: "Covenant; the word used in Scripture for a legally binding contract." This definition, in one form or another is the definition that almost everyone I have ever talked to has given me. This definition is accurate, but incomplete when it comes to the Gospel. If you aren't extremely careful and thorough in the way you define this word, it can have you groveling at the foot of mount Sinai instead of being in joyful assembly on Mt. Zion! (see Heb. 12:18-24).

"Diathēkē" Defined

The Strong's Exhaustive Concordance defines this Greek word as follows:

"G1242; "diathēkē; properly a disposition that is (specifically) a contract (especially a devisory Will): - covenant testament."

Reading that definition we can get the idea that this word is to be interpreted specifically as a "contract" or "covenant." I would argue that this word should be interpreted differently from what it has been by most Christians. Before you give up this book as having reached a point where we are going to start splitting hairs: I'll tell you that the way in which we view this word's interpretation will have a serious impact on our faith. Remember, we are saved by grace through faith alone. A correct faith is essential for our final salvation. We have already seen that a misapprehension of what constitutes a covenant has tripped up God's people before!

When we think of this word "covenant" we think of the covenant that God made with Abraham in the Old Testament. The promise He gave Abraham was that He would give him and his descendants the whole world! (See Rom 4:13) We think of the covenant that God made with Israel at Mt. Sinai when He spoke the law in their hearing. We think of the "new covenant" in the New Testament.

Question: Is this "covenant" a contract or agreement <u>between</u> two parties?

Contracts

What do we mean today when we say a covenant is a contract? In our day we still have covenants. In real estate they are called CC&Rs (Covenants, Conditions & Restrictions). These CC&Rs are certain rules and regulations imposed on those who would live in the communities where they are in force. They are something we agree to abide by or do while under, say, a home owner association's authority. We also have business contracts – written agreements that specify the work one party will do for the other party for such and such financial compensation. Is this what we are looking at here?

Was the promise of God to Abraham a contract? Was it God saying *"if you do this,"* say the rite of circumcision, *"I'll give you and your descendants the whole world"*? The Scriptures say unmistakably that the promise was not earned by Abraham through the fulfilling of a contract or agreement. It was a gift. *"For the promise, that he should be the heir of the world, was not to Abraham, or to his seed, through the law, but through the righteousness of faith"* (Rom. 4:13). It was not by keeping the law that Abraham received the promise. In other words, God did not say to him, "Here's the deal Abraham: If you will undergo the rite of circumcision, I'll give you the world as a payment for services rendered!" No, the rite of circumcision came later and was an outward sign which showed that Abraham was an heir according to God's promise. The covenant promise was not based on an exchange. It was not a transaction of payment for services rendered. It was a promise to Abraham and his Seed. This covenant came solely from the unmerited love of God. It came exclusively from His grace.

A Different Type of Contract

Let's go back now and look at the definition of this word that is almost everywhere translated "covenant": *"G1242 "diathēkē: properly a disposition that is (specifically) a contract (especially a devisory Will): - covenant testament."*[28]

28 Strong's Exhaustive Concordance

Let's unpack this definition by a simple perusal of our dictionary. (I know, more groans...)

1) It says this word *"diathēkē"* is properly a *disposition"* What is a disposition? Since it doesn't seem that this word can be referring to a person's sparkling "traits of personality,"[29] I'll have to go with Webster's other definition;

Disposition: The act of disposing...distribution; a giving away or giving over to another; as, he has made disposition of his effects"[30]

2) The definition goes on to say this is "(specifically) a contract"[31] "Aha! See!" some will say, "it is a contract after all!" Yes, it is a contract... contract... contract... thumbs through the massive volume known as Webster's Dictionary and...AHA!

Contract: *"An agreement or covenant between two or more persons, in which each party binds himself to do or forbear some act!"[32]* Here we have to be careful! This word *"contract"* is defined by those other words *"a disposition"* So what the word *"contract"* tells us is that this is a *contract of disposition!* It is an agreement or covenant to dispose or give away to another.

3) It is "especially a devisory Will."[33] When I read this I didn't know what *"devisory"* meant, so I looked it up and found this handy definition from old Mr. Webster.

Devisory: "of or relating to <u>division</u> or distribution."[34]

---

29 Noah Websters 1828
30 Noah Websters 1828
31 Strong's Exhaustive Concordance
32 Noah Websters 1828
33 Strong's Exhaustive Concordance
34 Noah Websters 1828

So in everyday speak the definition is telling us that this word *"diathēkē"* is specifically a contract of disposition that divides and distributes the assets of the one who wrote and signed it. Today we call these contracts "Wills."

Now, working from the assumption that you are still with me and that Mr. Strong, Mr. Webster and I haven't scared you off, it seems obvious from the definitions above that when we see this word, *"diathēkē"* it is not referencing a reciprocal agreement between God and ourselves. It is referring to a Last Will and Testament made by God. We have this same word, *"diathēkē,"* translated as "Testament" when we read Christ's words to His disciples at the last supper. *"For this is My blood of the new Testament, which is shed for many for the remission of sins"* (Matt. 26:28). This word "testament" we see here is the same Strong's *"G1242 "diathēkē,"* that we see so often translated as *"covenant."* I trust one last teeny-weensy definition for this section won't send you screaming into the hills, right?

Question: What is a "Testament?"

4) Testament:
"A solemn authentic instrument in writing, by which a person declares his will as to the disposal of his estate and effects after his death. This is otherwise called a Will."[35]

Alright, so a "Testament" is what we commonly refer to as a "Last Will and Testament" these days. While studying the meaning of *diathēkē* I had a great struggle when it came to relying on the definition of the word alone. I wrestled hard and long with this. Was basing my conclusions simply on a definition safe? Surely, the Scripture I was studying must harmonize with that definition.

I was finally given the reassurance that *"diathēkē"* indeed meant a Will of distribution, when I read in Hebrews; *"That is why He is the one who mediates a new covenant between God and people, so that*

---

35 Noah Websters 1828

all who are called can receive the <u>eternal inheritance</u> God has promised them. For Christ died to set them free from the penalty of the sins they had committed under that first covenant. Now when someone <u>leaves a Will</u>, it is necessary to prove that the person who made it is dead. <u>The Will</u> goes into effect only after the person's death. While the person who made it is still alive, <u>the Will</u> cannot be put into effect" (Heb. 9:15-17 NLT). Here it is spelled out clearly and unmistakably that what we are dealing with in Hebrews is a Last Will and Testament. The definition in the Greek is in harmony with the text's body. By the way, for future reference, please remember that there are conditions that make a Will binding and valid. Were those conditions met by Christ? We should see them fully met. If we do, it will be further evidence that this "New Covenant" is a "Will." More on those requirements and their fulfillment later.

So I ask, "What's in a word?" Very much indeed! Armed with this definition we will now apply it to the New Covenant/Will/Testament. We see it most clearly delineated in the book of Hebrews!

Of Hearing Aids and Eye Salve
A Warning

"Take heed unto thyself, and unto the doctrine;
continue in them: for in doing this thou shalt both save thyself,
and them that hear thee."
1 Timothy 4:16

I think it is safe to say we have all read Hebrews chapter eight. It is known as the new covenant chapter in the Bible. What Jesus said to His disciples I have found to be so true of myself, and to judge by appearances it is also true of many of my dear brothers and sisters: *"'You have eyes... can't you see? You have ears... can't you hear?'"* (Mark 8:18 NLT) Of the Israelites, the most "religious" nation then existing, Jesus said, *"For this people's heart is waxed gross,* [Meaning thick and calloused, not yucky!] *and their ears are dull of hearing, and their eyes they have closed; lest at any time they should see with their eyes and hear with their ears, and should understand with their heart, and should be converted, and I should heal them"* (Matt. 13:15). People have a tendency to believe what has been handed down to them. We think we have things all figured out and don't need any more understanding. We often don't stop to inquire of the Lord as to what is actually being said in the Scriptures we are reading. When things don't seem to fit or appear odd and out of place, we are often content to shrug our shoulders and settle back into our comfortable hand me down understandings.

There is something I have noticed about the inspired word of God. The Spirit presents the truth in ways that should make us sit up, scratch our heads, and say, "What? That makes no sense!" Sometimes we are reluctant to do this because we may believe that God wants us spiritually dull and submissive. Spiritually submissive, yes! Spiritually dull? Not so much! There are difficulties presented in the Word of God that, in our own strength, we are completely incapable of resolving. With the aid of God's Spirit, however, it is a completely different matter. To every prayer of... *"Open thou mine eyes, that I may behold wondrous things out of Thy law"* (Ps. 119:18), God eagerly responds!

Once, after preaching two sermons on this vital chapter and depriving the saints of their Sabbath afternoon repose, I had a lady say to me, "Oh, I've understood this since I was a little girl, it's nothing new!" "Wow," I thought! "If you knew this why have you not shared it with the rest of us?" My dear wife, God bless her, decided to pursue the matter a bit further. She found out in short order that this dear sister had not understood what was said at all! She had heard the familiar Scripture texts, and her default understanding had clicked into place so that she stopped paying prayerful and close attention. Our minds can do this to us. We've heard this, we know this, and "CLICK" (cue the sounds of our attention switching tracks). Before we know it we find ourselves wondering what will be served for dinner, or what sister so and so was thinking with that hat...

Paul seems to have had the same problem with his hearers.

He actually makes a, "Don't commit the sin against the Holy Spirit/unpardonable sin" type speech in the last part of Hebrews 5 and the first part of chapter 6. He says, *"You have been believers so long now that you ought to be teaching others. Instead, you need someone to teach you again the basic things about God's word. You are like babies who need milk and cannot eat solid food. For someone who lives on milk is still an infant and doesn't know how to do what is right. Solid food is for those who are mature* (Heb. 5:12-14 NLT). It's as if Paul is saying, "You guys are happily stuck in a rut of going over the same things again and again." Paul is here calling for God's children to awake from their "lazy-doze-eean" condition. It is time to start moving forward towards the heavenly Promised Land. He goes on, *"So let us stop going over the basic teachings about Christ again and again. Let us go on instead and become mature in our understanding"* (Heb. 6:1).

Have you ever noticed that though the flavor is changed in the "milk" we are fed every Sabbath, it still remains largely milk? Paul then gets serious brothers and sisters. Here, if we refuse to go on and *"... grow in grace, and in the knowledge of our Lord and Saviour Jesus Christ"* (2 Pet. 3:18), we run the risk of being forever lost!

Paul warns that, *"it is <u>impossible to bring back to repentance</u> those who were once enlightened—those who have experienced the good things of heaven and shared in the Holy Spirit, who have tasted the goodness of the word of God and the power of the age to come and who then turn away from God. <u>It is impossible to bring such people back to repentance;</u> by rejecting the Son of God, they themselves are nailing Him to the cross once again and holding Him up to public shame"* (Heb. 6:4-6). Here we are told that a refusal to go on to further understanding in our personal experience is akin to rejecting Christ!! But now it gets even worse (if it can). We read, *"When the ground soaks up the falling rain and bears a good crop for the farmer, it has God's blessing. But if a field bears thorns and thistles, it is useless. The farmer will soon <u>condemn that field and burn it</u>* (Heb. 6:7, 8 NLT). WOW! It seems that a spiritually static, lukewarm and self-satisfied condition is very sinful and dangerous indeed.

This warning is repeated at the end of Hebrews also: *"I urge you, dear brothers and sisters, to pay attention to what I have written in this brief exhortation!"* (Heb. 13:22 NLT). Do you think God is serious about us listening to what is being said in Hebrews? Does it sound like it is important that we move on in our understanding of truth? Well, when I read these passages they came home to me as a rebuke. I went to God and asked Him for hearing aids and eye salve, and I found it to be true that *"the same Lord over all is rich unto all that call upon Him"* (Rom. 10:12).

Chapter 9

The Will According to W5

And I say unto you,
Ask, and it shall be given you;
seek, and ye shall find;
knock, and it shall be opened unto you."
Luke 11:9

When I was a kid growing up in Canada, there was an investigative news magazine on CTV television called "W5". On this program, they would take a current news item and ask five questions about it that started with a "W." The questions were usually structured to fit the topic being examined. They were;

1) Why?
2) Where?
3) Who?
4) When?
5) What?

The order in which the questions were asked, varied from show to show as I recall and for our purposes I have also listed them above in a particular order to suit our needs. As a young man I thought "W5" was a clever way to investigate a topic. I think it will serve us very well as we investigate the Lost Will and Testament of Jesus Christ. For such a Will does indeed exist!

W1

1st Question: Why?

*"For finding fault with them, He saith, Behold,
the days come, saith the Lord, when I will make a new
covenant with the house of Israel
and with the house of Judah:"*
Hebrews 8:8

First up question #1 of the five: *"**Why**?"* Why was there a need for a "Will" to be written? I know it can be considered bad form to answer a question with a question but I'm going to do it anyway.

Question: "What is the purpose of a "Will?" The purpose of most Wills is to leave to one's offspring one's own possessions. By the legal instrument of a Will we transfer our substance to our children. It is important to note that a person can only leave their heirs something that they actually possess. It wouldn't matter if I was to bequeath to my two daughters, Rebekah and Rachel, the royal palace of Versailles in France. I don't possess it to give as an inheritance. I can't afford to buy it, and even if I could, it is not for sale! The same is true when it comes to holiness. We can only pass on to our children what we possess. We are not able to give them what we do not have.

Our Heritage

Question: What did our parents have to pass on to us? I don't ask this because I want to know about Grandma's china or Grandfather's clock. What I mean here is what, from a spiritual standpoint, did we inherit from our parents? Well, we inherited what they received from their parents, who received it from their parents, who received it from their parents... and so on and so forth right on back to old father Adam. He was the first of our human family to pass something on to his children. Spiritually speaking what was it that he had to pass on to us? Well, folks, it wasn't good! The only thing that Adam could pass on to his descendants, was what he possessed. What did Adam possess? A God-hating, love destroying, selfish, sinful nature. (see Rom 3:9-18) Every single one of us has that same nature as well. It is our legacy of sin from our first parents.

We are by nature, part of this vicious cycle; this dysfunctional family! I know that what I just said sounds harsh but that is what the Scriptures declare. (See Rom 3:10) Adam's children could, and still can, only inherit what he had to leave them. Adam could not pass on to his children a selfless, spotless, sinless nature because he no longer possessed one. He lost it at his fall and ever after *"That which is born of the flesh is flesh"* (John 3:6). What the human family needed was a change; a breaking of the endless inheritance of sin. What we needed was a new father. A father who could pass on a different inheritance to his children. We needed an adoption into a different family; and so Jesus came and died... *"To redeem them that were under the law, that we might receive the adoption of sons"* (Gal. 4:5). It was to break the cycle of sinful inheritance that Jesus came. We needed to be grafted into a different family tree.

A New Heritage

"Wherefore when He cometh into the world,
He saith, Sacrifice and offering Thou wouldest not,
but a body hast Thou prepared me"
Hebrews 10:5

Isaiah prophesied, *"Unto us a child is born, unto us a Son is given"* (Isa. 9:6). God entered the human race when He took on our nature in that stable in Bethlehem. We were adopted into God's family, not just in name, but in flesh and blood! *"Forasmuch then as the children are partakers of flesh and blood, He also Himself likewise took part of the same"* (Heb. 2:14). What incomprehensible love and condescension! How absolutely mind boggling that God would become man! It is through this incredible gift that we have adoption.

Through the unmerited love and favor of God, we have a different parent, a different Father. This is what the Scriptures mean when they say that there is a different Adam: *"The first man* [Adam] *is of the earth, earthy: the second man* [Adam] *is the Lord from heaven"* (1 Cor. 15:47). This second Adam does not possess a sinful spiritual nature, but a sinless one! This is the Good News, the very heart of the gospel! Jesus Christ can now write a "New Testament," a new "Will of Disposition," a "Devisory Will." He can break the dysfunction of the sons and daughters of men because He has made them children of God by becoming a partaker of flesh and blood. This new divine family that has adopted humanity is a tight knit and loving family of three. In this family there is no dysfunction whatsoever! God, adopting sinful fallen man into their family is what the incarnation of Christ is about! What love is here displayed! It makes you want to weep for wonder, joy, and gratitude!

It was so that we could become the sons and daughters of God that Christ came as a man. As a man, the Creator of all men, including Adam, could die and leave all of us, including Adam, the inheritance we so badly need: *"All praise to God, the Father of our Lord Jesus Christ. It is by His great mercy that we have been born again, because God raised Jesus Christ from the dead. Now we live with <u>great expectation,</u> and we have <u>a priceless inheritance</u>—an inheritance that is kept in heaven for you, pure and undefiled, beyond the reach of change and decay. And through your faith, God is protecting you by His power until you receive this salvation, which is ready to be revealed on the last day for all to see* (1 Peter 1:3-5 NLT). Thank God that He came in the flesh so that we can have such an adoption and such an inheritance!

W2

Question 2: Where?

<u>*Where:*</u> Where was this Will written? This is the second of our five questions. Along with this question comes the obvious additional

question of when. For a full contextual understanding we need to know not just where something happens but also when. I know it's cheating a bit to sneak another "W" question into my "W5" illustration, but please indulge me. There is a whole chapter coming up titled "When," but here we'll take a sneak peek at a truth which we will explore more fully in that coming section.

There are two ways that a Will can be said to be "executed." Firstly it is executed when it is written, and secondly it is also said to be executed when it is carried into full and final effect. We will look at where and when Christ's Will was written and signed throughout this section. We will look at when it will be brought into full and final force and the assets distributed to the heirs in the section titled: **"W4 When?"**

Let us now look at the writing and signing of the Will of Christ. In the book of Hebrews we read; *"For finding fault with them, He saith, Behold, the <u>days come</u>, saith the Lord, when I will <u>make</u> a new covenant with the house of Israel and with the house of Judah"* (Heb. 8:8) We need to note two things in the above text.

First: Please note that the underlined word "days" in Hebrews 8:8 is plural, as in a period of days, such as "the days of the week" So the text is saying that during a period of days a new covenant would be made.

Secondly: Where it says in Hebrews 8:8 that He would "make" a new covenant the original Greek word there is "sunteleō," pronounced *"soon-tel-eh'-o."* It means to: *"complete entirely*; generally *to execute* (literally or figuratively): end, finish, fulfill, make."[36]

So what we really read in Hebrews 8:8, is: The days come when I will complete entirely, finish and execute, a New Covenant/Will of Disposition. The word "covenant," here again is our new word friend *"diathēkē,"* which means a "Will of Disposition" Now let's take a look at "where" this new covenant was completed entirely and executed.

36#G4931, Strong's exhaustive Concordance

It was prophesied through Daniel that the anointed one would *"...confirm the covenant with many for one week: and in the midst of the week He shall cause the sacrifice and the oblation to cease"* (Dan. 9:27). This word "confirm" means to strengthen, make strong etc. It means almost the same thing as the Greek word "sunteleō" which we have just defined. In our day we might say that to confirm a covenant is to make it sure, water tight, and rock solid. What Daniel declared is, that during the seventieth week, Christ would establish and make strong His covenant or "Will," making it unchangeable, rock solid, and everlasting!

Question: Where was this Testament or Will that breaks the cycle of a sinful inheritance executed? We read in Hebrews, *"...Jesus is the great Shepherd of the sheep by an everlasting covenant signed with His blood. To Him be glory forever and ever. Amen"* (Heb 13:20, 21 NLT). Here we find our answer as to where the Will was executed, or written, and signed. Since it was signed with His blood, it must have been signed where the blood of Christ Jesus was spilled, on the cross of Golgotha.

A Legal Process

There is a process to be adhered to when confirming or making a legally binding Will. This process requires four main legal steps. If they are not followed, the Will is not valid and can be successfully challenged in court and overturned. It is vital to the testator (the one making the Will) and also to the heirs, that the proper legal steps are taken in the execution of a Testament. Once a Will has been established by the proper procedures, it is unchangeable and legally binding. It must be, and will be, carried into effect with no changes! The meeting of these requirements is very important. It is important because there could be some greedy or malicious person who might want to thwart the Will of the testator. However, if the Will is established the right way, it ensures that the desires of the one who wrote it will be carried out. Paul says in Galatians 3:15, *"Brethren, I speak after the manner of men; Though it be but a man's covenant,* [Will] *yet if it be confirmed, no man disannulleth, or addeth thereto!"*

Does the "New Covenant of Disposition" meet the legal requirements of confirmation? Let's take a look at the four main steps needed to execute a Will that is rock solid and can be legally confirmed. Some of these steps have stipulations within them which must also be met to fulfill the main requirement itself. We see this in our first step or requirement.

Step 1-Testamentary Intent and Testamentary Capacity

That's a jaw full isn't it! The above legal jargon just means that anyone who executes a Will must be capable of understanding what they are doing. The one making the Will must understand that:

a) The following proceedings are taking place to legally establish the individual's wishes regarding their property after death.

b) They must express their intention of making a Will, and

c) They must be found mentally capable of doing so, or of sound mind in other words.

Do we find evidence in the Scriptures that Jesus met the above criteria? If we do, then we can be sure that this first requirement for a rock solid and unchangeable Will was met at the cross. This question is important. If we are sure that the Will is valid, we can have every confidence that it can defeat any and all challenges that may be brought against it. We can have the absolute assurance that it will be carried out and implemented in the end. Let us see if the above criteria were met in the ministry of Jesus and especially in the events surrounding the cross.

Requirements. A, and B: First up, did Jesus understand what He was doing? Did He express His intention to execute a Will? Yes, He did. Christ Jesus even established a memorial to the proceedings. We call it "The Lord's Supper." Here we see Jesus gathering His friends in an upper room at the Passover feast. This was the festival which memorialized the slaying of the Pascal lamb and the application of its blood, which saved the life of all the first born of Israel in Egypt.

Christ was about to fulfill that foreshadowed death for the salvation of mankind. When He took the cup He said to the disciples, *"This cup is the New Testament in My blood: this do ye, as oft as ye drink it, in remembrance of Me"* (1 Cor. 11:25). Did He know that His death would give something to His children? Yes, *"... He took the cup, and gave thanks, and gave it to them, saying, Drink ye all of it; For this is My blood of the New Testament, which is shed for many for the remission of sins"* (Matt. 26:27, 28).

We see in the institution of the "Lord's Supper" that Jesus knew that by His death the sins of many would be remitted. The angels at the tomb on the morning of Christ's resurrection told His disciples, *"He is not here, but is risen: remember how He spake unto you when He was yet in Galilee, "Saying, The Son of man must be delivered into the hands of sinful men, and be crucified, and the third day rise again"* (Luke 24:6, 7). These texts, along with many others show that Christ expressed His intentions of executing a Will. They show that He knew what He was doing and that He knew what He would pass on to His children by His death. So far so good with regards to the requirements for A and B of step one in executing a valid Will.

Requirement C): Did Jesus have the mental capacity to execute a Will? Was He of sound mind? Some of the greatest exchanges of wit recorded in the Gospels, those that make you want to stand up and cheer, are the exchanges between Christ and His persecutors. In the last week of His life, just before the cross, we find Jesus facing a confederacy of the most subtle and brilliant religious minds of His day. All the intellect of the Jewish Sanhedrin was arrayed against Him, and we see Him calmly and quietly springing all their traps and leaving them silent, embarrassed and baffled. The inspired account says that when it was over, *"...no man was able to answer Him a word, neither durst any man from that day forth ask Him any more questions"* (Matt. 22:46). His mind was as sharp as a tack! He was of sound mind.

And there is also this: When He hung on that cross, enduring unimaginable agony of body, mind, and emotion, those who pitied Him ran and brought Him a sponge dipped in vinegar and gall. This was a small concession of mercy granted to those condemned to crucifixion. It was a stupefying mixture, or as we might say today, a mild anesthetic: *"They gave Him vinegar to drink mingled with gall: and when He had tasted thereof, <u>He would not drink</u>"* (Matt. 27:34). He would not accept anything that would impair His mental capacity. No one could say His mind was in a fog as He hung on that cross. He was of sound mind when He yielded up His life. Jesus met all the requirements in the first step of executing a Will! He demonstrated both His intent and His capacity to execute the new testament!

Step 2- Absence of Fraud and Undue Influence

Here we have the second requirement to execute a valid Will. It must be demonstrated that the one executing the Will was in full possession of the facts and not deceived or forced into anything. We might say in everyday language that he must have entered this contract of disposition willingly and with his eyes wide open.

Was there fraud of undue influence brought to bear on Christ when it came to making His New Testament/Will? The answer is no. He left His Father's throne voluntarily. We read; *"Who, being in the form of God, thought it not robbery to be equal with God: But made Himself of no reputation, and took upon Him the form of a servant, and was made in the likeness of men: And being found in fashion as a man, He humbled Himself, and became obedient unto death, even the death of the cross"* (Phil. 2:6-8). When it comes to any undue influence being exerted on Christ, we have direct testimony from Himself on the subject. To ensure that no one could say that He had been surprised, captured and killed, Christ foretold His betrayal and death to His twelve disciples. He said, *"Therefore doth My Father love Me, because I lay down My life, that I might take it again. No <u>man taketh it from Me</u>, but I lay it down of Myself. I have power to lay it down, and I have power to take it again"* (John 10:17, 18). Christ gave Himself to die willingly. There was no arm twisting, no coercion. Do you remember the murderous mob sent to arrest Him? Then you will also remember the angel that dropped that same mob at His feet as if they were dead. It was done as a witness to all, that if Jesus had so wished, He could have escaped their clutches. This same thing was also demonstrated by His act of pointing out Judas as His betrayer in the upper room. He knew perfectly well what was about to happen, and He permitted it willingly.

When it comes to the spiritual side of the equation, did Christ know just what He was consenting to? Again, decidedly, yes. He knew the Scriptures that say, *"But He was wounded for our transgressions, He was bruised for our iniquities: the chastisement of our peace was upon Him; and with His stripes we are healed. All we like sheep have gone astray; we have turned every one to his own way; and the LORD hath laid on Him the iniquity of us all"* (Isa. 53:5, 6). Jesus knew that God was to *"put Him to grief: when Thou shalt make His soul an offering for sin"* (Isa. 53:10). He knew all this when in the garden of Gethsemane He sweated great drops of blood. And yet we are told; *"He went away again the second time, and prayed, saying, O my Father, if this cup may not pass away from Me, except I drink it, Thy will be done* (Matt. 26:42). In fact, not once, not twice, but three times, He could have refused to drink that cup, but He submitted to that *"horror of a great darkness"* (Gen. 15:12) and He willingly became "sin *for us...that we might be made the righteousness of God in Him"* (2 Cor. 5:21). No one executed Christ! He freely and lovingly gave Himself up to die in order that He might execute a Will for His adopted children.

Step 3- The Signature Of The Testator

There is a third requirement to establish a binding Will. Every Will and testament must be signed by the one who executed it. In our day, we would take a ballpoint pen and scribble down our name. When it comes to what is allowed as an acceptable signature, the courts take a very liberal view of what constitutes a legal signature. Anything from an illiterate person making an X to a verbal declaration is considered valid. The important thing is the intent to sign. As long as the individual making the Will desired and intended to sign the Will it is considered a valid signature, even if they are physically handicapped.

Question: When did Jesus sign His Will? Again, let's go to the cross. At the cross we see the Saviour hanging on the tree of cursing. His hands pinioned by the cruel nails, He is panting in agony under the rending chastisement due to us for our sin. Is He able to reach out His hand and sign? Of course not. But what is His intention? Is He here by His own free will? Is it His desire to see this execution through? Does He really wish to die under the weight of our guilt so that we might receive blessing from God? Yes, He did, *"For ye know the grace of our Lord Jesus Christ, that, though He was rich, yet for your sakes He became poor, that ye through His poverty might be rich"* (2 Cor. 8:9).

We also know that He remained hanging there of His own desire. It is written: *"And the people stood beholding. And the rulers also with them derided Him, saying, He saved others; let Him save Himself, if He be Christ, the chosen of God"* (Luke 23:35). Christ was not helpless. He could have saved Himself. Do you remember what Jesus told Peter right after Peter tried to prevent Christ's capture by slicing off an ear? He said, *"Thinkest thou that I cannot now pray to My Father, and He shall presently give Me more than twelve legions of angels?"* (Matt. 26:53) He could have come down from that cross and stopped His execution and the execution of the New Testament as well, but He did not.

There is a song my father-in-law and I sang around the piano a long time ago. It asked the question; "Who Killed Jesus?" Why did He have to die? It was for love that He died. His love and His promise held Jesus on that tree. No other power in heaven or on earth compelled Him to stay there! He said that no man took His life from Him, but that He laid it down voluntarily. There can be no stronger evidence of Christ's intent to sign than His voluntary endurance of the unimaginable torture. Even when..." *at the ninth hour Jesus cried with a loud voice, saying, Eloi, Eloi, lama sabachthani? which is, being interpreted, My God, My God, why hast Thou forsaken Me?"* (Mark 15:34), He did not forsake His purpose! Even while those two hearts, hearts that had beat as one from all eternity, were being torn apart, His wishes did not change. No stronger evidence could be found than this free will offering! *"And when Jesus had cried with a loud voice, He said, Father, into Thy hands I commend My spirit:*

and having said thus, He gave up the ghost" (Luke 23:46).

Concerning the covenant that was sealed, or as we would say, signed with blood, we read: *"Because of the covenant I made with you, sealed with blood, I will free your prisoners from death in a waterless dungeon"* (Zech. 9:11 NLT). This is a prophecy foretelling the final deliverance of God's people. We see the sealing here is with blood. This is repeated in Hebrews, as we have already read, *"Jesus the great Shepard of the sheep by an everlasting covenant signed with His blood"* (Heb. 13:21 NLT). This laying down of His life when He had the power to stop it shows beyond doubt His intention to execute this devisory Will. This was Christ's signing of the New Testament. The signing before witnesses of His Will. His wishes were expressed by His actions.

Step 4- The Witnesses

We now come to the last main requirement in the execution of a Will as far as its legal structure goes. To make a legally binding Will, it must be witnessed by others. They must make and sign statements that they saw the testator (the one executing the Will) comply with the three previous steps.

As soon as Christ gave up His life a witness was immediately produced. The Roman Centurion bore witness *"that this man was the Son of God"* (Mark 15:39). This witness given by Christ's executioner identified the testator. It stated beyond any doubt that the One who was hanging lifeless on that tree was the Divine Son of God. It was the creator of the universe hanging there in death!

There were other witnesses as well. Christ said to His disciples after He rose again, *"But ye shall receive power... and ye shall be witnesses unto Me both in Jerusalem, and in all Judaea, and in Samaria, and unto the uttermost part of the earth"* (Acts 1:8). These disciples of Christ were His witnesses, and we have their written statements on record. Affidavits we would call them today. Here we must call Mr. Webster back into the room for a moment to give us another definition...

Affidavit: "A declaration upon oath... more generally, a declaration in writing, signed by the party, and sworn to, before an authorized magistrate."[37]

The gospels are the Apostles declarations in writing of what they witnessed. They are even called the "New Testament." Peter speaking later said *"And we are <u>witnesses</u> of all things which He did both in the land of the Jews, and in Jerusalem; whom they slew and hanged on a tree: Him God raised up the third day, and shewed Him openly; Not to all the people, but unto witnesses chosen before of God, even to us, who did eat and drink with Him after He rose from the dead"* (Acts 10:39-41). This insistence upon eye witnesses is seen in the selection of a replacement for Judas by the disciples before Pentecost. Peter said, *"... it is written in the book of Psalms, Let his habitation be desolate, and let no man dwell therein: and his bishoprick let another take. Wherefore of these men which have companied with us all the time that the Lord Jesus went in and out among us, beginning from the baptism of John, unto that same day that He was taken up from us, must one be ordained to be a witness with us of His resurrection"* (Acts 1:20-22). The lot which was cast fell on Matthias. He had been one of only two who were qualified to be witnesses of the confirming of the Devisory Will that had been executed by Christ during the seventieth week prophesied of through Daniel.

The Signature of the Witnesses

*"...when thou shalt be old, thou shalt
stretch forth thy hands, and another shall gird thee,
and carry thee whither thou wouldest not."*
John 21:18

Now there are some who might try to discredit these witnesses. They might say that they were lying. Were they? The evidence speaks for itself. People lie for many reasons. Sometimes it is to get them out of the hot seat. Sometimes it is to gain some earthly

37 Noah Webster 1828

advantage, whether financial, political, or social. Sometimes it is to save their very lives that people will lie. It is also true that every liar will reach a point at which he or she will no longer maintain the lie. When it becomes too costly to themselves, they will admit its untruthfulness. What do we see with the disciples of Jesus?

Did their testimony get them out of the hot seat? No indeed, it did the exact opposite! They found themselves hauled before the courts, thrown in jails, whipped and murdered. Maybe there was financial or social gain to be had from their written statements? Again, decidedly no! They were poor, homeless preachers like their Master. Maybe they gained politically? Definitely not. They were a despised and hated sect, chased from city to city. They were social outcasts as far as mainstream, religious society was concerned! Whether Jewish or Pagan, the "churches" of the day considered them a cult of deceivers following a so-called prophet! In short, they had nothing to gain by lying and they "lost" everything earthly in maintaining their witness about Jesus!

If you look at the lives of the disciples, tradition tells us that 12 of the 13 apostles (if you include Paul, the Apostle to the Gentiles) were martyred for maintaining their witness about Jesus. All 13 would have died if God had not preserved John, as tradition tells us, from attempted murder by boiling oil. Instead he was exiled to the penal colony of Patmos, there to serve a life sentence in a bleak and terrible prison. He could have rescinded his testimony and walked away, but he did not! These disciples, just like their Master, signed their witness statements with their blood! Their steadfastness in their assertions, even to the point of death, constitute their signatures as well.

There were many other witnesses to the death and subsequent resurrection of Jesus, and one can spend many fruitful hours looking into these affirming accounts. We must move on, but as for me, I am fully satisfied that the legal requirements for executing a Will were met during the seventieth week of Daniel's prophecy. Christ's Will has been legally confirmed! This is the best of news. We can have every confidence that this Will is binding and that it can never ever be changed or amended. God has made sure that we can rest in the absolute assurance that the heirs named in His Will are going to receive the inheritance left to them!

One last thing to note before we move ahead. In Hebrews it states that *"In the case of a Will, it is necessary to prove the death of the one who made it, because a Will is in force only when somebody has died; it never takes effect while the one who made it is living."* (Heb. 9:16, 17 NLT) At Calvary, the very next scene we see at the cross after the testimony of the centurion, is the thrusting of a spear up through Christ's side and into His heart. Here we find the required proof of death. The Blood and water that poured from His wounded side testify to the fact that the testator has died and that His Will has come into force! The gospels testify that the last words of Christ on the cross were a shout of victory! That cry, *"It is finished"* (John. 19:30) secures our salvation forever! *"For by that one offering He forever made perfect those who are being made holy"* (Heb. 10:14).

So there we have the first and second "W"s of our "W5" questions, the "why" and the "where." It (His Will) was *"confirmed with many for one week"* (Dan. 9:27), so that we could receive a different inheritance from a different Father. An inheritance from a sinless Saviour instead of a sinful Adam.

W3

Question W3

Who are those named as the beneficiaries of the Will?

"Know ye that the LORD He is God:
it is He that hath made us, and not we ourselves;
we are His people, and the sheep of His pasture."
Psalms 100:3

Question: How can we determine if someone is a real child and heir of God? This question must come home to each of us personally. We must candidly, with the eye salve of the Spirit examine ourselves in relation to this all important question. Let us take a look at what spiritual DNA will be seen in the lives of all those who, *"shall be heirs of salvation"* (Heb. 1:14 NLT).

When someone dies and leaves a Will, most everyone even remotely concerned with the Will, asks the same question: "Who is going to inherit?" This is especially true if the inheritance is large. In fact, the larger the inheritance is the more people want to know who the inheritors are. The inheritance we are talking about here is staggering in its richness. It is beyond comprehension or price. *"...we have a priceless inheritance, an inheritance that is kept in heaven for you, pure and undefiled, beyond the reach of change and decay"* (1 Peter 1:4). This inheritance is vastly greater than any inheritance that has ever been promised. All earthly riches pale in comparison to it. No matter what riches one may acquire in this world, in the end they all come to nothing with the death of their possessor. Not so with the riches promised to God's heirs. These riches will last forever because the inheritors of those riches are promised eternal life. They will never die! How important then that we *"Labour not for the meat which perisheth, but for that meat which endureth unto everlasting life, which the Son of Man shall give unto you"* (John 6:27).

Let's examine some passages in the book of Hebrews. In that book Christ's Will is most fully explained. There we read the following; *"For this is the covenant that I will make with the house of Israel after those days, saith the Lord; I will put My laws into their mind, and write them in their hearts: and I will be to them a God, and they shall be to me a people: And they shall not teach every man his neighbor, and every man his brother, saying, know the Lord: for all shall know me, from the least to the greatest. For I will be merciful to their unrighteousness, and their sins and their iniquities will I remember no more"* (Heb. 8:10-12 NLT).[38]

In these passages about the "New Will of Disposition," (*"diathēkē"*) we have not only clues, but decisive statements given that tell us "who" this Will was executed for. There are many nuances here, but for the sake of simplicity we'll look at only four of the defining characteristics that are given. The Scriptures will define for us "who" the heirs of Christ are. There are tell-tale signs that will always be found, to a greater or lesser degree, in God's children; *"And if children, then heirs; heirs of God"* (Rom. 8:16, 17). Please remember this idea of "paternity." It has everything to do with this subject as we shall see.

Who #1

The House of Israel

Our first clue or decisive statement as to who the heirs of God are is; *"For this is the covenant that I will make with the house of Israel"* (Heb 8:10 NLT). Who are the house of Israel? "Oh," you say, "now you've opened a can of worms right there!" This is a hotly debated topic in our world today. There are so many human theories running around about this. Fortunately, we do not need to worry about human theories and speculations. What we want is an understanding that is based on the plain statements of God's word. The Bible will tell us who they are that constitute the *"house of Israel."*

---

38 Also see Hebrews 10:14

Genealogy?

In Scripture we find a rebuke to all who would think or say that salvation is by genealogy. When John the Baptist was preaching, many of the leading physical descendants of the "house of Israel" came to see him. In this encounter God gives us a look into the hearts of these Scribes and Pharisees. John said; *"O generation of vipers, who hath warned you to flee from the wrath to come? Bring forth therefore fruits meet for repentance: And think not to say within yourselves, We have Abraham to our father: for I say unto you, that God is able of these stones to raise up children unto Abraham"* (Matt. 3:7-9). The "house of Israel," at Christ's time on earth were depending on their physical connection with Abraham. They completely missed the spiritual connection. It was not their descent by birth from Abraham that in God's eyes made them the "house of Israel." It was something else entirely. On the basis of a physical connection, God could make the stones as much Abraham's children as the Israelites were. God was/is here stating that the thing that makes one a member of the family of promise isn't a physical connection, it is a spiritual one. This will become more evident when we look at "Who #2."

Jesus later restated this same principle to the Jews when He compared their spirit to that of Abraham's. Jesus based a real connection to God not on a physical descent from Abraham but on a spiritual likeness to the patriarch. The contrast between the spirit which motivated the Jews and the Spirit that motivated Abraham was unmistakably displayed when Jesus said to them; *"Your father Abraham rejoiced to see My day: and he saw it, and was glad"* (John 8:56). The Jews immediately displayed a spirit exactly opposite from Abraham's. They immediately tried, not to see His day, but to end His "day" then and there. The fact that they were not, like Abraham, happy to see His day was evident. They didn't throw a joyful party; they picked up stones to throw at a certain party!

So if being an heir of God is not by genealogy how does God reckon things? Who in His sight are of the "house of Israel?

Spiritual Paternity

When it comes to showing us who the "house of Israel" are, the Scriptures spell it out very plainly. We are told in no uncertain terms what it is that constitutes the spiritual Israel of God. Paul states; *"For he is not a Jew, which is one outwardly; neither is that circumcision, which is outward in the flesh: But he is a Jew, which is one inwardly; and circumcision is that of the heart, in the spirit, and not in the letter"* (Rom. 2:28). The Jews were very proud of the rite of circumcision: However they failed to realize that what makes one a child of God is not what is on the outside. What makes us His children is His life in our hearts: *"For in Christ Jesus neither circumcision availeth any thing, nor uncircumcision, but a new creature. And as many as walk according to this rule, peace be on them, and mercy, and upon* <u>*the Israel of God*</u>*"* (Gal. 6:15, 16). Here we are told that the "Israel of God," are those who are new creatures in Christ Jesus. This passage of Scripture was written to the churches of Galatia, to Jews and Gentiles alike. Paul tells them plainly that: *"There is neither Jew nor Greek, there is neither bond nor free, there is neither male nor female: for ye are all one in Christ Jesus. And if ye be Christ's,* <u>*then are ye Abraham's seed,*</u> *and* <u>*heirs according to the promise*</u>*"* (Gal. 3:28, 29). Here we see again, even more clearly, that those who are Christ's are not depending on their physical descent, for their inclusion in the "house of Israel." Every one of them are depending on the promises of God. They count their inclusion in the "house of Israel" based on what Jesus has done and not on what they themselves have done or (importantly) are doing. Too often mankind has not done this. Too often we have based our inclusion in God's family upon our works, our sanctification, and our striving to overcome our sinful nature. Many are, like the patriarch Jacob, attempting to wrest a blessing from God.

Impossibilities!

"Even in the womb, Jacob struggled with his brother;
when he became a man, he even fought with God."
Hosea 12:3 NLT

So many of us are wrestling with our sinful nature. We think we can subdue it if God just gives us the power! We, laboring under a delusion, set out to conquer ourselves. We know it will take a terrible fight, we know that "we have met the enemy and he is us!"[39] We may attack our sinful nature with great zeal calling on God to aid us in this warfare. We may be ever so earnest in our attempts but we will only fight on and on in ever growing failure, disappointment, and dread. All the while, Satan is standing by encouraging us, shouting "atta-boys" while he laughs up his sleeve. What is it that is so funny? What gives him such kicks? Just this: He knows that *"the natural man receiveth not the things of the Spirit of God: for they are foolishness unto him: neither can he know them, because they are spiritually discerned"* (1 Cor. 2:14). He knows, though he tries to deceive us to the contrary, that our human nature is wholly corrupt. It can't receive the things of God or even really know them. Whether we know it or not we are spiritually dead unable to fight ourselves. We are prisoners of our own fallen natures. Our attempts to subdue our very personal adversary are all doomed to fail. Why? *"Because the carnal mind is enmity against God: for it is not subject to the law of God, neither indeed can be"* (Rom. 8:7). The underlined portion of that verse says it all. What the Devil finds so funny is that he is able to make us believe that we can do the impossible! That is, that we can subject our carnal minds to the law of God. We may wrestle and fight until we are mentally, physically, and emotionally exhausted but however much we fight, it will all be to no avail. We must sooner or later end up spiritually devastated and weeping under our beds. Just as we had no part in our physical birth, so too we cannot by our striving make ourselves children in the "the house of Israel."

---

39. Walt Kelly...AKA Pogo

Israel

"Thy name shall be called no more Jacob, but Israel "

Genesis 32:28

Do you remember the story of how Israel got his name? Then you will remember how and from whom this family name came. His name was not always Israel, it had been Jacob. It is a well known story. Jacob, after his sin in stealing a blessing had fled his home. At Bethel, he had received God's promise that He would bring him back to the land of inheritance. Years later on the way back home, as God was keeping that promise, Jacob received word that his brother Esau was coming with an army to meet him. He saw Esau, the one who stood as a witness and reminder of his sin of deception and theft, standing armed between him and his father's house.

Jacob goes off by himself to plead with God to keep His covenant promise, made to him here at Bethel. We see him struggling with his fears. He sees the danger approaching and under the night sky he pleads with God for deliverance. Suddenly a man lays hands on him. Jacob instantly thinks that he is being attacked and turns on his assailant. All night long he wrestles with his "enemy." Jacob cannot overpower his attacker. No matter how much strength he exerts, no matter how hard he tries, the other is his match, or so he thinks.

The God of heaven is the one who came to him that night. Not to fight him, but to bless him. As the day dawns, God makes Jacob aware of his human frailty with a simple touch. Now Jacob knows who he has been wrestling with, and he falls on the angel of the Lord and clings to Him. He will not let Him go until he receives the blessing he so desperately needs! It is written, *"he wrestled with the angel and won. He wept and pleaded for a blessing from Him. There at Bethel he met God face to face, and God spoke to him the Lord God of Heaven's Armies, the Lord is His name So now, come back to your God. Act with love and justice, and <u>always depend on Him</u>"* (Hosea 12:3-6 NLT). Here God makes an earnest call to each of us to stop our life of struggling, and instead, to live in clinging dependency upon Christ.

We, like Jacob, are guilty of sin and know that the coming of Christ is near. We know that He is coming *"To execute judgment upon all, and to convince all that are ungodly among them of all their ungodly deeds which they have ungodly committed"* (Jude 1:15). We too need God's help and blessing, but many of us are still wrestling, trying in our own strength to overcome our sinful natures. Oh, how you and I need a crippling touch. Oh, how we need to understand our own weakness and spiritual inability. That knowledge would end the laughter of the Devil. We must have the life of Christ continually dwelling within us. We must have Christ abiding within us, willing and doing of His good pleasure. We must cease looking partly to ourselves, and partly to Him. Christ must become all and in all. He must overcome in us by His Spirit (see Romans 8:9)

Do you see how Jacob was victorious? It wasn't until almost daybreak, prefiguring the second coming of Christ, that Jacob quit striving to overcome his assailant and started clinging to God. It was then that he prevailed with God. We, too, must rest in the power and work of Christ. It was not by fighting that Jacob overcame, but by a trusting, clinging dependence upon the power of God. It was then that Jacob received the name *"Israel... because... as a prince hast thou power with God and with men, and hast prevailed"* (Gen. 32:28). It was by utterly despairing of himself that Jacob prevailed! So it will be with those who are of the *"the house of Israel."* This will be the experience of those who are God's heirs. They will be those whose religion is not based on their striving, their fighting, or their righteousness/sanctification. Their religion will finally become a religion of clinging, prevailing dependency upon God! They will place themselves in the nail-scarred hands of Jesus, and in His power over sin, they will rest.

There is coming a day, very soon, when we will see the prophecy of Isaiah fulfilled: *"And it shall come to pass in that day, that the remnant of Israel, and such as are escaped of the house of Jacob, shall no more again stay upon him that smote them; but shall stay upon the LORD, the Holy One of Israel, in truth"* (Isa. 10:20). This word "stay" means to depend, or rely upon.

Question: Who have these remnant people been relying on? Who is he *"that smote them?"* Ezekiel, speaking of the king of Babylon, representing Satan and the false system of work righteousness which he has set up, says that *"He... smote the people in wrath with a continual stroke"* (Isa. 14:6). A religion of rule keeping which vainly attempts to subdue the carnal mind and subject it to the law of God is a terrible torture. There is coming a day when the remnant will no longer believe Satan's lies. They will rely on God and not upon the false doctrine of Christ/self-salvation.

To those who overcome by clinging, the promise is also given: *"To him that overcometh will I give... a white stone, and in the stone a new name written, which no man knoweth saving he that receiveth it"* (Rev. 2:17). They also like Jacob/Israel, will someday receive a new name and meet God face to face!

How is it with you, dear reader? Are you in a real, life-changing, clinging, and dependent relationship with Christ? Or are you still wrestling, trying to subdue your sinful nature because you think that is what God requires of you? Are you looking partly to Christ and partly to your good deeds, correct choices, and character development? There is only One who can save you. Have you entered into a restful dependence upon His power over and protection from sin? To every son and daughter of Adam, God extends a loving, wounded hand, saying *"...let him take hold of <u>My strength</u>, that he may make peace with Me; and he shall make peace with Me"* (Isa. 27:5). Those who do not reject that saving hand through pride or indifference are the spiritual "house of Israel" and heirs according to the promise.

Who #2

"The Least to the Greatest"

Question: Will it only be the greatest that are accounted heirs of Christ Jesus? Some seem to think that to be saved we need to have achieved a spiritual standing of this or that height. This idea runs completely contrary to Hebrews 8. When speaking of the new "Will of Disposition" we read that the heirs will be of various sorts. It says that, *"... all shall know Me, <u>from the least to the greatest</u>"*(Heb. 8:11).

Here we see a variety of Christian experiences and not a uniformity of perfect attainment spoken of. What is it that distinguishes those who are the least from those who are the greatest?

The Human Standard for the Least to the Greatest

Question: What is the <u>human standard</u> when it comes to greatness in the church? We know what it is in the world. I do not want to go over the worldly standard, it seems obvious enough. But what is the human standard that we see in the church for deciding who is the least and who is the greatest? A long time ago, conflict arose in the new church over this very issue. Contention grew between the twelve disciples over who would be the greatest, and by implication, who would be the least in the new kingdom. Jesus knew what was up, and one day *"...He came to Capernaum: and being in the house He asked them, What was it that ye disputed among yourselves by the way? But they held their peace: for by the way they had disputed among themselves, who should be the greatest. And He sat down, and called the twelve, and saith unto them, If any man desire to be first, the same shall be <u>last of all</u>, and <u>servant of all</u>"* (Mark 9:33-35). A servant of all? Last of all?

Self-exultation and selfishness is that deadly seed of sin which has reproduced itself throughout history. It has perpetuated this terrible harvest of suffering and death that we experience and witness all around us. This seed originated with Lucifer. He planted, nurtured, and watered it until it bore fruit in the destruction, not only of himself, but of all those whom he has deceived. We read of Lucifer: *"Thine heart was lifted up because of thy beauty, thou hast corrupted thy wisdom by reason of thy brightness"* (Ezek. 28:17). And Isaiah tells us more, *"For thou hast said in thine heart, I will ascend into heaven, I will exalt my throne above the stars of God: I will sit also upon the mount of the congregation, in the sides of the north"* (Isa. 14:13). This attitude of self love and climbing to the "highest" position, is what sin is all about. This self-exultation is what stamped Lucifer with his new name,"Satan."[40]

This dreadful rebellion is seen in every descendant of Adam. Speaking to the religious leaders of His day Christ said; *"Ye are they which justify yourselves before men; but God knoweth your hearts: for that which is highly esteemed among men is abomination in the sight of God"* (Luke 16:15). And He warned His disciples, *"... all their works they do for to be seen of men: they make broad their phylacteries, and enlarge the borders of their garments, and love the uppermost rooms at feasts, and the chief seats in the synagogues, and greetings in the markets, and to be called of men, Rabbi, Rabbi"* (Matt. 23:5-7). The religious leaders desired to exalt themselves. They were very exacting in their outward observances and ceremonies. The result of this outward piety was that the people looked up to them and reverenced them. The people were almost wholly unable to entertain any spiritual ideas that weren't endorsed by their "great" religious leaders. This power and prestige, this raising of oneself up above others, is the sinful human idea of greatness in the church. This was the greatness which the disciples desired when they disputed among themselves along the way.

The exclusiveness of the Jews in Jesus' day was proverbial. They considered themselves so much greater than the "heathen," that they wouldn't even enter a Gentile's house. Rebuking this false idea of greatness, Jesus said, *"I say unto you, that many shall come from the east and west, and shall sit down with Abraham, and Isaac, and Jacob, in the kingdom of heaven. But the children of the kingdom shall be cast out into outer darkness: there shall be weeping and gnashing of teeth"* (Matt. 8:11, 12). I look around at the beloved church of Christ, and I fear that nothing has really changed. Too often we see in the church a standard revered that is nothing more than that sin of respecting the persons of men. If this standard is held on to, what Jesus said to the proud exclusive Israelites will come true for us. I trust that by the grace of God this idea will not wholly

---

40 Again we see in Scripture the changing of a name reflecting the changing of a character, this time denoting a change for the worst

prevail. If we will listen to the lessons He gave to His grasping, place-seeking disciples, there is hope. Christ was about to give them a different standard to measure greatness by. A heavenly standard. It is this heavenly attitude that will be seen in the hearts of all His children, from the least to the greatest.

God's Standard for the Greatest

"But [He, Christ] *made Himself of no reputation,*
and took upon Him the form of a servant
and was made in the likeness of men."
Philippians 2:5, 6

Jesus, who knew the ongoing conflicts over position that His disciples were engaged in, decided it was time to call another family meeting! He had to set them straight about what constitutes greatness in the eyes of heaven. Of Christ it is said that *"...God also hath highly exalted Him, and given Him a name which is above every name: That at the name of Jesus every knee should bow, of things in heaven, and things in earth, and things under the earth"* (Phil. 2:9, 10). To Christ Jesus will be given the highest place and the most exalted name. This is not some arbitrary bestowal of power and majesty. It is the position that must be His because of heaven's standard of greatness. This standard of greatness is exactly opposite of what His disciples' idea of greatness was. We have a transcript of that family meeting: *"... Jesus called them to Him, and saith unto them, Ye know that they which are accounted to rule over the Gentiles exercise lordship over them; and their great ones exercise authority upon them. But so shall it <u>not be</u> among you: but whosoever will be great among you, <u>shall be your minister</u>: And whosoever of you will be the chiefest, <u>shall be servant of all</u>. For even the Son of Man came not to be ministered unto, but to minister, and to give His life a ransom for many"* (Mark 10:42-45).

Here is presented an entirely different standard of greatness. Here we see loving, self-forgetful service used as heaven's standard of true greatness. The reason that Christ's name is greater, and the reason that He is exalted above all others, is because He is the minister of all! He is the Creator who works lovingly and tirelessly, for all His creatures, whether friend or foe. Of Christ it is said, *"for through Him God created everything in the heavenly realms and on earth. He made the things we can see and the things we can't see—such as thrones, kingdoms, rulers, and authorities in the unseen world. Everything was created through Him and for Him. He existed before anything else, and He holds all creation together"* (Col. 1:16, 17 NLT). Christ is great because of who He is and how much He serves all others! This is not an arbitrary declaration of worth, it is a fact.

If we apply this principle to our passage in Hebrews we can see that those who are heirs of the new "Will of Disposition" will display, to a greater or lesser degree, a spirit that is entirely other-worldly. By the grace of God, what was later seen in the apostles will be seen in them: genuine Christ-like love, and a desire for the happiness and uplifting of others. This desire for the salvation of others will be manifest even if it means suffering and pain for themselves. This desire will also be something that they are almost completely unaware of. In the parable of the sheep and the goats Christ said, *"He shall set the sheep on His right hand, but the goats on the left. Then shall the King say unto them on His right hand, Come, ye blessed of My Father, <u>inherit</u> the kingdom prepared for you from the foundation of the world: For I was an hungred,... I was in prison, and ye came unto Me. Then shall the righteous answer Him, saying, Lord, <u>when saw we Thee an hungred, and fed Thee? or thirsty, and gave Thee drink?</u>"* (Matt. 25:33-37). The sheep will be oblivious to their own greatness. They will be unconscious of their own likeness to their master; but the likeness will be there.

This genuine love and self forgetfulness is divine DNA. It is something that only God can produce. *"God is love; and he that dwelleth in love dwelleth in God, and God in him"* (1 John. 4:16). Only in the hearts that are inhabited by God through the Spirit is such self forgetful love seen! The heirs of Christ will be great by heaven's standard, not by the standards of fallen religious reasoning.

Non Uniformity

When we read that the *"least to the greatest will already know Me,"* it is a definitive statement that there will be <u>different degrees</u> of this selfless love displayed in the lives of God's children. It does not say that there will be uniformity of attainment. These heirs cannot be said to be equal in selfless service if there is a discrepancy in their greatness. Was the thief on the cross, who knew Jesus for something like three and a half hours, as like Christ in reality as say John, who walked with Jesus for three and a half years? I don't think so. The thief on the cross wasn't the greatest of all Christ's followers, but he will be with Christ in paradise! <u>We must always remember that our salvation is a gift from God, not a payment for services we have rendered.</u>.

To sum up Who #1 & 2

1) The heirs to this new "Will of Disposition," will be found in a relationship of clinging dependency upon God, His power, and His promises!

2) The heirs of Christ will come in all spiritual heights. No one will be banned from the kingdom because they are not up to a certain level of goodness. However, they will all bear, to a greater or lesser degree, Christ's spiritual DNA. His selfless love for others will be seen in them for He will be in their hearts.

Who #3

Knowing God

"And they shall not teach every man his neighbour, and every man his brother, saying, <u>Know</u> the Lord: for all shall <u>know Me</u>, from the least to the greatest.
Hebrews 8:11

Knowing God. What does that mean? We are told that *"this is life eternal, that they might know Thee the only true God, and Jesus Christ, whom Thou hast sent"* (John 17:3). The religious leaders of Christ's time on earth had their ideas of what it meant to know God. They thought that by the acquiring of religious knowledge they could secure eternal life. Christ confronted them on this assumption one day. Jesus, in His love for them, told them plainly that they were in error. He said, *"Search the Scriptures; for in them ye think ye have eternal life: and they are they which testify of Me"* (John 5:39). What was He saying to them? They had searched the Scriptures. They knew them so well that if the old stories can be believed some of them could put a pin into their Torah and tell you what word the pin would hit based on where it was on the parchment and how far down the pin had penetrated. I'm not so sure I believe the story, but if it is an exaggeration regarding the exactness with which they had studied the Scriptures, it's not much of an exaggeration! These sons of Abraham "knew" the word of God! Christ desired them to rethink their ideas of what it meant to "know" the "Word"[41] of God. Those Scriptures that they were so proud of knowing, testified of Jesus Christ. They were written so that those who heard them might receive the faith, which is a gift of God. It was with sadness that Jesus added, *"And ye will not come to Me, that ye might have life"* (John 5:40). In the end it was demonstrated that all the scriptural/spiritual "knowledge" in the world did not help them. Without the life which only Christ can give they were spiritually dead. They ended up crucifying the Lord of glory!

It seems that this problem keeps coming up again and again. James confronts the same problem later in the Christian church. He was dealing with the opposite side of the coin, but it was the same problem. In the book of James we see a people who professed to believe in Jesus. They appear to have had the idea that they only had to "believe" and they were "saved!" They said they had faith. They said they "knew" God. James commends them for acknowledging there was a God, saying, *"Thou believest that there is one God; thou doest well: the devils also believe, and tremble"* (James 2:19). The devil knows God;

---

41 John 1:1

he was a covering cherubim after all. Even though he spreads everywhere the lie that God is a myth, he knows that God is, and Satan trembles.

Knowing God is not just acknowledging that He exists. It means something much more. Really knowing God has very profound and personal repercussions. John said the same thing as James when he wrote, *"He that saith, I know Him, and keepeth not His commandments, is a liar, and the truth is not in him"* (1 John 2:4). I can hear the Jewish rulers pipe up here and say, "Oh ya! Well, we know the Scriptures, AND we keep the commandments! Why! We have myriads of rules on how to keep the fourth commandant alone, so there!"

Well, how about it? Jesus said that *"many will say to me in that day, Lord, Lord, have we not prophesied in Thy name? and in Thy name have cast out devils? and in Thy name done many wonderful works? And then will I profess unto them, I never knew you: depart from Me, ye that work iniquity"* (Matt. 7:22, 23). Jesus says, that sadly, many will think they know Christ when in fact they don't. Professing to "know" Him, they will have done many wonderful works, some of which have even appeared to be supernatural, but what does Christ say? I never "knew" you. It is obvious, that a correct understanding of what it means to really "know" Christ is very important.

If knowing Him isn't just having a thorough knowledge of the Scriptures, believing there is one God, doing many great works, and following the rules, then what is it? Knowing and doing all these works is a good thing as far as it goes but it seems that something more is needed. The fountain of all these "good works" is missing. What do the Scriptures say a real knowledge of God is?

Intimacy

We read in Hebrews 8 that all the heirs to the "Will of Disposition," share a universal trait. They "know" God. The word "know" here, is something very different from our modern word "know." Let's take a look at the original language... (I can hear some readers squeaking, No... "know," no! Not again with the Greek? ...Yup! ☺). The word here translated as "know," in Hebrews 8:11, is the Greek word ginōskō which means to allow knowledge to be taken into one's self. It does not only mean the possession of information; it is more in line with the idea of an intimate connection. We have already seen, through the experience of the scribes and pharisees, that more is needed than mere knowledge. This word "know," is used in many instances as a hebraistic euphemism. A phrase which could do with a definition:

"**Euphemism:** a figure in which a harsh or indelicate word or expression is softened, or rather by which a delicate word or expression is substituted for one which is offensive to good manners or to delicate ears."[42]

This word "know," is a word used by the Hebrews to, ummm... describe an intimate connection of a rather private nature. This desire to soften and veil delicate subjects we find in modern examples, such as when we hear people say things like, "This will be the bride and groom's first night 'together,'" or when we say "love making...," etc. If we don't understand what this word "know" means, we will have an incomplete picture of the relationship being alluded to. Our hebraistic euphemism is telling us that "knowing" God involves an experience of intimacy with God. Not a physical intimacy, but a spiritual one. It is a union between Christ and the church, and remember that the church is made up of us as individuals.

A Great Mystery!

It is written: *"...we are members of His body, of His flesh, and of His bones. For this cause shall a man leave his father and mother, and shall be joined unto his wife, and they two shall be one flesh. This is a great mystery: but I speak concerning Christ and the church"* (Eph. 5:30, 31). In this passage of Scripture Paul says he speaks of a great mystery. I don't know about you, but I like a great mystery. Let's see if we can't, by the grace of God, figure this one out.

42Noah Webster 1828

Do you know who Paul was quoting when he says; *"For we are members of His body, of His flesh, and of His bones?"* He was quoting another man, not Christ, the *"the last Adam,"* but he is quoting *"the first man Adam"* (1 Cor. 15:45). Speaking of Eve, his wife, who was made from his rib by Christ, *"Adam said, This is now bone of my bones, and flesh of my flesh"* (Gen. 2:23). It was from *"Adam the first"* that God brought forth a wife or spouse. As Eve was created from Adam's wounded side, so too with the Church of God. It is from Christ's wounded side, from which flowed blood and water, that we see the church being created on Calvary.

Speaking to the Church in Corinth, Paul said, *"for I have espoused you to one husband, that I may present you as a chaste virgin to Christ"* (2 Cor. 11:2). The Church is seen everywhere in Scripture figured as the bride of Christ. In Ephesians 5, we read that to be one with his bride is why a man would leave his father and mother. So it was with Christ. He left His Father, His throne, and His home to come down here and become *"one flesh"* with us; fallen, unfaithful, and treacherous mankind. What a bride to marry! And what a price to be paid for such a bride!

The Wife

"O Israel and Judah, what should I do with you?' asks the LORD.
'For your love vanishes like the morning mist
and disappears like dew in the sunlight."
Hosea 6:4 NLT

In the Scriptures it is written, *"If we deny Him, He will deny us. If we are unfaithful, He remains faithful, for He cannot deny Himself"* (2 Tim. 2:12, 13 NLT). Christ is always faithful. He has always been faithful. The same can't be said for His bride! We have already established that the things which happened in the Old Testament happened as examples of what would/will happen later. It is also written that, *"The thing that hath been, it is that which shall be; and that which is done is that which shall be done"* (Eccles. 1:9). There is a long and sad history of unfaithfulness by Christ's bride, the church. This adultery was prefigured in the history recorded in the Old Testament and it has and is being played out in the history of the Christian church.

In the book of Hosea we read the following words: *"I know what you are like, O Ephraim. You cannot hide yourself from Me, O Israel. You have left Me as a prostitute leaves her husband; you are utterly defiled. Your deeds won't let you return to your God. You are a prostitute through and through, and you cannot not know the Lord... They have betrayed the honor of the Lord, bearing children that are not His. Now their false religion will devour them..."* (*H*osea 5:3, 4, 7 NLT 1996). Here we see the heartbroken accusations of God, figured as a betrayed husband. He likens His church to a prostitute who is committing crimes of intimacy with false religion. He says that it is the deeds, or works of His people that will not let them return to Him. It is this false religion, a religion of works righteousness, that prevents intimacy with God.

The whole system of paganism is a system of works, it is a system of doing things for your "god" in exchange for blessings. This is not the religion of Christ. The Bible says that *"God was in Christ, reconciling the world unto Himself, not imputing their trespasses unto them; and hath committed unto us the word of reconciliation"* (2 Cor 5:19). This is the true Gospel, <u>God</u> reconciling man to Himself, not the other way round! The religions that Israel went whoring after taught, and still teach, the opposite. This false "gospel" teaches that it is from man that salvation is to be expected. So, too, with the Christian church. Aping paganism, we have believed and taught for ages that we must, through our choices and works, reconcile God to us. This is what keeps us from "knowing" God. If we continue in a religion of works reliance we will end up writing ourselves out of our inheritance. When this adulterous and rebellious spirit resides in the church there will be no progress seen in her. There will be no fruitfulness, no new life, only barrenness.

New Life Given

"For in Christ Jesus neither circumcision
availeth any thing, nor uncircumcision,
but a new creature."
Galatians 6:15

What happens when the church does not depend on itself or on its good works and choices; but instead depends entirely upon her husband, Christ! In the Scriptures we read that, *"Adam knew Eve his wife; and she conceived, and bare Cain"* (Gen. 4:1). Here we have the recipe for the creation of a child. God created a wife for a man, and from a man. When Adam entered into that woman whom God had made from Adam's wounded side the two became one. When that union happened, the potency that he, Adam, brought into her, Eve, resulted in the bringing forth of new life. It resulted in a new birth and the creation of a child that carried Adam's very own DNA. Here we have an illustration of God's desired relationship with His Church. Here is depicted the spiritual results of Christ, the second Adam's work. By His life giving and vital connection to His church, children are born unto eternal life. If the Church does not "know" Him who is her real husband, she will be barren.

There is a beautiful prophecy in Isaiah foretelling what will happen to the church just before Christ Jesus returns the second time: *"Sing, O childless woman, you who have never given birth! Break into loud and joyful song, O Jerusalem, you who have never been in labor. For the desolate woman now has more children than the woman who lives with her husband,"* says the Lord. *Enlarge your house; build an addition. Fear not; you will no longer live in shame. Don't be afraid; there is no more disgrace for you. You will no longer remember the shame of your youth and the sorrows of widowhood. For your Creator will be your husband"* (Isa. 54:1, 4, 5 NLT). Not until Christ becomes the source of life to His people will we have His life in us. Knowing God means that the life which we have in us, both physically and spiritually is the life of God. We must be created by Him from barrenness. All that man has within himself is impotence. We can produce nothing but death. We must have an intimate, life-giving connection with God through the Spirit. We must be born from above. This is what Jesus meant when He told Nicodemus, *"Humans can reproduce only human life,* [our fallen and unholy natures] *but the Holy Spirit gives birth to spiritual life... 'You must be born again"* (John 3:6, 7 NLT).

It is not enough to have a profession; to say, "I am Christ's child, I am a sheep of His pasture." Anyone can say that. What must be seen in every true son or daughter of God, is the actual presence of His life, His vitality. This is why the Psalmist said, *"Search me, O God, and know my heart: try me, and know my thoughts: And see if there be any wicked way in me, and lead me in the way everlasting"* (Ps. 139: 23). We must have a look at our hearts. *"Christ is not weak when He deals with you; He is powerful among you...Examine yourselves to see if your faith is genuine. Test yourselves. Surely you know that Jesus Christ is among you; if not, you have failed the test of genuine faith"* (2 Cor. 13:3, 5 NLT). The God-assisted and heart searching question must be asked: "Is Christ a mighty power living within me? Or is my experience a human concoction and of my own making?" For millennia man has only been able to make lifeless images from clay by the works of his own hands. Only God has ever made an image of clay and brought it to life. So too in our hearts. Only God can give us real spiritual life. The true children and heirs of God will "know" Him. Through an intimate connection His life will be their life and Christ's life in them will always produce the fruits of real righteousness!

Willful Rebellion

One more point needs to be made. John writes: *"... hereby we do know that we know Him, if we keep His commandments. He that saith, I know Him, and keepeth not His commandments, is a liar, and the truth is not in Him"* (1 John 2:3, 4). Does this statement mean that anyone who falls short of God's glorious standard does not "know" God? When it says the "truth" is not in him it is a reference to Christ, *"...the way, the truth, and the life... "* (John 14:6)

Question: Is it true, that if we are sinful, weak, and fall short of perfect obedience to His commandments, that Christ is not in our hearts? No. If this was the case, then all, including John himself, do not know God. Furthermore, no one could know Him because the Scriptures declare that *"... all have sinned, and come short of the glory of God"* (Rom. 3:23).

So what does John mean then? James gives us a clue. He says, *"Therefore to him that knoweth to do good, and doeth it not, to him it is sin"* (James 4:17). If one knows the commandments of God and willfully, habitually and persistently ignores or violates even one of those requirements, he thereby shows that he does not have Christ living out His life within him. Please don't mistake me here, I'm not talking about weakness. John and James are talking about open rebellion. A sin which we will not confess to be sin, even when we are convicted by the Holy Spirit again and again, is what is being talked about here. To all people, no matter how far they have fallen, repentance and forgiveness is freely offered. Peter speaking of Christ said, *"Him hath God exalted with His right hand to be a Prince and a Saviour, for to give repentance to Israel, and forgiveness of sins"* (Acts 5:31).

Refusal of this gift of repentance, however, is evidence that He who is the Truth is not in us and that we do not "know" God. John clarifies his previous statement when he says, *"Those who have been born into God's family do not make a practice of sinning, because God's life is in them. So they can't keep on sinning, because they are children of God"* (1 John. 3:9 NLT). That text really sums up in a nut shell what knowing God really is. It is written that at the end of this world's history, A.K.A. "now," there will be only two groups of people. The Scriptures declare, *"Then shall ye return, and discern between the righteous and the wicked, between him that serveth God and him that serveth Him not"* (Mal. 3:18). There is coming a test in the very near future. This test will reveal who does and who does not "know" God. Jesus said, *"I am the good Shepherd, and know My sheep, and Am known of Mine"* (John 10:14). When the good Shepherd calls all to follow and obey His commandments, and not the commandments of man, those who "know" God will know that voice and follow Him.

So to Sum Up Who 1-3

The Heirs will be:

1) Found clinging to Jesus in dependence upon His strength.

2) Comprised of anyone, spiritually small or great, but they will be like Him. They will exhibit the same Divine spirit of selfless love!

3) His children. They will all "know" God. His life will be the origin and sustenance of their lives. They will have an intimate, life giving connection with Him.

The last of the Who's #4
The Sanctified of Christ

"Moreover also I gave them my Sabbaths,
to be a sign between me and them,
that they might know that
I am the LORD that sanctify them."
Ezekiel 20:12

We now come to our last distinguishing characteristic of those who will *"be heirs of salvation"* (Heb. 1:14). All who are children and heirs of God will be in a sanctifying relationship with Him. In Hebrews it says, *"For by that one offering He forever made perfect those who are being made holy"* (Heb. 10:14 NLT). Please notice something here. Ezekiel 20 states that it is the Creator, the Lord, who makes us holy. Many think that God requires perfect sanctification from them, and as a result, they are trying to make themselves holy. There is only One who can make them holy, but Christ speaks to all as He did to the Pharisees of old saying, *"...[you] make clean the outside of the cup and the platter; but your inward part is full of ravening and wickedness"* (Luke 11:39). Many of us have the idea that real righteousness consists in doing things right; keeping an outward correctness of behavior. We forget that, *"...man looketh on the outward appearance, but the LORD looketh on the heart"* (1 Sam. 16:7).

It is holiness of heart that God regards, but like the Pharisees, who "being *ignorant of God's righteousness, and going about to establish their own righteousness, have not submitted themselves unto the righteousness of God,"* (Rom. 10:3) many of us attempt to manufacture our own goodness of character. We think that by doing this we can achieve righteousness. We seem unaware that, "No man can look within himself and find anything in his character that will recommend him to God, or make his acceptance sure. It is only through Jesus, whom the Father gave for the life of the world, that the sinner may find access to God. Jesus alone is our Redeemer, our Advocate and Mediator; in Him is our only hope for pardon, peace, and righteousness."[43] To the poor blind Pharisees of yesterday and today Christ says, *"Thou blind Pharisee, cleanse first that which is within the cup and platter, that the outside of them may be clean also"* (Matt. 23:26).

Question: If we are told to clean the inside of the cup, i.e. our hearts, why can't we do that by our will power and works? The Scriptures ask a rhetorical question to answer this, *"Can the Ethiopian change his skin, or the leopard his spots? then may ye also do good, that are accustomed to do evil"* (Jer. 13:23). It is a pointed question, and it gives us a definitive answer as to why we can't sanctify (make holy) ourselves. Sin is more than outward acts. It is not just something we can wash off with enough scrubbing. It penetrates much deeper. It is a disease which permeates our entire being. Regarding our sinful condition the Word of God declares, *"the whole head is sick, and the whole heart faint. From the sole of the foot even unto the head there is no soundness in it; but wounds, and bruises, and putrifying sores: they have not been closed, neither bound up, neither mollified with ointment"* (Isa. 1:5, 6).

---

43 1ˢᵗ Selected Messages pg.332

We are a rotten mess. Like the lepers in Israel we are spiritual outcasts and mortally sick to our very marrow. We are doomed in ourselves to wander in desolate places shut out from Heaven and estranged from God crying unclean, unclean! We cannot clean ourselves up. Our sinful natures are like a deadly virus which only attacks and destroys all that is good and pure. We are helpless! As it is written; *"Who can bring a clean thing out of an unclean? not one"* (Job 14:4). Like Baldwin IV, the leper king of Jerusalem,[44] we may be capable of outward "victories" but we are spiritually blind and paralyzed. We can't make ourselves clean.

What every leper needs, and what we need, if we are to live, is our Creator's touch. *"And, behold, there came a leper and worshiped Him, saying, Lord, if Thou wilt, Thou canst make me clean. And Jesus put forth His hand, and touched him, saying, I will; be thou clean. And immediately his leprosy was cleansed"* (Matt. 8:2, 3). It is only Christ that can cleanse our hearts, only He can make us whole again. It is by His will that we have life and health. (see James 1:18)

Any "sanctification" not produced by His life-giving presence within us is false pretense and sin. As it is written; *"whatsoever is not of faith is sin"* (Rom. 14:23).

Emmanuel!

Just as it is true that we can never save ourselves, so it is also true that there is a Saviour! The angel told Joseph, *"And she shall bring forth a son, and thou shalt call His name JESUS: for He shall save His people from their sins"* (Matt. 1:21). Many today are deceived into thinking that Christianity is simply a sentiment. They are told that Jesus paid it all so don't worry about your sins. You are "Saved!" They are told, by implication, that God will save them not from their sins but in them. This makes no sense. What kind of a salvation is it which leaves you in the grip of sin? It is no salvation at all!

If you were the slave to a brutal master would it be helpful to you if I were to pass by your torture chamber one day and say; "Cheer

---

up, I've saved you!" That might cheer you up for a moment but if I then just went on my way whistling a happy tune and left you locked in your misery would I have saved you from anything? No, and you would be correct in assuming that I was a cruel liar. When the angel said that Jesus would save His people from their sins God meant just that. God is in the business of releasing prisoners from sin, that cruelest of tyrants. He came to set us free from the shackles of sin's slavery and bring us back into light, liberty, and the communion of His love! Of this work that Jesus alone can do, it was prophesied, *"The Spirit of the Lord is upon Me, because He hath anointed Me to preach the gospel to the poor; He hath sent Me to heal the brokenhearted, to preach deliverance to the captives, and recovering of sight to the blind, to set at liberty them that are bruised"* (Luke 4:18). In every genuine child of God will be seen a growth in grace and holiness, an ever growing freedom from the domination of sin. There will be witnessed empirical evidence of sanctification, a genuine growing likeness to their new Father. This will be because His life is in them, willing and doing of His good pleasure.

To sum up this entire section, the third of our five "W" s

God's word tells us "who" the heirs of God are, they alone will *"inherit all things"* (Rev. 21:7). They will be:

1) Clinging to Jesus in dependence upon His strength and power, as Jacob did;

2) Comprised of anyone, small or great, but they will be like Him. There will exhibited in them the same Divine Spirit of selfless love

3) His children. They will "know" God. Because of the intimate life-giving relationship which He is living out in them, His life will be seen in their lives. They will have His spiritual DNA;

4) In a sanctifying relationship with Jesus. He will be living out His life in them. He will be making them ever more pure in heart.

So, there we have defined for us in Hebrews chapters 8 and 10 "who" shall be accounted heirs of God, and entitled to the gift of inheritance: that inheritance which He has died to give them. This now brings us to the fourth of our five "W's."

W4

W4 When

"When will these things be?"

Luke 21:7

So far we have seen that there was a need to provide a new inheritance for sinful man. We have seen that what man inherited from father Adam was not good and that it is an existence of living death, *"For to be carnally minded is death"* (Rom 8:6). We have seen that a Will of Disposition was executed by Jesus Christ and made strong against all the assaults of Satan. It was signed and finished when Christ died on the cross of Calvary.

I hope as we went through the characteristics which define who the heirs of God are that you found yourself pictured there. If you didn't, then I hope that you admitted this to the loving God of heaven. I pray that you have asked Him to make you His child, in reality and not just in name.

I know that those of us who have found ourselves lacking this true living connection to Christ have had the devil in our ear, tempting us to either excuse or ignore our need. He may have also tempted you to try and "make" yourself a true child of God. This is not something any of us can do. I have never yet met or heard of anyone who was able to give themselves birth. It is just as impossible to give yourself spiritual birth. That being said, the devil is a master salesman and knows how to play on our fallen natures. I sincerely hope that you did not listen to him, but that you ran to the One who can and *"... shall supply all your need according to His riches in glory by Christ Jesus"* (Phil. 4:19).

Now, moving forward on the very safe assumption that God answered any and all of our prayers for adoption. We can now ask the burning questions that I would safely bet all heirs ask: "What was left to me?" and "When will I receive my inheritance?" As to "<u>what</u>" was left to you in His Will, keep reading, because that amazing answer will be in the next section, the fifth "W5." In this section we will be dealing with "<u>when</u>" we will receive our inheritance. An important consideration in its own right, wouldn't you agree?

Time Stamps

"I am God, and there is none like Me,
Declaring the end from the beginning, and from ancient times the
things that are not yet done, saying, My counsel shall stand, and I
will do all My pleasure"
Isaiah 46:9, 10

A time stamp is a stamped or printed record telling the time when some particular action or event has taken place. An example of this would be a taxi meter. We can use time stamps to tell us when an event occurred. In this case, the moment when the taxi meter started running and you started paying. Or perhaps you have used a time clock to punch into and out of work? This tells the paymaster how many hours you worked on a particular day.

God has given us time stamps in His word also, but because He knows the future He has the unique ability to issue time stamps on future events! On occasion, these glimpses into the future have had very precise dates connected with them. We see this in the wonderful prophecies of the seventy weeks and the 2300 days that we find in the book of Daniel.

Sometimes however, prophecies have no specific dates connected to them but they do have very specific <u>circumstances and events</u> described within them that give us a time stamp. I would like to look at some time stamps in the book of Hebrews which will answer the fourth of the five "W" questions: "When?" When will we receive our inheritance?

Puzzles

The Scriptures say that: *"It is the glory of God to conceal a thing: but the honour of kings is to search out a matter"* (Prov. 25:2).

In Hebrews 8 and Hebrews 10 we have a puzzle! I like puzzles and from the text just quoted it seems that God does too! He has made us intelligent beings and has endowed us with a mind which, when filled with, and taught by His Spirit, is capable of solving spiritual puzzles. So now, with a prayer that His Spirit will teach and guide our investigations, let's take a look at these time stamps!

Days Daze

Okay, so, run around the house in the snow three times, splash ice water on your face, or do something to sharpen your wits, because this next section will require some close attention! There will be a summary at the end of this section but you will need to pray and screw your thinking cap down tight here for a bit.

In Hebrews Paul writes: *"...Behold, the <u>days come</u>, saith the Lord, when I will <u>make</u> a new covenant with the house of Israel and with the house of Judah"* (Heb. 8:8). He then states right after that: *"this is the covenant that I will <u>make</u> with the house of Israel <u>after those days</u>, saith the Lord;"* (Heb. 8:10) Later, in chapter 10 he writes: *"Whereof the Holy Ghost also is a witness to us: for after that He had said before, This is the covenant that I will <u>make</u> with them <u>after those days</u>, saith the Lord"* (Heb. 10:15, 16).

There are a lot of the same words in the verses above. We have no less than three "<u>makes</u>" and three "<u>days</u>!" The problem is that when we read these passages it is not immediately clear what days are being talked about. Are all three references referring to the same set of days? Also, we have another problem muddling the waters. When the translators rendered those words *"make"* into English, they forgot to tell us that the words we read as *"make"* are not actually the same words in the original language! This is kind of a big deal, as we will see!

Now the first question is: why do we see three different sets of "days" mentioned? Let's break this up into manageable bites.

First Set of "Days"

"...Behold, the <u>days come</u>, saith the Lord, when I will <u>make</u> a new covenant with the house of Israel and with the house of Judah" (Heb. 8:8). Here we have the first set of "days" that <u>would come</u>. These days are not the same days spoken of in Hebrews 8:10 and Hebrews 10:15, 16. How do we know they are not the same? Well, we established something in the section we studied dealing with the question of "where" the Will was executed. Do you remember that I apologized for sneaking a "when" into that section? In that discussion we looked at this little word *"make"* and found it was the Greek word "sunteleō." We discovered that it really didn't mean to <u>make,</u> but to *"complete entirely*; generally to *execute."*[45] We saw that during the seventieth week spoken of by Daniel, Christ executed, established, and made a strong and unchangeable contract of disposition, or a Devisory Will.

45Strong's Exhaustive Concordance

Second Set of "Days"

The second two mentions of "days" we find in Hebrews 8:10 and Hebrews 10:15, 16: *"This is the covenant that I will make with the house of Israel after those days, saith the Lord;"* (Heb. 8:10) and; *"Whereof the Holy Ghost also is a witness to us: for after that He had said before, This is the covenant that I will make with them after those days, saith the Lord"* (Heb. 10:15, 16).

Please note that in these verses we have a difference. The above two passages say that "after those days," something will happen. There are two clues that tell us that both verses are talking about the same time period and should be linked in our understanding, and that they are speaking about a different time than Hebrews 8:8 is. They are:

Clue 1) The Spirit had already said this once before through Paul: *"Whereof the Holy Ghost also is a witness to us: for after that He had said before,"* (Heb 10:15). This is an old English way of saying, "The Spirit told you this before" in Hebrews 8:10.

Clue 2) The word "make" itself. In these last two passages the word "make" is not the Greek word that we saw in Hebrews 8:8. That word was "sunteleō," and meant to "complete." These last two "make"(s) are "diatithemai" pronounced, dee-at-ith'-em-ahee. "Diatithemai" does not mean to execute, or write and confirm and make strong a Will, but to: *"dispose by assignment compact or bequest."*[46]

Ding Ding Ding....Dictionary time again (you should be used to this by now!) In Websters 1828 dictionary we find the following definitions for the underlined words above:

---

46 Strong's Exhaustive Concordance #G1303

1) Dispose: "To give away or transfer by authority."

2) Assignment: "In law, the conveyance of the <u>whole</u> <u>interest</u> which a man has <u>in an estate</u>."

2 a) Here we need a sub definition for the word "interest" so we know what is being conveyed. **Interest:** "To have a share." So we could say that an <u>assignment</u> is the act of transmitting from oneself to another, the whole share which a man has in an estate!

3) Bequest: "Something left by Will; a legacy."[47]

So what we are really reading, in these last two passages, where we find this word "diatithemai," is; *"after those days"* I [God] will convey, from Myself to My children, the "<u>whole inheritance</u>"[48] which I have promised to them in the Will that I executed and made unchangeable at the cross!" We've now sorted out two pieces of this puzzle, we know what doesn't go together. We know that the making of the Will was at a different time than the distribution of the inheritance will be. One was a Will, executed (or made) during the seventieth week. The other is yet future and will entail the bestowal, or giving <u>in full</u>, of an inheritance to the children of God. By the way, from the following Scripture we know that we have not yet received our full inheritance: *"We believers also groan, even though we have the Holy Spirit within us as <u>a foretaste of future glory</u>"* (Rom. 8:23 NLT).

After Those Days – What Days?

We now know that when Paul says *"after those days"* he is referring to the time when God will give to all of His heirs their full

---

47The above four definitions, taken from Noah Webster 1828.

48 See footnote 46

inheritance. The next logical question is, "After which days?" When I first started to study these passages in Hebrews I worked under the assumption that when it says the covenant would be made *"after those days,"* the days being spoken of were the days which followed the death of Jesus on the cross. I assumed that this was when God would tell the world about His gift of salvation and give them a period of time to accept it, along with the new heart He promised them through His sanctifying Spirit. In my mind the narrative ran something like this; '... after those days when I make a new covenant I will make a new covenant....' It didn't make sense, but for a long time I thought "Hey, the Bible is sometimes hard to understand" and left it at that.

As stated at the beginning of this section, God likes puzzles, and for a long time the understanding I had regarding *"those days"* progressed no further, and I remained very "puzzled" indeed. I was however, quite disturbed by some of the things God said right after these new covenant passages. In the subsequent verses, I found four puzzle pieces which didn't seem to fit anywhere. After asking God what in the world He was talking about, the answer came back. God is saying something like this: "When I give the full inheritance to My children, these are the spiritual conditions that will exist and the results that will follow." All of a sudden a light went on and I realized, that what I was looking at were time stamps! Let's look at these time stamps, one by one and underscore the four puzzling parts which we especially need to note. Let's see what the conditions will be, spiritually speaking, when God gives His heirs their full inheritance.

First Puzzling Passage – Evangelism Ended

"For this is the covenant [Will and Testament] *that I will make with* [dispense fully to] *the house of Israel after those days,... they shall be to Me a people: And they shall not teach every man his neighbor, and every man his brother, saying, Know the Lord"* (Heb 8:10, 11). This word "and" is a primary particle which indicates that

what follows this word is the direct result of the action just taken. The action just taken is God giving the full inheritance to His children.

As I've just related, I always thought, and many others do too, that the time being spoken of as *"those days"* was the time of the gospel commission. This is not the case, as we shall see. The great Gospel commission is recorded for us in Matthew: *"Go ye therefore, and teach all nation,...: Teaching them to observe all things whatsoever I have commanded you..."* (Matt. 28:19, 20). Do you see an inconsistency here? If the complete disposal of the inheritance being spoken of in Hebrews was done during the Gospel time period, that is to say over the last two thousand or so years, how could it be said that the results of the full disposition of the new covenant would be that no one would need to go into all the world and teach everyone any more?

Hebrews clearly says that they, (God's children) would not need to teach either their neighbors or family to "know" the Lord after the inheritance had been given in full. We would have a direct conflict with the command of Christ to preach the Gospel if the time being spoken of was immediately after the cross.

What Paul is saying in Hebrews is that when the heirs receive their full inheritance, it will result in the end of evangelism! There will be no more calls of mercy, and the message of God's mercy is what the preaching of the good news is all about! This must mean that the gift of inheritance is received after the last call to join God's family has gone out. It is saying that the inheritance will be distributed at the end of that evangelistic time!

Second Puzzling Passage – *The Judgment Ended*

Next, we read this, concerning "when" the inheritance will be given: *"For I will be merciful to their unrighteousness, and their sins and their iniquities will I remember no more"* (Heb 8:12). This is repeated again in Hebrews 10 *"... their sins and iniquities will I remember no more"* (Heb. 10:17). Now where it says God will *"remember no more"* in verse 17, that word "remember" in the original Greek means that God will never "bear in mind" or "recollect."[49] God will forget forever our sins and iniquities! WOW!

In the ninth chapter of Hebrews we read that *"...it is appointed unto men once to die, but after this the judgment"* (Heb. 9:27). Also in another place it is written, *"For we must all appear before the judgment seat of Christ; that every one may receive the things done in his body, according to that he hath done, whether it be good or bad"* (2 Cor. 5:10). Since the Bible says there is an individual judgment, there must also be a record kept of each life, there must be evidence to submit in court, right? It would be a pointless exercise to bring a case to trial and then tell the judge that all the evidence pertaining to any wrong or right doing had been lost/forgotten, correct?

It says, *"and their sins and their iniquities will I remember no more"* (Heb. 8:12). Again we have this word "and" as a primary particle, and again it indicates that what follows is the direct result of the disposal of the inheritance. This means that <u>the reception of our inheritance must be after the judgment of God's people is finished</u>. All those who receive the inheritance will have their sins blotted from existence at the end of that process. The time referred to here cannot be during the Gospel time period, for the judgment of God's people is part of that time. Jesus also said, *"...behold, I come quickly; and My reward is with Me, to give <u>every</u> man according as his work shall be"* (Rev 22:12). If the reward is with Him for every individual, then it logically follows that the reward has already been determined by God in the Judgment of Investigation. The time for the disbursing of the inheritance must be after that judgment has ended.

Third Puzzling Passage – *The Empty Throne*

For our third time stamp we find this statement, part of which we have already examined: *"And their sins and iniquities will I*

---

49 See Strong's Exhaustive Concordance

remember no more. Now where remission of these is, there is <u>no more offering for sin</u>" (Heb. 10:17, 18). If you look at the underlined portion of this Scripture in the original Greek you will find that it says, in essence, something like the following: "Their sins and iniquities I won't ever call to mind or mention again and when I have finished My work, and done all I have promised, there will no longer be a need to offer up any sacrifice for sin." This means that the mediation of Christ will then be finished! The anti-typical day of atonement will be over. There will no longer be a need for *"... the blood of sprinkling, that speaketh better things than that of Abel"* (Heb. 12:24). Here Paul is speaking of the time when Christ will stand up and step down from the role of mediator. This is when He will take up His power as King of kings and Lord of lords. The throne of mercy will then be vacant. There will be no more opportunity for repentance. There will be no more justifying blood pleading for the sinner before God! Heartbreaking will be the position of those, who, realizing too late their lost condition, will seek for reinstatement into their birthright/covenant blessing. They will be like Esau, who for worldly considerations sold his inheritance and *"... afterward, when he would have inherited the blessing, he was rejected: for he found no place of repentance, though he sought it carefully with tears"* (Heb. 12:17).

Fourth Puzzling Passage – *Of Footstools and Their Making*

"But our High Priest offered Himself to God as a single sacrifice for sins, good for all time. Then <u>He sat down</u> in the place of honor at God's right hand. <u>There He waits until His enemies are humbled and made a footstool under His feet</u>" (Heb. 10:12, 13). Here we have a direct statement telling us which days are being spoken of when the Spirit says, *"after those days"* (Heb. 8:10, and Heb. 10:16). This raises some questions. Let's take a look:

- First, it says that after He (Christ), had offered Himself, He sat down. When Did Jesus offer Himself? At the cross.

- Second, we read that He sat down on His Father's throne and has remained there ever since (see Rev. 3:21). If you look back through the beginning of Hebrews 10 you will see that He could do this because His sacrificial death was full and complete. He didn't have to offer a lot of different sacrifices as the earthly priests did. His sacrifice covered all the bases, so to speak. His offering of Himself was/is all-sufficient for the salvation of mankind.

- Third, we are told that He will remain seated there on the throne until His enemies are humbled under His feet as a foot-stool.

So when we read, "*...this is the covenant* [Devisory Will] *that I will make,* [dispose of by a bequest to]*...the house of Israel after those days,*[those days of sitting and waiting until the humbling of His enemies] *saith the Lord"* (Heb. 10:16), we obviously need to ask another question.

Question: When will His enemies be humbled? The answer to that question will tell us when God's children will receive their full inheritance.

The words of Paul, where he writes, "*until His enemies are humbled and made a footstool under His feet,*" are a quotation from Psalms 110:1. Let's examine the original Scripture; "*The Lord said to my Lord, 'Sit in honor at My right hand until I humble Your enemies making them a footstool under Your feet.' The Lord will extend Your powerful dominion from Zion; You will rule over Your enemies. In that day of battle Your people will serve you willingly...The Lord stands at your right hand to protect you. He will strike down kings in the day of His anger. He will punish the nations and fill them with their dead; He will shatter heads over the whole earth*" (Ps. 110: 1-3, 5, 6 NLT). Here we need to note three points especially:

- **First,** Christ will sit at the right hand of the Father until His dominion is extended from Zion. When will that be? The answer is found in Psalms 110:1-3, which Paul was quoting. It will be in the day of battle when Christ's dominion extends from Zion, the heavenly city of God. *"The LORD shall roar from on high, and utter His voice from His holy habitation; He shall mightily roar upon His habitation; He shall give a shout, as they that tread the grapes, against all the inhabitants of the earth. A noise shall come even to the ends of the earth; for the LORD hath a controversy with the nations, He will plead with all flesh; He will give them that are wicked to the sword, saith the LORD"* (Jer. 25:30, 31). In the Lord's prayer we read *"Thy kingdom come. Thy will be done in earth, as it is in heaven"* (Matt. 6:10). Here we are urged to pray that God's kingdom will come and His will be done here on earth just like it is in heaven. We do not see this yet, but when God's enemies are made a footstool Christ will return, and then His will shall be done on earth as it is in heaven. [50]

- **Second:** Christ will sit at the right hand of the Father until the day of battle! It will be a day of battle and great trouble. *"He will strike down kings in the day of His anger. He will punish the nations and fill them with their dead"* (Ps. 110:5, 6 NLT) Isaiah prophesied of this when he said: *"For, behold, the LORD cometh out of His place* [Zion] *to punish the inhabitants of the earth for their iniquity: the earth also shall disclose her blood, and shall no more cover her slain"* (Isa. 26:1). When Christ comes out of His place He will have at this time risen from the seat of mercy[51] and will be going to war!

Third: This trouble will be universal! *"He will shatter heads over the <u>whole earth</u>."* (Ps. 110:6 NLT)

The Scriptures declare that Christ will sit at the right hand of God until that day of battle and universal trouble, and then He will stand

---

50 As an example of the defeated under the feet of the conqueror see
    Vercingetorix's surrender to Julius Caesar: *Plutarch's Lives*; *Caes.* 27.8-10;
    Flor. 1.45.26; Dio 40.41.3.

51 This seat is the anti-type of the ark of the covenant with it's mercy seat.

up: *"And at that time shall Michael stand up, the great prince which standeth for the children of Thy people: and there shall be a time of trouble, such as never was since there was a nation even to that same time: and at that time thy people shall be delivered, every one that shall be found written in the book"* (Dan. 12:1). Hebrews clearly states that *"After those days"* of sitting and waiting, Christ will give His children, all those found written in the book, their inheritance. Then He will come back to this sin ravaged world to make an end of suffering and death and receive us unto Himself, that where He is, we may be also! (see John 14:3)

To Sum Up The Fourth of Our Five "W" s

Our full inheritance will be received *"after those days"* of ministry by Christ. He is now seated on the throne of power and judgment in heaven and He will remain there until His work of salvation is done. He will then stand up and deal with this sinful, rebellious world; *"Behold, the Lord cometh with ten thousands of His saints, to execute judgment upon all, and to convince all that are ungodly among them of all their ungodly deeds which they have ungodly committed, and of all their hard speeches which ungodly sinners have spoken against Him"* (Jude 1:14, 15).

When God gives His children their inheritance it will be at a time when there will no longer be any need for evangelism. At that time the sins of God's children will be blotted out and will never be remembered or mentioned again. This means that the giving of the inheritance must also be after the close of the Judgment! The result will be that the spiritual salvation of His chosen ones will be complete: *"... they shall be Mine, saith the LORD of hosts, in that day when I make up My jewels"* (Mal. 3:17). This will result in the end of Christ's intercession. There will be no more need to offer up sacrifice, no more need for a mediator/intercessor between God and man! Once Christ stands up the Scripture will be fulfilled: *"When once the master of the house is risen up, and hath shut to the door, and ye begin to stand without, and to knock at the door, saying, Lord, Lord, open unto us; and He shall answer and say unto you, I know you not whence ye are"* (Luke 13:25). As it was in the days of Noah, the door of salvation will then be shut! *"That is why the Holy Spirit says,* "*Today when you hear His voice, don't harden your hearts as Israel did when they rebelled"* (Heb. 3:7,8 NLT). Now, happily, the door is not closed! We may still come to Him and request the adoption He died to give us, assured that *"He that spared not His own Son, but delivered Him up for us all, how shall He not with Him also freely give us all things?"* (Rom. 8:32) And Christ said, *"All that the Father giveth Me shall come to Me; and him that cometh to Me I will in <u>no wise cast out</u>"* (John 6:37). **Today**, dear reader, is the day to come to Him. **Today**, is the day, of salvation.

W5
The Fifth of Five "W" s
What?

*"Moses commanded us a law,
even the inheritance of the congregation of Jacob."*
Deuteronomy. 33:4

Now we come to it, the fifth of our five "W"s. "Finally" you say, "finally I can discover what has been left in the Will of Christ Jesus for me!" To which I reply, "Yes...but... We first need to lay a ground work of understanding." "What!?" You say! "I've waited this long, and you want me to wait even longer?!" Well, yes, but only so that your understanding and appreciation of what God has done will be deeper, and your confidence in what He will shortly do will be greater.

The Purpose of the Pictures

*"Then verily the first had also ordinances of divine service,
and a worldly sanctuary... Which was a
figure for the time then present..."*
Hebrews 9:1, 9

This section is <u>very important,</u> because it tells us something we <u>must understand</u>. It tells us <u>why</u> the sanctuary was made, and what the ultimate point of all the symbolism was. <u>It tells us "the purpose of the pictures,"</u> These pictures are all the illustrations and symbols found in the earthly sanctuary and its services. There was one overarching purpose to that whole intricate parable, and that purpose was to illustrate to us, the way God would/will save fallen humanity.

Speaking of the yearly service Paul says that when the whole Tabernacle was finished it was consecrated by the sprinkling of blood and water.[52] Paul also says that, *"... when these things were thus ordained, the priests went always into the first tabernacle, accomplishing the service of God. But into the second went the high priest alone once every year, not without blood, which he offered for himself, and for the errors of the people"* (Heb. 9:6,7). Paul then states that the earthy sanctuary was an illustration or figure to represent something. He says the purpose of that earthly service was to show, in illustrating pictures, the plan of redemption. He says; *"Which [Sanctuary] was a figure for the time then present,* [before the death of Christ] *in which were offered both gifts and sacrifices, that could not make him that did the service **perfect, as pertaining to the conscience**"* (Heb. 9:9).

Here we have the purpose of the sanctuary spelled out clearly. It was an illustration to the people living then and to us as well: It was an illustration in symbols of how God would make those who believed in Christ, *"**perfect, as pertaining to the conscience**."* The pictures show us how God would do a seemingly impossible work through the new covenant. It was/is an illustration of how God will make the believers in Jesus perfect through a "Devisory Will" which He wrote and confirmed on Calvary!

---

52 Read John 19:34 & Heb 9:19-21, here again it states that the execution and confirmation of the new covenant was done at the cross!

Conscience

If the purpose of the plan for our salvation was to make our consciences perfect, then shouldn't we:

a) know what it is that needs to be made perfect?

b) then ask the question; why isn't it perfect? What has defiled this "conscience," so that it needs cleansing?

I would like to ask you to stop reading now and write out your definition of the word "conscience"...When you're done, keep on reading. (Again, no dictionary or concordance please, and no cheating and reading ahead! ☺)

Conscience:

_____

_____

_____

There are many answers given to the above question. Many, myself included, at one time or another have thought that their conscience was/is the Holy Spirit. Now while it is true that the Spirit speaks to and troubles our consciences, it is not true to say that He <u>is</u> our conscience. If He was our conscience, then how could the purpose of the sanctuary be to cleanse our conscience? God is holy and He does not need cleansing. The work of the Spirit is to arouse us to a sense of our danger from sin, as it is written, *"... when He is come, He will reprove the world of sin, and of righteousness, and of judgment"* (John 16:8). I have asked many people to tell me what their "conscience" is. Most people who did not say it was the Spirit, answered, not by defining <u>what</u> the conscience was, but by telling me what it <u>did</u>. They have/will say something like, "The conscience is that little voice inside that tells you if what you are doing, thinking, or feeling is right or wrong." Not a bad answer... There is a great deal of confusion and debate as to just what the conscience is among scholars. If you look up the definition in the Websters 1828 dictionary, you will see this debate even there.

CONSCIENCE, *noun* [Latin, to know, to be privy to.]

1. Internal or self-knowledge, or judgment of right and wrong; or the faculty, power or principle within us, which decides on the lawfulness or unlawfulness of our own actions and affections, and instantly approves or condemns them... Others question the propriety of considering *conscience* as a distinct faculty or principle. They consider it rather as the general principle of moral approbation or disapprobation, applied to ones own conduct and affections; alleging that our notions of right and wrong are not to be deduced from a single principle or faculty, but from various powers of the understanding and will.[53]

Okay... so when it comes to this definition, I really must excuse you if you feel pained after having to read it!! But "no pain, no gain," as they say! Please pay attention to the underlined portions of the definition. They will help steady us as we explore what our conscience is.

We see in the above definition that the conscience is that part of us which we use to determine if we are thinking, acting, or feeling "rightly" or perhaps I should say, "righteously!" It is a faculty placed within us by our Creator. It is a kind of moral compass to approve or condemn our behavior. That behavior can be an outward act, an inward thought, a feeling or an impulse. This all functions well and good as long as the moral compass of our hearts and minds are in harmony with goodness. But what if that moral compass has been defiled and is broken or skewed?

---

53 Noah Webster 1828

A Skewed Course!

A story is told of a WWI fighter pilot who was home in England on a recruitment tour to that country's institutions of higher learning. He flew a Sopwith Camel fighter plane from school to school, and at the last stop on his tour he found himself in the extreme north of England. There he spoke to a group of likely young men about king and country, duty and the war effort. In that group of mostly, eager, patriotic young men, one face disquieted him. This young man seemed to have an intense dislike for our hero from the start. The captain did his best to shrug off the feeling of apprehension which he vaguely felt at their meeting and wished that the unpleasant lad would just go away. He was relieved when not long after his speech this young man left the group, and he was able to spend the rest of his time pleasantly.

He had thought that he was shot of him for good, but just before he flew south for a well earned leave in London, the disquieting young chap reappeared. The expression of dislike was still on the lad's face but it was now augmented by a more disconcerting and knowing smile! The Camel pilot was more than happy to climb into his cockpit, fire up the engine, and be rid of him.

Once England's "Ace" was airborne, he set a compass heading to the south and settled back for an afternoon's flight in the peaceful skies above Britain. The trip was supposed to be over the green countryside the whole way, so you can imagine his surprise when; looking down through the haze some time later he discovered that he was flying, not over the pastures of his native land, but over the ocean! This was all wrong! He checked his compass, and it seemed to be reading the correct heading. He knew, however, that on his original heading he should have been nowhere near water! After a few bewildering minutes he was wise enough to reverse his course 180 degrees. He barely made it back to the shores of England without running out of fuel! Upon further investigation he found, hidden in the heart of his aircraft near his compass, a large magnet. This magnet had skewed his compass 180 degrees from true and had given him the false heading which he had nearly flown to his death!

It was then that he understood the absence and sly smile of that disquieting young man!

Now when it comes to our consciences, or our "moral compass," we too will be in serious trouble if it is skewed from what is true. We hear a lot of advice thrown at us every day from every quarter and through every medium. We are constantly told that we should "trust our feelings" or "follow our hearts." The Bible clearly warns us against this course. It plainly tells us that there is something wrong with our thoughts, feelings, and intentions. It says, *"The heart is deceitful above all things, and desperately wicked: who can know it?"* (Jer. 17:9) The Bible plainly declares that each of us thinks that what we do is okay, even when it is not. *"Every way of a man is right in his own eyes: but the LORD pondereth the hearts"* (Prov. 21:2). If you use your own thoughts and feelings to decide if your behavior is good or bad, you will be in big trouble.

The Word of God says the reason that the Law was given was because of transgressions. (See Gal. 3:19) We will look at what transgression and sin is shortly, but please note this: the law was added to give us a course correction. Just as that pilot was warned that he was in big trouble when he looked down and saw water where land should have been, so it is with the Law. It was given so that man could have a true statement of what is really righteous and good. The moral compass we inherited from Adam is skewed 180 degrees from truth. We need an unerring reference point with which to compare our own course of action. The Law of God is that benchmark of righteousness. It was given to us so that we can have a true standard by which to check our "moral compass."

Our Agents of Control

"...the carnal mind is enmity against God:
for it is not subject to the law of God, neither indeed can be."
Romans 8:7

The word conscience originates from the "Old French" **conscience:** "conscience, innermost thoughts, desires, intentions; feelings."[54] These are the controlling agents, or senses, if you will, of the conscience. They tell us if we are right or wrong. Now, as in the story above, if these *"innermost thoughts, desires, intentions; feelings"* are skewed from what is really right and true, we are in big trouble if we follow them. *"There is a way which seemeth right unto a man, but the end thereof are the ways of death"* (Prov. 14:12). So the question must be asked: Is our moral compass skewed?

The pointed statements that we are about to read will show us who, and what, we really are. It is only possible for us to acknowledge these facts because of the power and grace of God. We do not like facing the truth about ourselves! We haven't ever since Eden. Remember, though, there is no need to despair. God has provided a lamb to take away the sins of the World. That includes your sin, and it includes mine!

The Condition of Our Conscience

"For we know that the law is spiritual:
but I am carnal, sold under sin."
Romans 7:14

What does the Bible have to say about our innermost thoughts, feelings, desires, and intentions? Well, first it says, *"My thoughts are not your thoughts, neither are your ways My ways, saith the LORD"* (Isa. 55:8). Now that is bad! Our thoughts are not the same as the thoughts of the God of love! But it gets worse: *"... we have already shown that all people, whether Jews or Gentiles, are under the*

---

54 etymonline.com

power of sin. As the Scriptures say, "No one is righteous—not even one. No one is truly wise; no one is seeking God. All have turned away; all have become useless. No one does good, not a single one" (Rom. 3:9-12 NLT). Here we have an unmistakable declaration of what our "innermost thoughts, desires, intentions; feelings" are! This sinfulness is what rules our conscience! Not one of us is righteous, wise, or even seeking God! We are sinful through and through! *"... we are all as an unclean thing, and all our righteousnesses are as filthy rags; and we all do fade as a leaf; and our iniquities, like the wind, have taken us away"* (Isa. 64:6).

Christ said to the "righteous" of His time: *"You brood of vipers, how can you who are evil say anything good? For the mouth speaks what the heart is full of"* (Matt. 12:34 NIV). You might object that He was speaking to the especially wicked Scribes and Pharisees and not to us "good folks." But remember, Romans says that *"No one does good, not a single one."* What comes out of our mouths shows what is in our hearts. Romans goes on to say: *"Their talk is foul, like the stench from an open grave. Their tongues are filled with lies. Snake venom drips from their lips. Their mouths are full of cursing and bitterness... They have no fear of God at all"* (Rom. 3:13-17 NLT). Since the Bible declares that the mouth speaks from what is in the heart, we must conclude that our hearts are foul like a rotten corpse, Our hearts are filled with lies and venom, cursing and bitterness! There is no fear of God in us at all! Looking at that sobering picture, do you feel you should "follow your heart?" I think I must agree with the Scripture that says, *"He that trusteth in his own heart is a fool"* (Prov 28:26).

If our consciences are controlled by our "innermost thoughts, desires, intentions; feelings," are they clean? Are they a safe guide for us? The work of God shown in the symbols of the sanctuary service on earth, and which is now being carried out for real in heaven, is all being done with one aim in mind. Do you remember what it was? It was an illustration of how God would make those who believed in Him, *"perfect, as pertaining to the conscience"* (Heb 9:9).

Question: How did we get into this mess? How were our "innermost thoughts, desires, intentions; feelings," defiled? By what were they defiled?

Eden

"But like Adam, you broke My covenant
and rebelled against Me."
Hosea 6:7 NLT 1996

If we want to find out how our consciences were defiled and what it was that defiled them, we must take a close look at the record of those events. We find the sad story of man's transgression in the book of Genesis. *"God created man in His own image, in the image of God created He him; male and female created He them"* (Gen 1:27). Man was made in the image of God. What did that entail? Well, it seems clear that in his physical form man resembled his creator. When we consider the spiritual, emotional, and mental capacities man was created with, they too, must have been created in the image of God. One thing is certain, man was in harmony with his Creator on all moral levels. Adam and Eve's "innermost thoughts, desires, intentions; feelings" were pure and innocent. The Bible says that *"...they were both naked, the man and his wife, and were not ashamed"* (Gen 2:25). I think God used this nakedness as a very powerful image so that we could understand what happened in the minds and hearts of Adam and Eve when they fell.

Have you ever had "that" nightmare? You know, the one where you dream that you are suddenly out in a crowded public place without a stitch of clothing or a barrel hoop to hide behind? You frantically try to cover up with anything you can but it somehow doesn't seem to cover you at all! In that dream you have the most acute feelings of utter shame, fear, and humiliation! The only desire in your mind is to be decent and away from the gazing, critical eyes of the friends and family who always seem to be present in "that" dream! Well, something like that, but much worse, must have been what Adam and Eve felt when they transgressed! The Bible says that

"... the eyes of them both were opened, and they knew that they were naked; and they sewed fig leaves together, and made themselves aprons" (Gen. 3:7). The shame and distress that resulted from sin drove them to try and cover up the truth. It drove them to hide from God.

Estrangement

"For the wages of sin is death;"
Romans 6:23

In the midst of paradise Adam and Eve experienced that death which they had been warned would find them on the day they transgressed! They did not die suddenly on a physical level. There was a plan in place based on God's foreknowledge of the fall. God had provided Himself a Lamb, *"the Lamb slain from the foundation of the world"* (Rev. 13:8). But as soon as man sinned there was a change. There was an estrangement between God and man, and an estrangement between man and woman. We see this demonstrated that evening when God came walking in the garden looking for His children. *"And the LORD God called unto Adam, and said unto him, Where art thou?"* (Gen. 3:9) The responses to the Lord's questions give us an insight into what transgression had done to mankind. *"And he [Adam] said, I heard Thy voice in the garden, and I was afraid, because I was naked; and I hid myself"* (Gen. 3:10).

On that first terrible day of sin and death man ran from the God who is love. All of us have been born running ever since. The oneness of thought and feeling with God, which had existed from man's creation, was destroyed! God had not changed, but man had. Man was now a deserter of good and a defender of selfishness! *"And He [God] said, Who told thee that thou wast naked?"* (Gen. 3:11) Who had told Adam that he was naked? Adam had said that he was afraid (an emotion), and the fact that they were ashamed (another emotion or feeling) is evidenced by their sewing fig leaf aprons to hide behind. We also see that Adam and Eve's thoughts had shifted from love to God, and love for each other, to thoughts of selfishness. This can be clearly seen in the conversations that followed.

God asks Adam: *"Hast thou eaten of the tree, whereof I commanded thee that thou shouldest not eat?"* (Gen. 3:11) Adam's first thought must have been something like, "How am I going to get out of this jam? I know...I'll blame Eve and God!" *"And the man said, the woman whom Thou gavest to be with me, she gave me of the tree, and I did eat"* (Gen. 3:12). God, not being deceived in the least, turned to Eve and asked, *"What is this that thou hast done? And the woman said, The serpent beguiled me, and I did eat"* (Gen 3:13). "It was the serpents fault!" Eve said, "Um, and by the way, why did you make that crafty serpent God?" Eve's first thought after Adam threw her under the bus, so to speak, must have been something like, "How could Adam do that to me, the horrid man...how am I going to get out of this jam? I know...I'll blame the serpent and (subconsciously perhaps) God..."

We can clearly see that after transgression their consciences or their *"innermost thoughts, desires, intentions; feelings"* were no longer pure, loving, and innocent. Transgression had warped their hearts and minds. It had corrupted and changed their characters! This is how man's conscience was defiled.

Now we need to take look at "what" had defiled them. What is this "sin" that it should be so terrible? Was eating one (well, two) pieces of fruit so bad? Is all the injustice, suffering, death, and horror that we see around us and throughout history really the result of eating a piece of fruit?

Transgression

"Who are ye? and from whence come ye?"
Josh 9:8

Have you ever asked yourself the questions,"What is sin anyway? Where did it come from?" "Why can't God tolerate sin, and why does He hate it so much?"

Many have the idea that sin is the breaking of some, no doubt just, but arbitrary rules. They think its a kind of failure to jump through all the hoops tha God has set up to test us to see if we will obey His law! Some of us think that "sin" is not obeying the "Big Boss!" The Israelites had this view. They looked at God's law as a set of rules to be obeyed in order to keep God "happy" with them Sadly this is the way most of the human race views sin. But what is sin really? There is one cogent and clearly spelled out definition of sin in the Bible. *"Whosoever committeth sin transgresseth also the law: for sin is the transgression of the law"* (1 John 3:4). So sin is the "transgression of the law."

Question: What does it mean to "transgress" the law?

If we can understand what it means to "transgress the law," it will help answer the question of what sin really is. And it will help us understand what needs to be cleansed from our consciences. If you look up "transgression" in a good dictionary it will say:

"TRANSGRES'SION, *noun* The act of passing over or beyond any law or rule of moral duty; the violation of a law or known principle of rectitude; breach of command."[55]

This may give us a clue as to what "sin" is, but it is not all that can be said on what "transgression" is. We find a lot more help when we look at the etymology of this word.

"Transgression: *late 14c., from Old French transgression "transgression," particularly that relating to Adam and the Fall"*[56]

This word "transgression" is made up of two parts: The first part, **trans:** is a word-forming element meaning; "across, beyond, through, on the other side of something. Secondly, we must add the past participle **"gressus,"** which comes from the PIE root[57]

---

55 Noah Webster 1828

56 online etymology dict.

57 Proto-Indo-European root

"ghredh"- which forms all or a part of; agress; agression![58] **"Agress"** means to "make an attack," and **"agression"** means "to make   an unprovoked attack."[59]

So to define "transgression" in simple terms, transgression means to cross over from one position to another, and then to make an unprovoked attack on the position you previously held! It would be something akin to treason, or like a soldier's betrayal and desertion to the enemy without cause.

Now let us apply this understanding of "transgression" to the definition of sin we just read, *"Whosoever committeth sin transgresseth also the law: for sin is the transgression of the law"* (1 John 3:4). This text is saying that sin is treason against God's law! It is a crossing over from a position where a son or daughter is in harmony with the law of God to a position where that person opposes, hates, and wars <u>relentlessly</u> against that law! This understanding of transgression brings up the inevitable question: What then is the law? What is it that sin opposes and fights against relentlessly? By understanding just what God's Law is, we will come closer to understanding why God hates sin so much, and why He will not, cannot, and should never tolerate the smallest particle of sin in His universe or in His creatures!

The Scriptures say, *"Owe no man any thing, but to love one another: for he that loveth another hath fulfilled the law. For this, Thou shalt not commit adultery, Thou shalt not kill, Thou shalt not steal, Thou shalt not bear false witness, Thou shalt not covet; and if there be any other commandment, it is briefly comprehended in this saying, namely, Thou shalt love thy neighbour as thyself. Love worketh no ill to his neighbour: therefore <u>love is the fulfilling of the law</u>"* (Rom. 13:8-10). So we see here that the Law is an expression in clear written form of what love is.

If we now take our definition of transgression and add in this understanding we find that sin is a crossing over from a position

---

58 online etymology dict

59 online etymology dict.

where a son or daughter is in harmony with love (the law of God) to a position where for no good reason that person opposes, hates, and wars relentlessly against that love (law)! Can you start to see why God will not, cannot, and should not tolerate sin in His universe or His creatures? As long as sin exists it will always relentlessly attempt to seek out and destroy love. It is like a mad dog whose only thought is to rend, infect, and destroy. This mad dog of sin must be put down! No one would think a parent loving if they kept a rabid dog in the baby's nursery, let alone in the neighborhood where their dear little children played. God's problem lay in the fact that His children were infected with this terrible disease of sin. So He provided a soul-saving transfusion for them which cost Him His life. This transfusion was left to them in His Will and Testament!

The Inheritance!

"His divine power hath given unto us
all things that pertain unto life and godliness"
2 Peter 1:3

So now at long last we come to it! We will now look in detail at what those who are found to be God's children are to inherit on the day when Christ stands up! *"Whereof <u>the Holy Ghost</u> also is a witness to us: for <u>after that He had said before</u>, This is the <u>covenant</u> that I will <u>make</u> with them after those days, saith the Lord, I will put my laws into their hearts, and in their minds will I write them"* (Heb 10:15, 16). Please remember what we have learned in the other four "W"s. Those studies told us that the above texts are saying that after the days of waiting, God will dispose and give fully and finally the inheritance to the heirs of Christ. Please note, it is specifically the Holy Spirit who is speaking here. There is coming, in the very near future, a bequest/inheritance from God by the Spirit.

Flip-Flopping Verses

Question: In Hebrews 8:10 and Hebrews 10:16 do we have the same promise being presented? The answer is "Yes," but we have some flip-flopping going on. Have you ever compared the two promises side by side? If you had you would have seen something odd. Let's take a look:

Hebrews 8:10
"For this is the covenant that I will make with the house of Israel after those days, saith the Lord; I will <u>put My laws into their mind</u>, and <u>write them in their hearts</u>:"

Hebrews 10:16
"This is the covenant that I will make with them after those days, saith the Lord, I will <u>put my laws into their hearts</u>, and <u>in their minds will I write them</u>;"

Do you see it? The order is reversed! In chapter eight the law is <u>put</u> into the mind, and in chapter ten, the law is <u>written</u> in the mind. Also, when it comes to the heart. In chapter eight the law is <u>written</u> in the heart and in chapter ten the Law is <u>put</u> into the heart! The fact that we are dealing with the same promise is clearly shown when we read, *"Whereof the Holy Ghost also is a witness to us: for <u>after that He had said before</u>"* (Heb. 10:15). In other words, Paul is saying that he is here referring us back to the words of the Spirit which Paul had already written down in Hebrews 8.

If we put the two texts together they would read something like this; "For this is the covenant that I will make with the house of Israel after those days, saith the Lord; I will <u>put my laws into their mind</u>, and <u>in their minds will I write them</u> and I will <u>put my laws into their hearts</u>, and <u>in their hearts will I write them</u>:" Or to make it less wordy, we might say God has promised to put and write His law in our hearts and minds.

Putting and Writing

You are by now no doubt familiar with what we are about to do. We are again going to take a look at the components of these Scriptures so that we can understand what they are actually saying. I hope by now, as a seasoned campaigner, you are starting to find this kind of thing fun. We have two actions being performed by God in His distribution of the inheritance to His heirs:

First: Putting (not to be confused with the game of Golf 😊) If you look up this word in the original Greek, you find it is the word "dídōmi,"[60] which means to bestow. This word "bestow" implies the "conveying of something as a gift and may suggest condescension on the part of the giver"[61] So one part of our inheritance will be the gracious conveyance of God's law from Himself as a gift into our hearts and minds! A great condescension of love indeed!

Second: Write (not to be confused with the author of this book 😊) This is the Greek word epigrapho, pronounced *"ep-ee-graf'-o,"* which means to "inscribe."[62] Websters 1828 Dictionary defines inscribe as follows:

> **"Inscribe:** To write on; to engrave on for perpetuity;" "To imprint on; as, to inscribe any thing on the mind or memory."[63]

Please notice that this writing is meant to be permanent or to last always. That is what "perpetuity" means. This writing or inscribing will have an existence that never ends. There will never come a time when it will be effaced or erased! This is what is being alluded to where the Scriptures say, *"He will make an utter end: affliction shall not rise up the second time"* (Nah. 1:9). So the second part of this disposition of the inheritance, which Christ died to leave His children

---

60 Strong's Exhaustive Concordance #G1325

61 Merriam Webster

62 Strong's Exhaustive Concordance #G1924

63 Noah Webster 1828

in His Will, is the permanent impressing, inscribing or sealing of His law into the hearts and minds of the *"heirs of salvation"* (Heb. 1:14). I hope the above helps to *"put write"* our understanding. 😊 Now we must take a look at the destination of this "putting" and "writing" of the Law.

Hearts and Minds

There is a song I listened to before Christ apprehended me, which should warn you that its morals were not the best. It was called "The Head and the Heart."[64] In this song a young man is trying to decide if he should stay in a relationship with his girl or if he should leave her. The battle in this decision was between his head, or mind, and his heart. Between his passionate, emotional feelings, and his cold, calculating intellect. When people use the words "heart" and "mind" today, this is almost always what they mean. We, as cautious Bible students, must not assume that this modern concept is what we are dealing with when we read these words in Hebrews. When it comes to the texts we have been examining, we must ask the question: "Is this what the Spirit meant when He said *"hearts"* and *"minds?"*

Would it surprise you to find that both these words "hearts" and "minds," which we find in Hebrews chapters 8 and 10, have aspects of intellectual thought in them? Only one of them contains the element of our feelings as well. Let's take a look.

First up, let's look at the word that has been translated as "minds."

Minds: This word in the original Greek is "dianoia" pronounced *dee-an'-oy-ah*. It means: *"deep thought"*[65] and comes from another word "dia" which *"denotes the channel of an act."* [66]

64Chris64Chris De Burgh The Head and the Heart lyrics © BMG Rights Management US, LLC

65 Strong's Exhaustive Concordance #G1271

66 Strong's Exhaustive Concordance #G1223

If we were to put this into modern language, we might say that this word "mind" means, that part of us which lies deep beneath our surface thoughts, and unconsciously channels and influences our thoughts and emotions. Some might call this our subconscious mind or the deep motives and intentions of the heart. Have you ever done, felt, or thought something horrid and immediately wondered, "What was I thinking?" or "Where did that come from?" Well, it was most likely a deep, unconscious impulse of the mind which did not register on the surface level. (Otherwise known as "foot in mouth disease!") Now, what about this word "hearts?"

Hearts: This is the Greek word "kardia" Strong's defines it as follows: "the heart that is (figuratively) the thoughts or feelings (mind)"[67] Notice the combining of two things. This word is dealing with our thoughts and/or feelings. This is not the same Greek word that is used for deep thought. This is a word used in the Greek for the conscious thoughts of an individual <u>and</u> his or her feelings.

Why are feelings included here with thoughts? Well, feelings are emotional responses that are driven by our thoughts, either consciously or subconsciously. On the flip side, feelings can also drive our thoughts. These thoughts or feelings can be rational or irrational, good or bad, happy or sad, righteous or wicked. In short, what we are dealing with here is our state of mind on a conscious, intellectual, and emotional level.

Here in our hearts (our conscious thoughts and feelings) and in our minds (our subconscious motives and impulses), God will, through a promised inheritance, "put" and "inscribe" His law permanently! His Law will again be the controlling element and the spring of our thoughts, actions, and feelings forever after!

So coming back to the lost Will and Testament. If you had been given an earthly inheritance in this world, and the executor of the Will told you he would be making a deposit into your account, wouldn't you like to know what that deposit was? I sure would. The Scriptures say that; *"Moses commanded us a law, even <u>the inheritance</u> of the congregation of Jacob"* (Deut. 33:4). This text

---

67 Strong's Exhaustive Concordance #G2588

brings up the next logical question: What is this law of God which He will deposit and impress permanently in our subconscious minds and our conscious thoughts and feelings?

The Law of God!

"Whereby are given unto us exceeding great and precious promises: that by these ye might be partakers of the <u>divine nature.</u>"
2 Peter 1:4

In order to understand what is to be given to God's children as an inheritance; in order to understand what is to be put into their hearts/ minds and inscribed/sealed there forever, we need to circle back and look again at just what the law of God is. If you remember, we talked about this briefly in our study of the word "transgression." We found that sin was transgression; an unaccountable element that hates and opposes God's Law. We discovered that sin constantly wars against, and tries to destroy love. As it is written: *"Owe no man any thing, but to love one another: for <u>he that loveth another hath fulfilled the law</u>..."* (Rom. 13:8). And again: *"Love worketh no ill to his neighbour: therefore <u>love is the fulfilling of the law</u>"* (Rom. 13:10).

The word of God tells us that the Law of God is a transcript, a written description of what love is. By extension, it is also a written transcript of what lies in the heart and mind of God. The whole law describes what love looks like. *"Beloved, let us love one another: for <u>love is of God</u>; and every one that loveth is born of God, and knoweth God. He that loveth not knoweth not God; <u>for God is love</u>"* (1 John 4:7, 8). This love is not that indulgent, sentimental emotion that passes for love in the world and many times in the churches these days. This love is a principle of self-forgetfulness for the good of others. Jesus wasn't held on the cross by nails and ropes, or Roman guards. He was held on that tree by self-sacrificing love!

Professor Edwards A. Park, an American Congregational pastor, once wrote, "Our most illustrious preachers gave a wonderful majesty to their discourses by following the example of the Master, and giving prominence to the law, its precepts, and its threatenings. They repeated the two great maxims, that <u>the law is a transcript of the divine perfections,</u> and that a man who does not love the law does not love the gospel; <u>for the law,</u> as well as the gospel, <u>is a mirror reflecting the true character of God.</u>" The Law of God is the standard of righteousness for time and eternity. It is a written declaration of goodness and love. *"And we have known and believed the love that God hath to us. <u>God is love;</u> and he that dwelleth in love dwelleth in God, and God in him"* (1 John 4:16). We read above from Pastor Park that the Law is a "transcript" of the divine perfections. This truth is seconded by the most prolific Christian writer of the nineteenth century. In the book "God's Amazing Grace," we read that, "<u>God requires perfection</u> of His children. <u>His law is a transcript of His own character.</u>"[68] And also that "<u>The law is but a transcript of the character of God.</u> Behold in your heavenly Father a perfect manifestation of the principles which are the foundation of His government."[69] The foundation of God's government is love. Self-forgetful, self-sacrificing love.

Some Last Definitions

So now are you starting to see what we are being promised as an inheritance? Two short definitions should flesh it out for us.

Transcript: What do I mean when I say the law of God is a transcript? The word "transcript" means *"A copy; a writing made from and according to an original".*[70] The Law of God given to Moses was written by His own finger, and is an exact copy of His holy, moral character. Okay, so what is the moral character?

Character: This is a fascinating word because it has two primary definitions. First is that a character is a "symbol marked or branded on the body; and comes from Greek "kharaktēr" "engraved mark.""[71]

---

68   *God's Amazing Grace* E.G. White pg.148
69   Thoughts from the Mount of Blessing pg.77
70   Noah Webster 1828

71 Online etym. Dict.

(This should make Revelation 7:2 mean a bit more, right?) It also means the <u>inherent qualities</u> of a person. When looking for a good definition of moral character I found this gem: *"The thoughts and feelings combined make up the moral character."[72]*

The Law of God is the written account of God's righteousness and is an expression of His perfect thoughts and feelings, or character. God has promised that the inheritance left to His children will be the putting into and permanent inscribing of, that perfect righteous character of love. It will be placed in and permanently impressed upon the subconscious mind and the conscious thoughts and feelings of ALL who are found to be His children!

This is the end goal of the plan of salvation, and the reason Christ died to give us another inheritance. An inheritance of perfect righteousness. A righteousness that is by the faith of Him (Christ) alone! (see Eph. 2:8) Do you now understand the Scripture which says, *"For we through the Spirit <u>wait</u> for the hope of righteousness by faith"* (Gal. 5:5). This is what the Spirit meant when Peter wrote: *"According as His divine power hath given unto us all things that pertain unto life and godliness, through the knowledge of Him that hath called us to glory and virtue: Whereby are given unto us exceeding great and precious promises: that <u>by these</u> ye might be <u>partakers of the divine nature</u>, having escaped the corruption that is in the world through lust"* (2 Pet. 1:3, 4). This word "nature" is the Greek word *"phusis,"* pronounced; "foo'-sis." It is a noun and means "the inherent or inner nature."[73] These are those "qualities that are considered permanent or cannot be separated from an essential character."[74] In this case we are promised Christ's perfect, inherent or inner nature. A character of absolute, flawless purity and love!

Paul, looking forward to this glorious day says Christ died so, *"that He might present it* [His church] *to Himself a glorious church, not having spot, or wrinkle, or any such thing; but that it* [His church] *should be holy and without blemish"* (Eph. 5:27). Through a

---

72 RH April 21, 1885, par.2

73 Strong's Exhaustive Concordance #G5449

74 Vocabulary.com

final crowning act of "putting" and "inscribing" the righteous character of Christ into the hearts and minds of God's true children, they will be made perfect. Not just considered perfect, not just perfect at any stage of growth and experience, but they will finally be absolutely, actually, morally perfect! They will think and feel about transgression the same way that God thinks and feels about it! They too, will hate and abhor anything and everything which attacks love!

Just before he sealed his witness for the truth with his blood, Paul wrote: *"I have fought a good fight, I have finished my course, I have kept the faith: Henceforth there is laid up for me a crown..."* Was this a crown of gold and gems? No, it was a very different kind of crown. It was a crown *"... of righteousness, which the Lord, the righteous judge, shall give me at that day: and not to me only, but unto all them also that love His appearing"* (2 Tim. 4:7, 8). I pray that God will cause you and me to love, not only His appearing, but the character that lies within that face which I have so long desired to see in peace!

Mission Accomplished!

"For, behold, the darkness shall cover the earth, and gross darkness the people: but the LORD shall arise upon thee, and His glory shall be seen upon thee.[75]"
Isaiah 60:2

This is the work of Christ in the sanctuary. This is the cleansing He has been working tirelessly for in that Holy temple *"not made by hands"* (Heb. 9:11). This inheritance is how He will cleanse our *"innermost thoughts, desires, intentions; feelings."* This is the final righteousness that is by the faith of Jesus, for which, *"...we through the Spirit wait for the hope of righteousness by faith"* (Gal. 5:5). By the distribution of this *"priceless inheritance,"* His children's hearts will again beat in perfect unison with the heart of Him who is Love We will hate only sin. We will love, always and forever, as He loves.

---

75 Also see Exodus 33:18-21 which defines God's "glory" as His goodness.

Then will the promise be fulfilled: *"...He will make an utter end: affliction shall not rise up the second time"* (Nah. 1:9). Never ever again! This understanding of the perfecting love and mercy of God towards undeserving and sinful men and women should drive out all fear. We no longer need to fear perfection and His coming but we may now joyfully and longingly say with John; *"Even so, come, Lord Jesus!...Amen!"* (Rev. 22:20)

> *"Beloved, now are we the sons of God,*
> *and it doth not yet appear what we shall be:*
> *but we know that, when He shall appear,*
> *we shall be like Him; for we shall see Him*
> [face to face] *as He is."*
> 1 John 3:2

PART III
The Problem of Perfection?

In the last section of this book, we must take this understanding of the Will and Testament of the Son of God and apply it to the problems of perfection we looked at in part one of this book. Let's see if these "problems" are still problems.

Actual Moral Perfection!

First up, let's revisit the frightening realization that to see God face to face and survive the experience we must be faultless. That seemingly insurmountable problem reared its head when we looked at what the Bible declares us to be, and what it says we must be. We saw that absolute actual moral perfection was the indispensable thing required to see God face to face. We must be absolutely perfect and we do not now possess that perfection!

Question: Will we possess that perfection when God distributes the inheritance, finally and fully to His children? Since it has been shown that the inheritance is His very character and perfect spiritual nature the answer is "Yes!" Now we can understand how we get a hold of, or "apprehend" that perfection. It is not a perfection which we attain by our own efforts and achievements. It is a victory given as a legacy by God. It will be given to those found to be the legitimate heirs of Christ!

That being said, the devil will certainly try and tempt some of us to act presumptuously! Don't be deceived! We must by the grace of God, test our faith. *"Examine yourselves to see if your faith is genuine. Test yourselves. Surely you know that Jesus Christ is among you; if not, you have failed the test of genuine faith"* (2 Cor. 13:5).

We must discover if it is Christ at work in us or if there is another, lying spirit who has set up shop in our experience! Does our "righteousness" come from the indwelling Christ alone or from our own efforts? Is there displayed in our lives a real, genuine, God-given heart righteousness; or just an outward lip service or rule-following and list-checking religion? Maybe our righteousness consists of a synthesized idolatry of faith/works? Are we partly trusting in God and partly trusting in ourselves? If you find self-righteousness, apathy or idolatry in your experience, I urge you to run to, and fall upon the Rock, Jesus Christ. Be broken while there is still a little time left!

A Dog's Breakfast Revisited!

As promised in the beginning of the second part of this book, we will now go back through our "dog's breakfast" and take a look at the problems that we saw there. Can our new understanding of the Lost Will and Testament of Christ reconcile these issues? We will be looking at them in a reverse order as follows:

6) Probationary Time
5) The Delayed Return of Christ
4) The Empty Throne
3) The Cheating Dead
2) A Perfect Remnant
1) The Judgment

Chapter 10

Dog's Breakfast #6

"Probationary Time"

When examining this spicy dish we saw that many of us have the idea that probation was God giving us enough time to prove that we had gotten our act together spiritually. We saw that many of us view probation as a "ready or not, here I come" proposition. How should we now view this idea of probationary time? If you examine the etymology of the word "probation," you will find that it comes from the same word as "probate" and "probationary." The word "probate" is especially interesting because it is the word used for the legal procedures that must be followed when a legally binding Will has come into force. This word probate means to "prove" or test in court.

Probate

Probate is a process of "proving" a Will. This process takes place over an indefinite period of time during which a probate court sits and oversees the process of testing and then implementing a last Will and Testament. We will now take a look at the steps in this process. As we do, we will ask the questions; do we see this process being carried out in the plan that God has made for our salvation? And do we see this process of probate kick into action after Christ wrote and executed His Will during that seventieth week prophesied of in Daniel? (see Dan 9:27)

Step 1 of Probating a Will,
"Opening the Process of Probate"

The first step taken to get the process of probate going after the testator of a Will dies is to file a petition with the court. This petition usually contains the following three things:

A) A valid Will must be submitted to the probate court.

B) Evidence must be submitted to the court which proves the death of the testator (the one who wrote the Will).

C) The court must appoint the executor of the Will.

Let's take a look and see if this has happened. Does the Word of God show that these steps have been taken in the case of the "Last Will and Testament" of Jesus Christ?

A. The Submission of a Valid Will

Question: After the death and ascension of Christ, do we find the submission of a valid Will to a court in heaven? We have already studied the validity of the last Will and Testament that Christ wrote and signed with His blood. (see the section titled: "Question W2: Where?") But we have yet to determine if this Will was submitted to the court of heaven after Christ's death.

The apostle John in the book of Revelation was told the following: *"What thou seest, write in a book, and send it unto the seven churches which are in Asia; unto Ephesus, and unto Smyrna, and unto Pergamos, and unto Thyatira, and unto Sardis, and unto Philadelphia, and unto Laodicea"* (Rev. 1:11). All of the cities mentioned in the above text were in Roman provinces. As such they were under Roman Law. God uses images in Revelation which would have been very familiar to the people and culture the book was being written to. In this case the audience is the seven churches of Asia; those living in a Roman province, under Roman law.

Roman Probate Law

There was a famous Roman jurist named Gaius (last name unknown). He was one of the five experts on Roman law whose opinions were to be used in deciding cases at law in the ancient Roman empire.[76] His writings shed very particular light on the legal proceedings necessary to execute and implement a last Will and testament under Roman law. Gaius wrote that a valid Will and testament must be sealed with seven seals and that the Will could not be opened unless at least four of the seven witnesses who had sealed the Will were present.[77]

In Revelation chapters 4 and 5 a scene is presented to John. Could it be that he was describing a legal proceeding such as the one mentioned by Gaius? Let's take a look. He wrote that *"...before the throne there was a sea of glass like unto crystal: and in the midst of the throne, and round about the throne, were four beasts full of eyes before and behind"* (Rev. 4:6). Here we have represented in imagery the four witnesses that people living under Roman probate law would have expected to see. The seven churches would have understood that their law required at least four witnesses to be present at the unsealing of a last Will and testament. Here was a scene, that though not familiar to us, was very familiar to the churches of Asia. They would have known instantly that the scene before them was a legal proceeding.

Question: Was a book with seven seals submitted to the court of heaven here in Revelation? Yes, indeed! We read, *"And I saw in the right hand of Him that sat on the throne a book written within and on the backside, sealed with seven seals"* (Rev. 5:1). This document from its description was undoubtedly a Will and Testament. Anyone reading John's description during his time would have instantly recognized it as such! Please notice that the book was written without and within. This was an ancient safeguard to prevent tampering. The contents of the document were written on one side and again on the other side. The document was then folded in half

76 See the "Law of Citations" issued by the emperor Valentinian III, AD 426.

77 See Giaus Institutes Vol II

and the front edge was stitched closed with papyrus. Then, the seals of seven persons were affixed to the outside sealing the document. These seals testified that what was written on the inside was the same as what was written on the outside. This procedure allowed people to understand what was in the Will without opening it and thus invalidating it. [78]

In Revelation 5 we are shown a legal document in the hand of God on the throne. It contains an inheritance beyond imagining. The wealth of God is infinite and the Scriptures declare that *"... if we are faithful to the end, trusting God just as firmly as when we first believed, we will share in all that belongs to Christ"* (Heb. 3:14 NLT).

B) Proof of Death

The next step in the probate process is the submission of the proof of death to the courts. The Will can only go into effect and into the process of probate once a person dies. We see this same requirement stated in the Word of God, *"Now when someone leaves a Will, it is necessary to prove that the person who made it is dead. The Will goes into effect only after the person's death. While the person who made it is still alive, the Will cannot be put into effect. That is why even the first covenant was put into effect with the blood of an animal"* (Heb. 9:16-18 NLT).

Question: Was the required proof of death submitted to the court in heaven? In Hebrews we read that we, by faith have come *"... unto mount Zion, and unto the city of the living God, the heavenly Jerusalem, and to an innumerable company of angels,...to Jesus the mediator of the new covenant,* [diathēkē/Will] *and to the blood of sprinkling"* (Heb. 12:22, 24). This blood of sprinkling is seen here in these passages of Hebrews, not on earth where it was spilled, but

---

78 The Old Testament covenant services in the sanctuary were a foreshadowing of the New Testament. Here in this imagery of a book written externally and internally is the same idea. The external sanctuary services on earth were <u>outward</u>, visible symbols, foreshadowing what Christ would do <u>internally</u> in the hearts and minds of His people; through the mediating/implementing of the "New Covenant," His "Devisory Will."

in heaven. Do you remember what Paul said when relating the story of the dedication of the earthly tabernacle? He stated, *"That is why blood was required under the first covenant as a proof of death"* (Heb. 9:18 NLT 1996). He was here referring to the <u>blood and water</u> which Moses took and with which he sprinkled the entire tabernacle and the people. This dedicated the earthly tabernacle and instituted the service of the sanctuary on earth.

The same was done in heaven where the real temple is. John says that *"... I beheld, and, lo, in the midst of the throne and of the four beasts, and in the midst of the elders, stood a Lamb as it had been slain"* (Rev. 5:6). The Lamb is Christ. He here appears as a slain lamb. This appearance of a slain lamb proves that the *"Lamb of God"*[79] has died. This happens at a crisis which had caused John to weep. What is that crisis? It happens amid the great courtroom scene of Revelation 5. The crisis is the inability of anyone to open a book! (More on this in a moment.) The comforting of John comes when the court, satisfied with the proof of death, allows the book to be opened! Here we have a proof of death being submitted to the court of heaven. This is what Christ meant when He told Mary, *"Touch me not; for I am not yet ascended to my Father: but go to my brethren, and say unto them, I ascend unto my Father, and your Father; and to my God, and your God"* (John 20:17). We read in Hebrews that when Christ went to His Father, *"Neither by the blood of goats and calves, but by His own blood He entered in once into the holy place, having obtained eternal redemption for us"* (Heb. 9:12). This was that <u>blood and water</u> which flowed from His pierced side! Here in Revelation we see that the proof of death has been submitted to the court and accepted.

C) The Appointing of the Executor

The next process when probating a Will is that the court must grant a petition which establishes who the legal executor of the Will is. It is vitally important that the executor of the Will carries out the wishes of the testator as if they themselves were the testator. This is the reason that we sometimes call both the person who wrote and

---

79 See John 1:29

signed the Will and the person who undertakes to carry out their wishes, the "executor." The courts will under almost all circumstances, appoint as executor the person who was named executor by the executor! (Sorry, I couldn't help myself ☺.)

Do we have anywhere in Scripture a record of who the executor of Christ's Will is? Yes, we do indeed! Jesus Christ is in a very unique situation when it comes to appointing an executor for His will. He is in the position to be His own executor. He can do this because He has died and yet has risen from the dead. He Himself can mediate His "diathēkē," His "New Covenant" or "Devisory Will." It says of Christ that He is *"...the mediator of the new covenant,"* or Will (Heb. 12:24).

Question: What is a mediator? When people say that "Jesus is our Mediator," have you ever wondered what that role actually entails on a practical level? Webster's 1828 dictionary defines mediator as: *"MEDIA'TOR, noun, One that interposes between parties at variance for the purpose of reconciling them."* [80]

Mediator

Whenever I've read the word "mediator" and its definition in the past, my mind would conjure up pictures of an offended God who needed someone to hold Him back so He didn't blast those evil sinners! It always came across as if we needed a protector in Christ so we weren't destroyed by the Father. This is the picture of God that the church of the Dark Ages held, and still holds. How my understanding has changed. It is through the Father's gift of His only begotten Son that we have the inheritance which Christ has promised us! We can now understand that the new covenant is the way that the Father has established to save us. Since it is through the inheritance of Christ's perfection that God's children will finally be perfect, it naturally follows that Christ's work in the sanctuary is to implement that Will. Christ's implementation of His new covenant will result in full and final atonement. It has/will reconcile two parties (God and man) that have been at variance.

---

80 Websters 1828 Dictionary

Atonement

The word "atonement" (at-one-ment), means the same thing as the word mediator. It is the work of God which results in <u>reconciliation</u> between two <u>parties that have been at variance</u>! Christ is the One who carries His own Will into effect. That Will is what brings about a complete and final at-one-ment between God and man. This assertion is supported by the Scripture that says: *"That is why He is the mediator of the new covenant between God and people, so that all who are invited can receive the eternal inheritance God has promised them"* (Heb 9:15). It is the job of an executor to open and execute the Will of the testator. It is the executor's job to bring the heirs into their inheritance! An inheritance of at-one-ment! An inheritance of perfection! So as you see, we should be able to interchange the word "mediator" with the more modern word "executor."

Authorization

Question: Is Christ the one who has been authorized to open and execute His Will and Testament? He is! In the great court scene in Heaven, which we have been looking at in Revelation, John says: *"And I saw in the right hand of Him that sat on the throne a book written within and on the backside, sealed with seven seals. And I saw a strong angel proclaiming with a loud voice, Who is worthy to open the book, and to loose the seals thereof? And no man in heaven, nor in earth, neither under the earth, was able to open the book, neither to look thereon. And I wept much, because no man was found worthy to open and to read the book, neither to look thereon"* (Rev 5:1-4). Here we see a Will in the hand of Him who sat on the throne and a question is asked, "Who is worthy, who is legally entitled to open the Will and to execute it?" It says that no man was found worthy, and it caused John to weep in abject distress.

What caused this grief and distress? If John had not recognized that scroll for what it was, do you think it would have disturbed him so much? He might have thought... "Oh well, it's probably a recipe for onion soup or something, no big deal!" But no, he knew what was in God's hand and the thought that this Will could not be read and executed nearly crushed him! Why was it that no man could open that scroll and read the will?

Question: Have you ever stopped to ask yourself if this declaration that <u>no man</u> could open the book included Christ? Was Christ then in heaven? It wouldn't matter, no man in heaven could open the book. Maybe this was when Christ was on the earth? That wouldn't matter either, no man on earth could open that book! Maybe He was resting at this time, maybe this was during the three days He was in the tomb or *"under the earth?"* This also wouldn't make any difference, because no man under the earth could open the book either. No matter where He was, Christ, too, could not have opened and read that document. "Whoa!...Why not?" you say (probably with a furrowed brow and a degree of elevation in your voice ☺) "Christ can do anything, He is God after all!"

Well, let's take a look at why not. In ancient times, if a Will had been written and sealed with seven seals it was called a testament under seals. The Will went into effect, or became legally binding, only upon the death of the one who wrote it. If someone were to break its seals while the testator was still living, the Will would have been rendered invalid! So you see, Christ couldn't open and execute the Will until He had died! That is why one of the elders said to John, *"Weep not: behold, the Lion of the tribe of Juda, the Root of David,* <u>*hath prevailed*</u> *to open the book, and to loose the seven seals thereof"* (Rev 5:5). Do you remember the cry of victory Jesus uttered on the cross? *"It is finished!"* By His death Christ has prevailed! By His death He has brought His Will into force! As stated already: *"...when someone leaves a Will, it is necessary to prove that the person who made it is dead. The Will goes into effect only after the person's death. While the person who made it is still alive, the Will cannot be put into effect"* (Heb. 9:16, 17 NLT 1996). In response to the elders statement of encouragement, John turns to the throne. *"And I beheld, and, lo, in the midst of the throne and of the four beasts, and in the midst of the elders, stood a Lamb* <u>*as it had been slain*</u>*"* (Rev. 5:6). By His death on the cross Christ has prevailed, and has put His Will into force! It can now be safely opened without invalidating it. Immediately following this scene we see Christ appointed as executor of His own testament. *"And He* [the Lamb] *came and took the book out of the right hand of Him that sat upon the throne"* (Rev. 5:7). Here the Will is delivered by God into the hands of Christ who shortly afterward opens the first seal and begins the process of executing His Will. Christ has been appointed as the executor, or mediator, of the new covenant. Next we need to take a look at the second step in this process of probate.

Step 2, of Probating a Will
"Notification"

As stated previously, when someone who has a legal Will dies the Will goes into force and can't be changed. After it is opened by the proper person at the proper time and place, it enters into the next phase of probate. If the heirs of the Will are unaware of their inheritance, this period of time is used to contact them with the "Good News" of their new-found prosperity! Do we see something similar in the gospel? Yes we do! *"And this gospel of the kingdom shall be preached in all the world for a witness unto all nations; and then shall the end come"* (Matt. 24:14). The good news must be published!

This Good News is to go to everyone since Jesus died to save all. There is no one, no matter what they have done, or how bad they may be, that is excluded. To all, God extends an invitation into His family: *"The Spirit and the bride say, Come. And let him that heareth say, Come. And let him that is athirst come. And whosoever will, let him take the water of life freely"* (Rev. 22:17). One of the most beautiful and inclusive promises in Scripture is this one, *"...as Moses lifted up the serpent in the wilderness, even so must the Son of man be lifted up: That whosoever believeth in Him should not perish, but have eternal life"* (John 3:14-15). Whosoever will, may be born again of the Spirit and made a child of God. By God's grace, anyone can become an heir of Christ.

This notification to all the world of an inheritance takes time, but it is not the only thing that must be done during this process of probate. There is more to be done when probating a Will. Now we must look at the other work Christ must do to implement His Will and it includes more than just notification.

Step 3 of Probating a Will
"The Calling in of Debts"

Another vital part of the probating of a Will and Testament is dealing with all the outstanding debts of the estate. All who have a claim against the estate are notified and are required to submit their debts to the court to have them paid. Any outstanding debts which are not submitted by the close of the probation process will remain unpaid, and the loss must forever be borne by the one who did not submit the debt for payment.

Now while God's children are heirs, they are also debtors along with all the world. We have a debt of guilt which we cannot pay ourselves. Was such a notification sent out after Christ ascended into heaven? Yes, the Spirit was sent to *"...convict the world of sin, and of righteousness, and of judgment"* (John 16:8). The Spirit came to convict all of us that we have a tremendous debt that needs to be submitted to Christ for payment. Jesus has provided the payment for our impossible debt, His estate will cover our poverty! The promise of grace is a beautiful one, *"If we confess our sins, He is faithful and just to forgive us our sins, and to cleanse us from all unrighteousness"* (1 John 1:9). If we decide to reject this offered mercy and cling to our sin, we will have to pay the debt ourselves.

That idea is kind of scary! It makes you want to bring all your debt to Him, right? Yes, but please note that we are not saved by our works here. Some of us might now be tempted to depend on our confession of sin for our salvation. This cannot be the case. The Scriptures say that *"it is God which worketh in you both to will and to do of His good pleasure"* (Phil. 2:13). This especially includes repentance and confession! "Repentance is as much the gift of Christ as is forgiveness, and it cannot be found in the heart where Jesus has not been at work. We can no more repent without the Spirit of Christ to awaken the conscience than we can be pardoned without Christ. Christ draws the sinner by the exhibition of His love upon the cross, and this softens the heart, impresses the mind, and inspires contrition and repentance in the soul."[81] Please do not yield to the temptation to look to yourself here, look to Jesus. It is He that has bought all of our debt. He now owns it and it is He alone who can clear our debts.

If, through the convicting Spirit of Christ, I find that I have anything, any attitudes, desires, thoughts, feelings, or tendencies in my life that are sinful, what am I to do? I cannot save myself. I cannot change my skin or my spots, but by God's grace I can confess these sins to Jesus.

Dealing With Sin, A Warning

"Ephraim is joined to idols: let him alone."
Hosea 4:17

Our God will never employ force or coercion to the conscience. Force is completely contrary to His nature. If God brings conviction to a person's heart and that person, though convicted of the sin, still clings to and cherishes whatever it may be; if they stubbornly refuse to admit that sin to God, God will not force His salvation on them. If they will not submit that debt of sin to Him so that His estate can pay it, they will have to pay it themselves. That is not a survivable experience for the debtor. Please note again, that I am not talking about weakness here. We all experience the battle between the sinful nature and the Spirit of God within us.(see Gal. 5:17) I am talking here about stubborn, persistent rebellion. There is another point as well. We do not need to fret about whether or not we have all our debts turned in. It says in the Scriptures, *"Let us therefore, as many as be perfect,* [through the justifying blood of the lamb, see Col. 1:22] *be thus minded: and if in any thing ye be otherwise minded, God shall reveal even this unto you"* (Phil. 3:15). We may pray with the Psalmist *"Search me, O God, and know my heart: try me, and know my thoughts: And see if there be any wicked way in me, and lead me in the way everlasting"* (Ps 139:23, 24). We may pray to

---

81   The Review and Herald April 1, 1890.

Him, and then rest in Him!

This need for a dependent rest is very important. On the last day of the annual typical service in the earthly sanctuary, called "the day of atonement," the people were required to afflict their souls before God. *"And this shall be a statute for ever unto you: that in the seventh month, on the tenth day of the month, ye shall afflict your souls, <u>and do no work at all</u>, whether it be one of your own country, or a stranger that sojourneth among you"* (Lev 16:29). This word "afflict" means to humble oneself or to cast ones eyes downward. During that day of atonement, they were to acknowledge their need of salvation and their utter inability to save themselves. By faith they were to gather around the Tabernacle and look to the mediation of their high priest. They were to trust in a salvation provided by God. Please note that they were to afflict their souls and rest! In Hebrews we read, *"There remaineth therefore a rest to the people of God. For he that is entered into His* [God's] *rest, he also <u>hath ceased from his own works</u>, as God did from His"* (Heb 4:9, 10). The Sabbath was given to remind us that it is God that makes us holy!(See Ezek. 20:12). We must/may rest in complete dependence on Him who always fulfills His promises!

Shortcomings

One last point I would like to emphasize is this. There are transgressions which fall under the *"come short of the glory of God"* category (see Rom. 3:23). What of these shortcomings? What of these sins which we all commit ignorantly? Well, our dear Saviour has us covered there as well. It says in Hebrews that *"... into the second* [Most Holy Place] *went the high priest alone once every year, not without blood, which he offered for himself, and for the errors of the people"* (Heb. 9:7). The word "errors" here is the Greek word agnoéma, pronounced "ag-no'-ay-mah," which means: "a thing *ignored* that is <u>shortcoming:</u> - error."[82] We have a Saviour who has, and will, cover and cleanse all our sins, even those that we are unaware of.

---

82 Strong's Exhaustive Concordance G51

Now, dear reader, is the time, before the process of probation ends, to submit your debts to Him for payment. He will pay your debt however monstrous it is. His estate is wealthy beyond any need. He can and will also give you a heart repentance, He can and will work miracles in your life to free you from your chains! If you have something, some sin which you love and feel you simply cannot give up and turn in, do not despair! It is written, *"Him hath God exalted with His right hand to be a Prince and a Saviour, for to <u>give repentance</u> to Israel, and forgiveness of sins"* (Acts 5:31). Confess it to Him. Be honest and tell Him the truth. He already knows. Tell Him that you do not want to turn in this debt. Tell Him that you love it and that you don't want Him to touch it!! Tell Him that your heart is rebellious. He is able to change your desires here! Ask Him to work the work of confession and repentance in your heart! He will never fail to do so! *"Therefore let all the godly confess their rebellion to you while there is time that they may not drown in the flood waters of judgment"* (Ps. 32:6 NLT). Give Jesus the chance to save you! Give Him the chance to pay your debts! All power has been given to Him in heaven <u>and</u> in earth. He is faithful and just to forgive you and to cleanse you!

Step 4 of Probating a Will
"The Examination of Claims"

"For the Father judgeth no man,
but hath committed all judgment unto the Son:"
John 5:22

The fourth step in the process of probate, before the disposal of the inheritance, is an examination of the claims made against the estate. The executor of the estate may and must discard any and all false claims! Imagine this scenario: A wealthy man dies and in his Will he states that anyone who comes forward with a legitimate claim as his child will be accounted as an heir to his possessions. It further states in the Will that any and all debts which they have incurred will be paid in full by his estate! Such a Will would put a great burden on the executor. It would also greatly prolong the time needed to probate the Will in court. I'm pretty sure any attorney connected with estate planning would strongly advise this wealthy man against such an open ended last Will and Testament! Why? Well, such a document would leave the estate of the testator open to all sorts of fraudulent attacks! How many shysters, liars and con-men would come calling, presenting bogus claims of paternity and pretending to be the decedent's children? How many crooks would be lined up around the block, demanding their "share" of the inheritance and the paying off of all their debts?

Question: Would this "delay" in the proceedings be chargeable either to the judge or the executor of the Will? No. Who would be to blame? Those who made the false claims against the estate and, importantly, anyone who had put them up to it! When it comes to God, however, He does not count time as we do. He is willing to take whatever time is needed and to incur any expense, to save all His children. *"The Lord is not slack concerning His promise, as some men count slackness; but is longsuffering to us-ward, not willing that any should perish, but that all should come to repentance"* (2 Pet. 3:9).

The most weighty trust and responsibility placed on an executor of a Will is the examination of the claims that are submitted against the estate. The executor must gather together all of the registered debts and determine if the persons submitting them to the estate have a valid claim to the riches of the estate and the inheritance. So it is with Christ and His Will. We read in the Scriptures, *"Blessed are they that do His commandments, that they may have right to the tree of life, and may enter in through the gates into the city"* (Rev. 22:14). Jesus had said earlier that, *"Not every one that saith unto Me, Lord, Lord, shall enter into the kingdom of heaven; but he that doeth the will of My Father which is in heaven"* (Matt. 7:21). Please bear in mind who Jesus was speaking to when He said this. He was speaking to the most religious nation on earth. These people were hyper-vigilant when it came to keeping God's "commandments." These were the tithers of garden herbs (...nine dill seeds for me, one for God... nine for me, one for...)!

Jesus went on to qualify His statement about keeping the commandments. I can easily imagine that some of His hearers were feeling pretty smug and secure right up to the point when He said, *"Many will say to me in that day, Lord, Lord, have we not prophesied in Thy name? and in Thy name have cast out devils? and in Thy name done many wonderful works? And then will I profess unto them, I never <u>knew you</u>"* (Matt. 7:22, 23). Did we ever discuss anywhere in this book anything about "knowing" Him? Yes, we did. I hope you remember what it means to "know" Him. Those upon whom He will bestow His nature and perfect character, will "know" Him, from the least to the greatest!

One last point. Since it is an essential part of the probate process to examine all claims, how important is it that the process be thorough and meticulous. How very important that every word be examined, even the idle ones (Matt. 12:36). How imperative that every thought and every motive of the heart be considered! If they were not, someone, some child of God, might miss out on their inheritance, and that is something God will never permit!

Step 5 of Probating a Will,
"Last Call"

As the final days of probating a Will approach, the judge who is hearing the case will instruct the executor or mediator of the estate to send out one final notice. This notice is in <u>two parts</u>.

Highways and Hedges

The first part of this notice: This last call, is a final opportunity for any missing heirs to declare themselves to the court so that the executor may write their names down in the records which will be submitted to the judge and finalized. This is a sort of "Executor's Book of Inheritors." Only those found to be legitimate heirs after an examination, by the executor or mediator of the estate, have their names recorded. Only they will receive the inheritance. Any names found during the probate process to be invalid will be disallowed and struck from the record book. The judge and the executor are both very keen to ensure that ALL the children and heirs are notified and have an opportunity to receive their inheritance!

Do we find a final notice, a last urgent call going out in the plan for man's salvation? Yes, we do. This final notification that goes out is illustrated at the end of Christ's parable found in Luke 14. In this parable a man made a great feast. He commanded His servants to go and tell those who were invited that the supper was ready. We pick up the story upon the return of the servant: *"So that servant came, and shewed his lord these things...* ["These things" being that those who were invited would not come to the feast]*...Then the master of the house being angry said to His servant, 'Go out quickly into the streets and lanes of the city, and bring in hither the poor, and the maimed, and the halt, and the blind"* (Luke 14:21). Here we see the first gospel call, or notification, that went out. It was sent out with the outpouring of the Spirit upon the disciples on the day of Pentecost. The unbelieving Jewish nation, as a nation, rejected the invitation to the marriage of God's Son and so the Gospel went to the "unclean," or lame and blind, gentiles.

Christ continued His parable by saying, *"And the servant said, Lord, it is done as Thou hast commanded, and yet there is room. And the lord said unto the servant, Go out into the highways and hedges, and compel them to come in, that My house may be filled"* (Luke 14:22, 23). Here we see a "last call," a last urgent compelling invitation to come to the banquet!

Do we see this last call prophesied of elsewhere in the Scriptures? In Revelation it says that just such a call is and will go out, not once, not twice, but three times! By this threefold message, an urgent notice is to be sent out to all the world. Right at the midnight hour of this planet (AKA now), God sends out one more plea. These notifications are found in Revelation 14, and are figured as three angels or messages that God sends into all the nooks and crannies of this world. They are sent to urge His people to declare themselves as His children, His heirs! This is done just before the process of probate finishes. All who answer this loving call will have their names retained in the "Lamb's Book of Life" (see Rev. 13:8). They, along with Abraham, will have a part in that *"...city which hath foundations, whose builder and maker is God"* (Heb. 11:10).

The second part of the notice: The probate court also requires one final notice to any remaining debtors. This notice is sent out to all those who may still have outstanding debts for the estate to cover. As stated previously, the loss incurred for any debt not submitted to the probate court and approved by the executor before the probate process ends, will have to be borne by the person who failed to surrender that debt to the estate for payment.

Do we see this idea presented in the Scriptures? Yes, we do. The Scriptures declare that *"If we confess our sins, He is faithful and just to forgive us our sins, and to cleanse us from all unrighteousness"* (1 John 1:9). This word "confess" means to confess, yes, but also to "profess."[83] To profess means that we make an open declaration to God that we are sinners, debtors to the Law of God. It means that when convicted of our lost condition and any particular sins, we candidly admit the truth to God, the idea being that we must not be found hiding behind fig leaf aprons, excusing our sins. By His grace we will not be playing the "Blame Game" that our first parents did in Eden. By the gift of repentance from Christ (see Acts 5:31), we will candidly confess our sins to Jesus so that He may forgive us and cleanse us from that unrighteousness.

When we read that He (Christ) is *"Faithful and just to forgive us our sins and to cleanse us from all unrighteousness,"* it means just that. Why? Because He is "faithful. The Scriptures declare, *"If we believe not, yet He abideth faithful: He cannot deny Himself"* (2 Tim 2:13). Have you ever felt that you were just too far gone for God to save? Have you ever despaired and thought that you had gone too far into sin and done things that were unforgivable, things that could never be undone? I have. To every one of us whose hearts fatally accuse us, Christ assures us that *"if our heart condemn us, God is greater than our heart, and knoweth all things"* (1 John 3:20). What is it that He knows? He knows the truth which Satan

---

83 Strong's Exhaustive Concordance #G3670

continually tries to hide from all mankind. He knows that *"the LORD hath laid on Him* [Christ] *the iniquity of us all"* (Isa. 53:6). He has been punished for all the sins which mankind has ever, or will ever, commit. That includes all the sins which you and I may have perpetrated. No matter how seemingly unforgivable the crime, the fact is that the price has been paid. Love has bought our entire debt! It would be terrible to waste this love and grace! Do you see? We can bring all our disasters to Him. He will forgive and cleanse them all. That is the reason that He paid such a terrible price. Since He took the guilt and punishment of all sin upon Himself, He has the right to clear away any debt of sin, and He longs to do so.

I know we have already seen the importance of giving all our sins to Him but in keeping with the final notice theme: I want to restate this one more time since it is so vitally important. When God reveals to us our need of forgiveness and cleansing we must, by the power of His Holy Spirit, freely and openly admit the fact to Him. You are not telling Him anything He doesn't already know. The Scriptures plainly declare that, *"Neither is there any creature that is not manifest in His sight: but all things are naked and opened unto the eyes of Him with whom we have to do"* (Heb. 4:13). This may seem scary at first read, but it is really just the opposite if you think about it. God knows the future. He sees the things which are not as though they were (see Isa. 46:10). He knew all about you. All your pride, selfishness, hate. All your lust, envy and any other defiling sin which you have done, currently commit, or will perpetrate. He saw them all, in all their horrid detail, before you were ever born. Knowing all this in advance, He still loved you. The Father, the Son, and the Holy Spirit gave themselves completely so that you might be saved! As it is written, *"God was in Christ, reconciling the world unto Himself, not imputing their trespasses unto them"* (2 Cor. 5:19). Please personalize this verse. He has been loving you with His eyes wide open! There is no need to be afraid, no need to hide! So please, do not hesitate to submit your sins to Christ. He longs to cover you and enter "pardoned" against your name. He longs to cleanse you and to have you, you yourself, with Him for all eternity! He does not want you to keep and pay the debt of sin yourself! That would re-break His heart!

Step 6 of Probating a Will
"The Last Act of the Executor, Distribution of the Inheritance and Closure of Proceedings"

The last act of the probate process is the submission of the executor's work and findings to the court. Once these findings are approved by the court, the debts which have been found to be legitimate are declared to be finally and fully paid.

Have you ever had a huge debt forgiven or blotted out? Have you ever experienced the relief that comes when you have freedom from indebtedness? So it will be when the plan of salvation is complete. When Christ's work is finished, all the debts of sin recorded in the sanctuary will be blotted out, including the *"sins the people had* [or have] *committed in ignorance"* (Heb. 9:7 NLT 1996). All our debts will be paid in full and God's children will have no more of guilt or indebtedness.

Standing up and Stepping Down

In our civil proceedings today, when the last call by the executor has gone out and been heeded or rejected, the executor of the Will asks the court to release him/her from the role of executor. They then step down as the representative of the estate. This is because the process is completed and the need no longer exists for their mediation before the court. When all is completed and done, the final ruling comes down, the proceedings are finished, the judge stands up and the decisions of the court become forever fixed and final.

It is the same with the mediation of Christ in heaven. We read in Hebrews, *"Now where remission of these is, there is no more offering for sin"* (Heb. 10:18). Here we see the end of the probate process. It was to ensure the completion of the plan for our salvation that Jesus was made the executor of His own will. It is by virtue of His death that He has an inheritance to give to fallen mankind. Once it is determined who the heirs of God are, the probate process will end and the inheritance will be given. Until this stage is reached the inheritance has only been a promise. But when the process of probation is over, that which has been promised to the heirs as a possession by inheritance becomes theirs in reality. At this time also, all their sins/debts will be separated from them and blotted out, and the ministry of Jesus will cease.[84] We will then stand before God as we truly are, our consciences cleansed, perfect not just by imputation, but in reality, and viewed forever by Him as though we had never sinned! Crazy wonderful, I know!

When all is completed the pronouncement will be heard, *"He that is unjust, let him be unjust still: and he which is filthy, let him be filthy still: and he that is righteous, let him be righteous still: and he that is holy, let him be holy still"* (Rev. 22:11). Here is a definitive statement that says, "It is done!" We read in Revelation: *"there came a great voice out of the temple of heaven, from the throne, saying, It is done"* (Rev. 16:17). The process of probate is over, probation is ended. This is not some arbitrary declaration meant as a threat. It is simply the fact that the work for the salvation of all mankind has run its course.

A Call to Rest

We are now living in the time of the last call. How is it with you? Are you a real child of God? Is His life manifest in you? If not, do you hear Him calling, *"Today if ye will hear His voice, harden not your hearts...For we which have believed do enter into rest,"* (Heb. 3:15 and Heb 4:3). There is the most desperate need for the professed people of God to prayerfully and humbly study this rest. It is found described in Hebrews 3 and 4. Especially should Hebrews 4:10 be considered: *"For he that is entered into his rest, he also hath ceased from his own works, as God did from His."* There is a rest for you and I today. We can rest in Christ's completed work. We must rest in His power to save us. We can rest from our attempts to sanctify/perfect ourselves and instead live

---

84 See the ceremony of the scapegoat: Lev. 16:21 and the forgetting of sins in Heb. 8:12 and 10:17.

in dependence upon our gracious God and the Will He has written. He will never fail any who do this. Will you have it so?

"So now come back to your God!
Act on the principles of love
and justice and always live in confident
dependence on your God."
Hosea 12:6 (NLT 1996)

Chapter 11

Dog's Breakfast #5

"The Delayed Coming of Christ"

"Son of man, behold, they of the house of Israel say,
The vision that he seeth is for many days to come, and he
prophesieth of the times that are far off."
Ezekiel 12:27

In this next section we must face the question concerning the long delayed return of Christ. We have seen in the portion just covered concerning the probating of a Will, that there is a process. This process takes time to progress through. Of Christ and His work, the Scriptures say, *"He is the Rock, His work is perfect: for all His ways are judgment: a God of truth and without iniquity, just and right is He"* (Deut. 32:4).

I am a cabinet maker by trade and I know that good, thorough work requires a lot of time to get right. I once had a fellow on a job site say to me, "You're good, but you are slow." My sinful pride was riled up a bit by his comments. He seemed to be saying that he was just as good as I was, but not a "slow-poke" like myself. As I finished my "slow" kitchen installation, I mollified my pride by reflecting that high quality fit and finish takes time.

A few weeks later, I was dropping off some extra hardware that had been requested at that same house. Imagine my surprise to find my critic there. He was not at all talkative or boastful this time however. I discreetly asked the home owner what had happened. He told me that this "expeditious" gentleman had put all the hanging mantles and a bunch of other trim in crooked. Only the power of God's Spirit kept me from observing this interesting fact to that "speedy" gentleman. The main point of my anecdote is that to do a thorough job takes time. God is not interested in half measures when it comes to sin. The prophet Nahum said, *"He will make an utter end: affliction shall not rise up the second time"* (Nah 1:9). It may seem to us mortals that the time has been long. But if we understand that a work has been going forward at full speed in heaven, and if we can understand that this work is absolutely essential for man's salvation and the eternal security of the universe, shouldn't this help us wait patiently? How long will two thousand years seem when we look back at the conflict say... two hundred billion years from now? We will then be living in a future that will never again be threatened with the dark shadow of sin and death. Will it seem a "long time" then?

We have already looked at Noah's building of an ark as a type. It seemed like 120 years was a long time, but it took as much time as it took to finish the work on that place of sanctuary. In Noah's day the amount of work was finite. It only took so much work to build an Ark. There were only so many logs to be milled, nails to be driven, and pitch to be daubed before there was no more work to do and the ark was finished. So, too, now. There is only so much work that Christ must do. One day soon it will be complete. Christ has almost finished the work of preparing a place for us. Very shortly He will stand up.

Contesting of the Will

When we looked at the process of probating a Will, I purposely neglected to cover one important point. During the time of probate, when the heirs are being called and registered in the books of record, a Will may be contested. A person of malicious intent may then present objections to the Will. Objections such as, "Is the Will valid?" "Are the heirs named in the Will legitimate?" etc... An example of this would be if the Will said something like: "I leave an equal share of my wealth to my legitimate children." (Which is just what Christ's Will says.) I have heard many stories of inheritance battles where people have contested a Will. This contesting of a Will can also occur when people fraudulently claim that they themselves should be entitled to the inheritance. Whatever the objection or claim is, the court must consider these challenges. This can impede the work of the court and can turn probate into a lengthy process.

Delaying Tactics

If all those involved desire to have the wishes of the testator carried out, the time required to prove a Will is usually very short. If, however, that is not the case, well, I hope you brought extra provisions and a comfy chair, because it is going to drag on for a bit!

Question: Can you think of anyone, anyone at all, who might possibly want to drag things out when it comes to the Will of God? Anyone who might be opposed to the Will of Christ? Is there someone who might come forward as an accuser of the heirs and question their legitimacy?

Satan has been contesting the Will of Christ ever since it was written and he was defeated at Calvary! (See Rev 12:9, 10 & Zech. 3:1) If we have so long a delay in the return of our dear Lord, shouldn't the blame rest where it belongs? Satan is constantly trying to accuse God of the delay; but he is the one responsible! It says in Daniel, that Satan would be given a certain time to make his case against God and His people. That time would last for 1260 years, and then the court in heaven would sit and the last stages of probate would commence. Brothers and sisters, that last work of determination is almost done. Soon, all of God's heirs will be registered. The delay is almost over!

Chapter 12

Dog's breakfast #4
"The Empty Throne"

I don't think we actually need to say much about this portion of our dog's breakfast. It seems pretty self-explanatory now doesn't it?

If you understand that the inheritance of God's children is His perfection, this empty throne ceases to be a problem. Understanding what the inheritance is the putting in and inscribing upon the hearts and minds of God's children, His perfection, clears this problem right up. When that gift of holiness is bestowed, and the sins of His people are blotted out, the mercy seat can be safely vacated. The need for God's mercy will no longer exist. One day Noah laid down his tools and his work on the ark was finished. Soon Christ's work, not on the ark, but "at" the Ark will be finished. Then Christ will stand up and come in His glory, the glory of the Father and the holy angels[85] to gather His waiting children and take us home.

85 Luke 9:26

Chapter 13

Dog's Breakfast #3
The Cheating Dead?

*"As for me, I will behold Thy face in righteousness: I shall be
satisfied, when I awake, with Thy likeness."*
Psalm 17:15

Let us now take a look at this problem of the cheating dead; those
who, like my dear father or the thief on the cross, went into their
graves loving and believing in Jesus, but who were not actually,
morally, perfect. If you remember, we asked two basic and then hard
to answer, questions:

1) Are there two ways of salvation? One for the dead and one
for the living?

2) Where will the dead find perfection, since they died imperfect?

Let's now take a fresh look at these seemingly irreconcilable
problems and apply the understanding we have gained regarding the
"Lost Will and Testament" of Christ to these issues.

First: We need to take a look at the eleventh chapter of Hebrews.
Do we read in this chapter that there is a separation of the dead and
the living when it comes to perfection? In other words, are the dead
made perfect one way, and the living another?

It is written, *"And these all,* [the righteous dead] *having obtained
a good report through faith, <u>received not the promise</u>: God having
provided some better thing for us, <u>that they without us should not be
made perfect</u>"* (Heb 11:39, 40). Here we see it clearly stated that the
dead, along with the living, will be made perfect. We do not find any
separation but quite the contrary. In this Scripture there is not seen
two different ways to perfection, but only one. We don't find the dead
cheating the perfection requirement through the grave while the
living are required to do the impossible, namely to achieve perfection
through attainment.

Also, please note that they all died in that saving faith which is a gift of God (See Eph. 2:8). This faith was clearly shown, not by a perfect life, but it was seen in the telltale outward manifestations of a true, Christ-created righteousness. These works were evidence of their living connection with Christ. By these acts of faith we see Christ's working within each of them. They "knew" Him.

Even though they died in faith, <u>they were not perfect</u>! I can't stress this enough! Abraham, Isaac, and Jacob all died imperfect, yet Christ said to His people, *"... ye shall see Abraham, and Isaac, and Jacob, and all the prophets, in the kingdom of God..."* (Luke 13:28). Here we are clearly told that the patriarchs and prophets will be in the kingdom of Christ; even though they died imperfect. In fact, Paul is here speaking not only of them but of all who are listed as heroes of faith in Hebrews 11. This same assurance is found in the story of Christ's promise to the dying thief. *"And Jesus replied, "I assure you today, you will be with me in paradise"* (Luke 23:43). This brings us to the second question.

Second: How then, are the dead to be made perfect? Where are they to obtain the absolute actual moral perfection which all must possess who shall see God's face in peace? The answer is now quite simple. They will obtain it the same way the living do. The Bible says that God inhabits eternity (see Isa. 57:15). To Him who lives always, and in all time, the dead are in no different a position than the living. But I'm saying it rather poorly. Here is someone who says the same thing, but much better:

"He [Christ] said, *'But as touching the resurrection of the dead, have ye not read that which was spoken unto you by God, saying, I am the God of Abraham, and the God of Isaac, and the God of Jacob? God is not the God of the dead, but of the living.'* God counts the things that are not as though they were. He sees the end from the beginning, and beholds the result of His work as though it were now accomplished. The precious dead, from Adam down to the last saint who dies, will hear the voice of the Son of God, and will come forth from the grave to immortal life. God will be their God, and they shall be His people. There will be a close and tender relationship between God and the risen saints. This condition, which is anticipated in His purpose, He beholds as if it were already existing. The dead live unto Him."[86]

God makes no distinction between the living and the dead. All are considered the same to Him. When the final determination of who God's heirs are is finished, then all the heirs, the living at the close of probation, and the dead at the resurrection of the just, will receive their inheritance. All will be given a crown of glory on that great day. All will be made righteous by faith. All will *"be partakers of the divine nature"* (2 Pet. 1:4). God sees my father as though he has not died and some day soon by the grace of God and the inheritance He has provided, my father, and all our loved ones who have died in Christ (see 1 Thess.4:16), will rise perfect from their graves. Gone will be the sinful nature that plagued them. By the unmerited grace of God, I, my father, and I pray you, too, dear reader, along with all *"who love His appearing,"* will look Him in the face with holy, undimmed, and eternal joy!

---

86 The Desire of Ages pg. 606

Chapter 14

Dog's Breakfast #2
A Perfect Remnant

So here we are again with the "Super Saints" issue. As stated before, many seem to think that the last remnant will have to <u>attain</u> perfection in order to be saved. Since we have now seen that the Scriptures teach that perfection is a gift of inheritance, most of these questions have been resolved. As I shared with you before; when I aspired to this special group, it was partly from pride and desire for the highest place, but mostly from necessity. I thought that if I had to be perfect to be saved, then I had to be in this 144,000 group of perfect saints. Now I have a vastly different view. Our perfection comes fully and finally from Jesus Christ's righteousness. It is not from our developed holiness. It is Christ who justifies. It is He who sanctifies through His indwelling by the Holy Spirit; and at last it will be His law/character/nature that He, through that same Spirit, will place and seal in our hearts and minds for eternity. This priceless inheritance comes to us by His blood. All four perfections; justification, sanctification, moral perfection, and finally, physical, bodily glorification, come from the righteousness of Christ alone! None of them come to us by creature merit! Our focus now, and the burden on every heart, should not be, "Am I good enough? Am I perfect?" The burning question should be, "Am I a real child of God?"

Terrible Evangelistic Results?

In this section we looked at a parable Christ gave when He told the story of the farmer who hired workers to work in His field. We saw that it was at quitting time that He once again went into town and found some others whom He sent out to work for Him. At the end of the day (a few minutes later in other words), the master paid all these workers the same wage. Here Jesus taught that it is from His grace that all receive the same thing. It didn't matter that some had been laboring longer than others. Those who were called at the last minute were in no inferior position from those that had labored all day long.

There is another parable which we have mentioned already. This is the parable of the king's supper. In the last command the king says to His servants, *"The wedding is ready, but they which were bidden were not worthy. Go ye therefore into the highways, and as many as ye shall find, bid to the marriage. So those servants went out into the highways, and gathered together all as many as they found, both bad and good: and the wedding was furnished with guests"* (Matt. 22:8-10). Have you ever stopped to look at this? The King said that those who were invited were not worthy.

Question: What was it that made them unworthy? Were they unworthy because they were not "perfect?" Was that why they couldn't come to the supper? No, they were unworthy because they themselves rejected the offered gift of communion. *"... they made light of it, and went their ways, one to his farm, another to his merchandise"* (Matt. 22:5). They were too busy with this world and the things in it. Either that or they really hated the King. The parable says; *"And the remnant took His servants, and entreated them spitefully, and slew them"* (Matt. 22:6). They rejected their king's loving gift to them. This rejection, and not their moral condition, is what unfit them for the communion feast. How can we be sure that this is the case? Because of what the king said next; *"Then saith He to His servants, The wedding is ready, but they which were bidden were not worthy. Go ye therefore into the highways, and as many as ye shall find, bid to the marriage"* (Matt. 22:8, 9). Here is plainly shown that the qualification required to come to the marriage supper wasn't/isn't perfection, or "Super Saint" status. All who did not reject by indifference or violence, the invitation, could come and were welcomed. Both the good and bad. This is the final nail in the coffin of the "only the good guys get in" attitude exhibited by some who hold the perfection by attainment/"Super Saint" doctrine.

We read further, *"So those servants went out into the highways, and gathered together all as many as they found, both bad and good:*

and the wedding was furnished with guests" (Matt. 22:10). You see? All types were gathered in at the end. There is no requirement that all must have been "good enough" to attend the feast. There was one requirement, however.

"...when the king came in to see the guests, He saw there a man which had not on a wedding garment: And He saith unto him, Friend, how camest thou in hither <u>not having a wedding garment</u>? And he was speechless. Then said the King to the servants, Bind him hand and foot, and take him away, and cast him into outer darkness; there shall be weeping and gnashing of teeth" (Matt. 22:11-13). Here was one who had come to the feast in his own righteousness. He was walking among the guests naked.

Nakedness

"Neither is there any creature that is not manifest in His sight: but all things are naked and opened unto the eyes of Him with whom we have to do."
Hebrews 4:13

Do you remember the garden scene in Eden? Adam and Eve were afraid because they were naked. That sense of nakedness was the result of transgression. It is no accident that to the last church in Revelation a call is given to be clothed. Here is pictured a self-sufficient, self-complacent church, smugly secure in its own wealth. *"Thou sayest, I am rich, and increased with goods, and have need of nothing"* (Rev. 3:17). This is the same situation referred to in the book of Hosea, *"the people are like crafty merchants selling from dishonest scales... Israel boasts, "I am rich, and I have gotten it all by myself"* (Hosea 12:7 NLT). This is the self-reliance seen in the last poor, naked, and blind church. The counsel of the true witness is *"buy of Me... white raiment, that thou mayest be clothed, and that the shame of thy nakedness do not appear"* (Rev. 3:18). How is this white raiment "bought"? *"Ho, every one that thirsteth, come ye to the waters, and he that hath no money; come ye, buy, and eat; yea, come, buy wine and milk without money and without price"* (Isa. 55:1). We are all without money with which to buy, even though we think we are rich! It is not our "Super Saint" attainments here depicted as "white raiment." No, for when speaking of our righteousness the Scriptures clearly say, *"But we are all as an unclean thing, and all our righteousnesses are as filthy rags"* (Isa. 64:6). This white robe is the righteousness of Christ, provided for us through His bequest. It is no coincidence that in Revelation 3 a picture of one last invitation is represented by Christ knocking at the door and offering communion and supper. It will not only be the "good" who are accepted, but whosoever will not reject the invitation to adoption. These will be the good and the bad, for *"the Spirit and the bride say, Come. And let him that heareth say, Come. And let him that is athirst come. And whosoever will, let him take the water of life freely"* (Rev. 22:17). It is through a gift of inheritance, the perfect holiness of Christ, that we will one day see our Saviour and blessed King face to face.

John wrote in Revelation, *"After this I beheld, and, lo, a great multitude, which no man could number, of all nations, and kindreds, and people, and tongues, stood before the throne, and before the Lamb, clothed with white robes, and palms in their hands; And cried with a loud voice, saying, Salvation to our God which sitteth upon the throne, and unto the Lamb"* (Rev. 7:9, 10). The song of the redeemed before the throne of God in heaven is one that ascribes all salvation to God and to the Lamb. "No power but that of Christ could have made them conquerors. In all that shining throng there are none to ascribe salvation to themselves, as if they had prevailed by their own power and goodness."[87] The Scriptures say that *"the life of the flesh is in the blood: and I have given it to you upon the altar to make an atonement* [at-one-ment] *for your souls"* (Lev. 17:11). The 144,000's "capes" flowing behind them may be white, but they will have been made that way by Christ Jesus alone! They will be white by virtue of the spotless life and holiness that is in His precious blood!

Before we break away and head to the last of our "dog's breakfast ingredients," We might want to take look at two quotes which we as Seventh-day Adventists have struggled with and which have terrified so many of us.

---

87 The Great Controversy pg. 665

First up is this staggering statement; "I also saw many do not realize what they must be in order to live in the sight of the Lord without a high priest in the sanctuary through the time of trouble. Those who receive the seal of the living God and are protected in the time of trouble **must reflect the image of Jesus fully.**"[88] In light of the inheritance presented in the book of Hebrews which we have studied, is this statement now so terrifying? Since it is the very nature of God, His perfection, His character/image that is to be put into and sealed in our hearts and minds, it seems this is now just a statement of what will then be a fact. It is certainly a serious appeal to be found a part of the "house of Israel." It is surely a solemn call to really "know" God and to be born again as His child, but for me this statement has lost its terror and now stands as a promise.

Second staggering quote: "I saw that none could share the 'refreshing' unless they obtain the victory over every besetment, over pride, selfishness, love of the world, and over every wrong word and action. We should, therefore, be drawing nearer and nearer to the Lord and be earnestly seeking that preparation necessary to enable us to stand in the battle in the day of the Lord. Let all remember that God is holy and that none but holy beings can ever dwell in His presence."[89] The Scriptures have a lot to say about victory. But one of the most important texts on the subject of victory is this one: *"For whatsoever is born of God overcometh the world: and this is the victory that overcometh the world, even our faith. Who is he that overcometh the world, but he that believeth that Jesus is the Son of God? This is He that came by water and blood,* [remember this was the proof of death and assurance of His unchangeable Will] *even Jesus Christ; not by water only, but by water and blood. And it is the Spirit that beareth witness, because the Spirit is truth"* (1 John 5:4-6).

Do you see that those who overcome, are those who are born of God? They have His life in them, overcoming this wicked world and keeping them secure. They are His children. Their spiritual life is actually His life within them, as it is written: *"I am crucified with*

---

88 Manuscript Releases pg. 41
89 Manuscript Releases pg. 41

Christ: nevertheless I live; yet not I, but Christ liveth in me: and the life which I now live in the flesh I live by the faith of the Son of God, who loved me, and gave himself for me" (Gal. 2:20). And also; *"it is God which worketh in you both to will and to do of His good pleasure"* (Phil. 2:13). The over-comers are those who are born again and have an intimate connection to God by the Spirit. They are His children. They depend on Christ to save them. They "know God" and are His heirs. It is faith that overcomes. A faith given to us by Jesus. His own faith (see Eph. 2:8). Perfection is found nowhere but in Christ Jesus. To the proud, self-righteous people of his day and ours, Peter said, *"Neither is there salvation in <u>any</u> other: for there is <u>none other name</u> under heaven given among men, whereby we must be saved"* (Acts 4:12). That includes your name and my name.

The author who wrote those preceding statements has been maligned as legalistic inside her own denomination and especially in the wider Christian church because she stated that to see God one must be perfectly holy. This is a truth which we have found stated and illustrated everywhere in the Scriptures. These Scriptures and illustrations show this accusation against her to be a false charge, brought about because people have not seen any way to the required perfection except either by:

a) Law righteousness, a hellish doctrine which I continually pray will be eradicated from the church of Christ regardless of denomination: A doctrine that has been shown to be a deception where mankind is expected to attain perfection through human efforts aided by divine power. Or...

b) by trying to remove the revealer of men's hearts, the law of God. That law which shows us what true goodness and disinterested love really looks like. Many of us buy into this "the law is no more" evasion of perfection and completely disregard the fact that, *"by the law is the knowledge of sin"* (Rom. 3:20). By removing the law this delusion also removes the need for God's grace and our need for Christ and His salvation from sin. Also reflect on this for a moment: if the law is no more...we have no inheritance!! Remember, the Word says that *"Moses commanded us a law, even <u>the inheritance</u> of the congregation of Jacob"* (Deut. 33:4).

The same author who wrote the previous statements regarding perfection, also wrote this when it comes to righteousness by faith in Christ alone; "I ask, How can I present this matter as it is? The Lord Jesus imparts **all** the powers, **all** the grace, **all** the penitence, **all** the **inclination, all** the pardon of sins, in presenting His righteousness for man to grasp by living faith—**which is also the gift of God**. If you would gather together **everything** that is good and holy and noble and lovely in man and then present the subject to the angels of God as acting **a part** in the **salvation** of the human soul or in merit, the proposition would be rejected as **treason.**"[90] In that statement there is not a thread of salvation by human attainment. Salvation and absolute moral perfection is not an achievement of our own. It is a free gift from God to all who are found to be His true children.

90 Faith and Works pg. 24

Chapter 15

Dog's Breakfast #1
"The Judgment"

Investigations!

...the judgment was set, and the books were opened.
Daniel 7:10

Finally we need to take a fresh look at this last ingredient in our "Dog's Breakfast." We can now ask a few questions that might not have been open to investigation before we understood that our perfection was an inheritance from God. As we have seen, there is a period of time at the end of the probate process when the court must make some judgments. The court must determine who are real and legitimate heirs. To accomplish this, the court must look at some basic facts. Foremost is the evidence which must be submitted to the court, <u>proving the relationship</u> of an heir to the testator. The courts will hear any evidence, however small, that might justify the claimant in their kinship to the testator. In reading the institutes of Gaius, that famous juror of ancient Rome, one gets the distinct impression that the courts were very keen to see that no legitimate heir was overlooked.

Right off the bat let me make something clear. In our discussion of the judgment we will not be dealing with the reward side of the issue. There is a reward for the righteous and the wicked. The righteous will receive a reward from God. *"Say ye to the righteous, that it shall be well with him: for they shall eat the fruit of their doings"* (Isa. 3:10). This reward is the result of God's work in them. This reward however, is not "salvation," for it is written, *"Salvation is not a reward for the good things we have done, so none of us can boast about it"* (Eph. 2:9 NLT). There is also a reward for the wicked. *"Woe unto the wicked! it shall be ill with him: for the reward of his hands shall be given him"* (Isa. 3:11).[91]

---

91 Please note that it is the wicked that receive a reward for their works, and that the righteous that will eat of the "fruit" of the Vine, produced by Christ in them.

We will not be looking at the results of the investigative judgment beyond asking the vital question of "how is God determining who is saved and who is lost?" It is essential that we understand the answer to that inquiry. A correct understanding of this question will sound the death knell of works righteousness.

Balance Scale Theory, or..?

Many find it is almost impossible to see how the judgment can be a survivable process when their names are called and their deeds are examined. This has led many to claim that the message of the 2300 days, the cleansing of the sanctuary, and the investigative judgment, are downright false teachings. Until I understood that perfection was by Christ's Last Will and Testament, I really only had one way to view the judgment: Which was by viewing the judgment as all heathen religions did and still do. As a balance scale, where all the evidence for and against me was compiled, sorted, and placed on the appropriate side of a giant scale or ledger. If all my good deeds and meritorious actions came up to at least 51% then whew! I was in! If not...

This is a disastrous view to hold. It promotes a striving after good works for the value they will have in tipping the scale, or "cooking the books" in our favor. All that these endeavors do is to deepen our condemnation (see Rom. 14:23). The Scriptures describe my goodness to a T in the first three chapters of Romans. I have already shown the false, pagan, hell-born philosophy behind this idea of a balance scale type judgment. We should know that we will not be saved by trying to balance things out. So what, then? What do all the seemingly conflicting Scriptures that we looked at previously in our pros and cons list mean? How are they reconcilable?

Paternity Test

*"Then shall ye return, and discern between
the righteous and the wicked, between
him that serveth God and him that serveth Him not."*
Malachi 3:18

If the judgment is not a matter of examining our righteousness or perfection to determine if we are good enough and make the cut, then how else can it be viewed? What is it that is being judged? Let's do an exercise and see if you can tell me the answer to two riddles. Well, they are not really riddles, more like a one-sided game of twenty questions:

Riddle #1: Who am I?
- I am a four footed animal with paws.
- I am furry and soft.
- I have an expressive tail and eyes.
- I am a domestic household friend of man.
- I can be haughty and arrogant. Independent, self willed, and dismissive at times.
- I love my master on my own terms. I treat his orders more like optional suggestions. Who am I?

Riddle #2: Who am I?
- I am a four footed animal with paws.
- I am furry and soft.
- I have an expressive tail and eyes.
- I am a domestic household friend of man.
- I am obsequiously loving and dependent upon my master. When we are parted I mope and pine away like someone has died!
- I love my master obsessively and am eager to follow his commands! Who am I?

There we have our two riddles! In case some require more evidence to solve the riddles, I'll set it up like tee-ball. The last clue in riddle #1, would be, "My favorite word is "Meow," The last clue in riddle #2 would be, "My favorite, and oft repeated phrase is "Woof!" Well now even a child can tell who is who, right?

Congratulations, you have just been through a mini-investigative judgment! The first animal is obviously a dog and the last one a cat, right?...No? I got it wrong you say? Well, I've known dogs who weren't as attentive to their master as they should be (I'm looking at one right now), and I've known cats that were loving and affectionate! "But," you say, "it is what comes out of their mouths that make it absolutely clear who is who!" You are right, of course. Jesus said something like this as well, *"Out of the abundance of the heart the mouth speaketh"* (Matt. 12:34), and *"...by thy words thou shalt be justified, and by thy words thou shalt be condemned"* (Matt. 12:37). You see, it is the words that come out of our mouths and that which is seen in our habitual actions that "tell the tail" (Yes, pun intended). These really show who and what we are. Is it possible that the investigative judgment referred to in Daniel (see Dan. 7:9, 10) is an examination, not of our merits or demerits, but of our paternity? Is it possible that the issue at question is not about how good or bad we are, but rather a determination of who our Father is? Is it God? Do we "know" Him? Are we really His children? Or are we, while bearing the sacred name of Christ, actually the children of an entirely different father?

Hosea, Uncertain Offspring!

"...as a wife that committeth adultery,
which taketh strangers instead of her husband!"
Ezekiel 16:32

The Book of Hosea is a fascinating book. It is a bit startling and alarming at the outset but it has some very important points to make which will help us resolve some of the seeming contradictions that we found in this "Dog's Breakfast." It begins with God telling poor

Hosea to go out and marry a whore. *"When the Lord first began speaking to Israel through Hosea, He said to him, "Go and marry a prostitute, <u>so that some of her children will be conceived in prostitution.</u> This will illustrate how Israel has acted like a prostitute by turning against the Lord and worshiping other gods"* (Hosea 1:2 NLT).

This story is hard to stomach at first! God tells one of His holy prophets to go marry a prostitute? This seems so wrong, but God had an important purpose in His strange command. He was, and is, trying to demonstrate, by way of an illustration, how the church has/is being unfaithful to Him. Just as Hosea's wife went whoring after other men and became pregnant by them, so God's church has tried to bring forth new life by associating with paganism. We have gone whoring after pagan gods and their ideas, philosophies, and teachings (doctrines of devils, really). We, the church and bride of Christ, have taken into ourselves the man-centric philosophies and methods of the religious systems of this unholy and fallen world. Everything from works righteousness and cheap grace to man-centered free will has "entered into" the church and defiled it. The results of this "criminal conversation"[92] with these "lovers" is that the church has produced "children" of a sort, but these converts are children from another father. They carry his DNA, not Christ's. The traits of self-love, self-dependency, and human exaltation and pride are seen in us/them.

When the self-trusting, self-righteous scribes and pharisees accosted Jesus with His, supposedly, ignoble birth, He told them plainly that their "paternity" was showing. He said, *"Ye are of your father the devil, and the lusts of your father ye will do"* (John 8:44). Despite their outward adornments and professions of holiness, their real father was not God, the true husband of the church. Christ declared their father to be Satan. And so it is today. Sadly, many of the "children" of the church have been and are being conceived in "prostitution." Many who have taken upon themselves the name of Christ are not in fact His. Their experience has not come from Christ but from another gospel- a false gospel, the gospel of man. This is

92 An old English term for adulterous relationships

getting so flagrant and terrible today that in the name of false charity or "love" if you prefer, the churches have fallen. They have sunk so low as to join openly with other religions which deny the Deity of Christ and the clear, exclusive salvation which the Scriptures say comes from none other name than that of Christ Jesus (see Acts 4:12). This is a terrible crime and blasphemy against the true God! He calls all who are His, to separate from such things (see Rev. 14:8)! Clearly with so much confusion and treachery there must be an investigation by the court of heaven to determine just who are, and who are not, the real children of God. There must be a paternity test.

The Parable of the Sheep and Goats
Who is Which?

"I beheld till the thrones were cast down,
and the Ancient of days did sit... the judgment
was set, and the books were opened."
Daniel 7:9 &10

When it comes to the judgment and really understanding what is going on we are given several parables by Christ. For many years, I thought that in the parable of the sheep and the goats, Christ was picturing His second coming. Now, I don't think so. "Why?"

The parable reads: *"When the Son of man shall come in His glory, and all the holy angels with Him, then shall He sit upon the throne of His glory: And before Him shall be gathered all nations: and He shall separate them one from another, as a shepherd divideth his sheep from the goats:...And He shall set the sheep on His right hand, but the goats on the left. Then shall the King say unto them on His right hand, Come, ye blessed of My Father, inherit the kingdom prepared for you from the foundation of the world"* (Matt. 25:31-34). Christ then goes on to enumerate the differences between the sheep and the goats.

Question: Why don't I think we have Christ's second coming pictured in this parable? Well, Jesus said, *"...behold, I come quickly;*

and my <u>reward is with me</u>, to give every man according as his work shall be" (Rev. 22:12). Christ says that when He returns the reward for every man and woman will be with Him. This must mean that the Judgment has been completed before He comes in glory to this earth. This becomes abundantly clear when you read the various descriptions of Christ's return. (see 1 Thess. 4:16, Ps. 50:3, Rev. 6:14-17 etc…) There is no mention of a judgment being held in these depictions.

There is another passage found in the book of Daniel. As you read it, please note the parallels and similarities between this scene and the story of the sheep and the goats: *"I beheld till the <u>thrones</u> were cast down, and the Ancient of days <u>did sit</u>, whose garment was white as snow, and the hair of His head like the pure wool: His <u>throne was like the fiery flame,</u> and His wheels as burning fire. A fiery stream issued and came forth from before Him: <u>thousand thousands ministered unto Him</u>, and ten thousand times <u>ten thousand stood before Him</u>: the judgment was <u>set</u>, and the books were opened"* (Dan. 7:9, 10).

Do you see the similarities? In the parable Christ sits on His glorious throne with His ministering angels (see Hebrews 1:14), and the nations are gathered before Him. Christ then performs a judgment of separation between the sheep and the goats. In the prophecy of Daniel, God sits on a glorious fiery throne, where millions minister unto Him (again see Heb.1:14), and hundreds of millions stand before Him; as it is written, *"for we shall all stand before the judgment seat of Christ"* (Rom. 14:10). The court is put into session and the books of record are opened.

In these two passages we have the same event taking place. Since this is so, we should be able to look at this parable of Christ's to help us determine what is going on in the judgment found in Daniel. What do we see regarding perfection in the parable of the sheep and the goats? Does it say that the "perfect" sheep are on one side and the goats and any blemished sheep on the other? No. The separation is based on a determination of who is what, just like my silly illustration of the cat and dog previously. This judgment is not based on merit but on the spiritual paternity seen in each one.

This is why, though not declared righteous before God because of our works (see Rom. 3:20), we will be seen to be God's true children when our lives are examined in the judgment. His life, and its very real manifestation, will be seen in us (see Rom. 2:13). Here, there is no works righteousness which merits us heaven. There will, however, be "tell-tale" indicators in the outward life which show that God, who alone can produce true holiness in the human heart, is our Father.

This reality of the judgment being a paternity test is found in many places in the Scripture. We'll take a look at just two more of Christ's parables. Let's see if the judgment is there also described as a simple determination of paternity.

The Parable of the Net,
Is it a Keeper?

"Who shall ascend into the hill of the LORD?
or who shall stand in His holy place?
He that hath clean hands..."
Psalms 24:3, 4

Jesus spoke a parable saying, *"the kingdom of heaven is like unto a net, that was cast into the sea, and gathered of every kind: Which, when it was full, they drew to shore, and sat down, and gathered the good into vessels, but cast the bad away. So shall it be at the end of the world: the angels shall come forth, and sever the wicked from among the just"* (Matt 13:47-49). Here is presented a judgment scene where the "good" are separated from the "bad."

Question: What in the Hebrew culture made a fish "good" or "bad?" Well in God's health instructions to Israel concerning clean and unclean animals He said, *"whatsoever hath fins and scales in the waters, in the seas, and in the rivers, them shall ye eat... And all that* have not fins and scales in the seas, and in the rivers, of all that move in the waters, and of any living thing which is in the waters, they shall be an abomination unto you" (Lev. 11:10). Consequently, when Christ told this parable, all His hearers, sitting there by the sea of Galilee, would have instantly recognized that Jesus was talking about this kind of sorting. This sorting was simply to determine if the fish in question was clean or unclean, nothing more.

Of mankind, apart from the new life and sanctifying presence of Christ, the Bible says, "*...the whole head is sick, and the whole heart faint. From the sole of the foot even unto the head there is no soundness in it; but wounds, and bruises, and putrifying sores: they have not been closed, neither bound up, neither mollified with ointment*" (Isa. 1:5, 6). It does not matter if we have a profession of "righteousness." What is vitally important is the question, "Do I know God?" Jesus said to the people, "*Many will say to me in that day, Lord, Lord, have we not prophesied in Thy name? and in Thy name have cast out devils? and in Thy name done many wonderful works?, And then will I profess unto them, I never knew you: depart from Me, ye that work iniquity*" (Matt. 7:22, 23). Without the entrance of the life of Christ into the soul temple, that temple cannot be cleansed, and in spite of any adornments of "good works," it remains "unclean" and will be cast away. On the other hand, if we, through the grace of God, acknowledge our condition and cry to Jesus as the leper did, "*If thou wilt, thou canst make me clean,*" Jesus will reach in and touch anyone who, by the Spirit, utters that cry. To all He will say, "*... I will; be thou clean*" (Mark 1:40, 41). He will begin to bind up and close our wounds. His life will enter into the soul temple, and begin to cleanse, and drive out the sin dwelling there. The life will reflect His presence, and it will testify in the judgment of investigation that we are His!

The Parable of the Householder.
Barn or Burn?

Do you remember the parable of the farmer? Christ said: "*The kingdom of heaven is likened unto a man which sowed good seed in* *his field: But while men slept, his enemy came and sowed tares among the wheat, and went his way. But when the blade was sprung up, and brought forth fruit, then appeared the tares also. So the servants of the householder came and said unto him, Sir, didst not thou sow good seed in thy field? from whence then hath it tares? He said unto them, An enemy hath done this. The servants said unto him, Wilt thou then that we go and gather them up? But he said, Nay; lest while ye gather up the tares, ye root up also the wheat with them. Let both grow together until the harvest: and <u>in the time of harvest</u> I will say to the reapers, Gather ye together first the tares, and bind them in bundles to burn them: but gather the wheat into my barn"* (Matt. 13:24-30). In this parable we have the same type of illustration presented that was given in the book of Hosea regarding his unfaithful wife. In this parable, the field was seeded by two different men. As a result, it contained a crop which had both wheat and tares. My farmer brothers tell me that it can be hard to discern between these two plants as they both look a lot alike. And so it is within the church. It can be hard to discern who are, and who are not God's children. In fact, because we cannot read the heart, we are incapable of telling who are and who are not genuine children of God. It was that way in the parable above. The householder said in response to his servants inquiry as to whether they should root up the tares; *"Nay; lest while ye gather up the tares, ye root up also the wheat with them. Let both grow together until the harvest"* (Matt. 13:29).

Question: At the harvest, what is being determined? What decides if the plant is bundled to be burned or whether it is saved into the barn? Is the decision based on how productive and "good" the wheat is? Maybe it has to do with how ripe it has become? No, the decision is based solely on the results of an investigation of the plant and a determination of whether it is a wheat or a tare. The question will be, "Whose work produced the plant?" Was it planted by Christ or the enemy?

Again, we see the judgment portrayed by Christ as a process of investigation and determination. The judgment is to clear up all doubt about who is and who is not a true child of God. This can be difficult to know now. Paul said to Timothy: *"Remember, the sins of some people are obvious, leading them to certain judgment. But there are others whose sins will not be revealed until later. In the same way, the good deeds of some people are obvious. And the good deeds done in secret will someday come to light"* (1 Tim. 5:24, 25 NLT). The judgment is an investigation to discover who are Christ's real children and who are not. Once this determination has been completed, the judgment, and process of probation will end. The inheritance contained in the new covenant will then be given to the saints of the Most High. This brings up the last issue we'll be dealing with as we close out our "Dog's Breakfast" segment. How is God to judge those that are alive and remain at His coming? How is He to judge the living whose life stories are not yet ended?

Problems of Choreography?

But the LORD of hosts shall be
exalted in judgment, and God that is holy shall be
sanctified in righteousness.
Isaiah 5:16

Here we must deal with the last problem we encountered in the judgment. This had to do with choreography. Remember that we <u>all</u> must stand before the judgment seat of Christ (see 2 Cor 5:10). This must also include the last men and women still living on this planet when the process of probation closes. They will not be able to be judged all at once, but all must appear individually before the scrutiny of Christ. Is there a way that God can complete the judgment of the living in a transparent way which can be seen to be fair and non-arbitrary?

Why a Last Crisis?

"Because thou hast kept the word of My patience,
I also will keep thee <u>from the hour of temptation, which shall come</u>
<u>upon all the world</u>, to try [test] *them that dwell upon the earth."*
Revelation 3:10

Have you ever wondered why there must be a last crisis on this earth? Yes, there has been a war between Christ and Satan. The controversy with Satan and the wicked must come to a head, but why do God's people have to go through it? Many have come up with non-Biblical ways to spirit the saints away before the trouble begins; but the Bible clearly states that the white-robed throng that stand before the throne came out of *"great tribulation"* (see Rev. 7:14 and Dan. 12:1). We are further told that there will be a great separating issue, an issue that will place all the world in just one of two camps. This issue is the "Mark of the Beast." Here is presented a scenario in which all are commanded to bow down to the spiritual authority of man instead of God. If they don't, then first they will be visited with economic sanctions and finally with a death penalty (see Rev. 14 & 13). Pretty serious stuff!

Question: Why a test? Why is it necessary to have God's people and the wicked tested in this way? After all, *"The Lord knoweth them that are His"* (2 Tim. 2:19). Well, I feel a typology coming on! Do you remember the story of the birth of Jacob and Esau? Before their birth, God in His foreknowledge told their mother Rebekah: *"Two nations are in thy womb, and two manner of people shall be separated from thy bowels; and the one people shall be stronger than the other people; and the elder shall serve the younger"* (Gen 25:23). The events that followed showed that God was correct in His assertion. The only way that the history of the twins could have been foretold was through the foreknowledge of God. He is the One who said, *"I am God, and there is none like me, declaring the end from the beginning, and from ancient times the things that are not yet done, saying, My counsel shall stand, and I will do all my pleasure"* (Isa. 46:9, 10). Through His foreknowledge God is able to tell what the future holds. He can declare what men will do because He inhabits eternity (again see Isa. 57:15).

Now, when it comes to the end of this world's history, we will have people still alive. Their last chapters will not have been written. As such, their history will be unfinished when the declaration goes out, *"He that is unjust, let him be unjust still: and he which is filthy, let him be filthy still: and he that is righteous, let him be righteous still: and he that is holy, let him be holy still"* (Rev. 22:11). How can

God make this final declaration of who is saved and who is not when the possibility of variation still exists? Some may object to the judgment of God. They may say, "Wait a minute! So and so is a good man, why is his name not found in the Lamb's Book of Life?" Or, some of my old acquaintances and teachers might say, "What is that Troy guy's name doing in the Lamb's book of life?"

Here we come to the reason that there must be a last crisis. In this last crisis there will be a great dividing into only two camps. *"Then shall ye return, and discern between the righteous and the wicked, between him that serveth God and him that serveth Him not"* (Mal. 3:18). The last great test will be God's way of saying, "Watch." "Here in the findings of the judgment is My determination regarding who are Mine. Cross reference My findings with what you are about to witness. See if I made any mistakes in My determinations of paternity." As the great crisis is sprung like a trap on this world, God's decisions regarding the hearts of all mankind will be vindicated. I can boldly assert that not one whom God has listed as an heir will be found on the side of the enemy. *"My sheep hear My voice, and I know them, and they follow Me: And I give unto them eternal life; and they shall never perish, neither shall any man pluck them out of My hand. My Father, which gave them Me, is greater than all; and no man is able to pluck them out of My Father's hand"* (John 10:27-29).

This last test with its perfectly predicted separation will show all that God's judgments in regard to the hearts of the living were/are just. God's justice in judging as He is about to, will be vindicated by subsequent events. At the end of the millennium, when all who have ever lived are assembled, everyone, the saved, and the lost, will declare, *"Who shall not fear Thee, O Lord, and glorify Thy name? for Thou only art holy: for all nations shall come and worship before Thee; for Thy judgments are made manifest"* (Rev. 15:4).

It is not for nothing, that God gives a last and decisive test to this world. It is a high honor that is given to the heirs of salvation now living. They, from the least to the greatest, will have the privilege of verifying that *"The Lord knoweth them that are His"* (2 Tim. 2:19). This last test is not to see if you can "make the cut," but a clear demonstration of paternity. And through everything that will come, we may say with Paul, *"...I know whom I have believed, and am persuaded that he is able to keep that which I have committed unto him against that day"* (2 Tim. 1:12). Jesus will be by His children's side through it all, they will pass through that great crisis the same way they have lived, by trusting implicitly in Him who has said, *"I will never leave you, nor forsake you"* (Heb.13:5).

Chapter 16
Unity in Christ

"There is one body, and one Spirit,
even as ye are called in one hope of your calling;
One Lord, one faith, one baptism One God and Father of all, who is
above all, and through all, and in you all."
Ephesians 4:4-6

So now we come to the end of this book; but before we finish, I would like to make an appeal to each of the four divisions of the church. If we truly grasp the significance of the "Lost Will and Testament," it should have a profound impact on those things which have separated us. In this truth lies the remedy to what ails us in each of the four camps we examined at the beginning of this book. If this truth is headed, the "Lord of hosts," can and will heal our divisions. Then it will be said of the church; *"Who is she that looketh forth as the morning, fair as the moon, clear as the sun, and terrible as an army with banners?"* (Song of Sol. 6:10)

An Appeal to the "Conservderate Army"

"For he that is entered into His rest,
he also hath ceased from his own works,
as God did from His."
Hebrews 4:10

I sincerely hope that it has become plain that there is another way to realize the condition of perfection, but it is not found in the rigorous keeping of God's Law. It is not found in *"...works of righteousness which we have done"* (Tit. 3:5). It is found in a gift of inheritance.

For those of us who have sentenced ourselves to a life sentence of hard labor, trying to attain perfection, rest is freely offered. If we can grasp what Christ has done and will shortly do, it will give rest to the works-burdened soul. It will do this without compromising the truth in the Scriptures that *"...without...* [holiness] *no shall see the Lord"* (Heb. 12:14). We can now lay down our burdens and rest in the promise of God. *"You will break the yoke of their slavery and lift the heavy burden from their shoulders. You will break the oppressor's rod, just as You did when You destroyed the army of Midian* (Isa. 9:4). It was God who broke the Midianite enslavement of His people. It is God alone who can/will defeat the armies of enslaving sin in the lives of His children. Through His power working in us we can be set free, and one day soon, by way of an inheritance, *"He Himself will free Israel from every kind of sin"* (Ps. 130:8 NLT 1996). Along with Paul, I appeal to you, *"Harden not your hearts, as in the provocation..."* for *"...we see that they could not enter in because of unbelief"* (Heb. 3:8, 19). God is able to cleanse us. Our perfection is a promised gift from His Will. You may now turn to Him and confidently *"...through the Spirit wait for the hope of righteousness, by faith"* (Gal. 5:5).

An Appeal to the "Non-Combatants"

"For as the body without the spirit is dead,
so faith without works is dead also."
James 2:26

In our study of the Scriptures I think it has been shown beyond a doubt that only those who who are the real children of God will inherit the blessing of the New Covenant/Will. Because of the problem of perfection, many have adopted a faith based on emotional feelings, impressions, and wishful thinking. In light of what we have studied, The question must be asked: Do we need to be afraid of perfection now? Is it something that we can only avoid by settling for a false gospel of presumptuous grace; an "Eat drink and be merry, heaven is our home" kind of gospel? I believe this truth regarding the Will and Testament of Jesus should have taken that weapon of fear out of the Devil's hands. We should now understand that this perfection, which all must possess to see God's face in peace, is only promised to those who "know" God. They will have the convicting Spirit of God living within them. His life in them makes them His children. I appeal every one of us to seek God's understanding here. Ask Him to reveal to you if you are, or aren't, really His. If the answer comes back negative, and you are shown that your faith is dead; If you find that Christ is not *"a mighty power within,"*[93] both *"willing and doing of His good pleasure,"*[94] don't despair, rejoice. "Rejoice?" you say! Yes, rejoice, because He is now able to help you. Go to Him. Admit that you need His life, and He will in no wise cast you out. *"The Spirit and the bride say, Come. And let him that heareth say, Come. And let him that is athirst come. And whosoever will, let him take the water of life freely"* (Rev. 22:17). That "water" is the life of Jesus Christ which we will all have welling up within us if we are His. To all of us this life-giving water is offered freely.

An Appeal to "The Deserters"

"Thus saith the LORD; Refrain thy voice from weeping, and thine eyes from tears: for thy work shall be rewarded, saith the LORD; and they shall come again from the land of the enemy."
Jeremiah 31:16

For those of us who have given up hope of ever being good enough and have wandered away looking for pastures less painful and barren, I hope this book has helped. Do you feel the call of God once more? He is a loving shepherd, not an exacting tyrant who demands the impossible of His people. I pray that you have seen that all our needs He will supply, including "perfection." What He requires from you is "you." This good God is real. He has the power to give us what this world of sin only promises and always fails to deliver: peace and companionship in this vale of tears and a future which, when all is over, will never know sorrow, sadness, or death. All that this world can ever offer is nothing compared to what He has promised. He is not a neutered God. He is able to give you life, and that life will be more abundant than anything you have ever known.

---

93 2 Cor 13:3
94 Phil 2:13

Jesus is seeking you. He is calling you by name. The Great God heaven has promised, *"I will search for My lost ones who strayed away, and I will bring them safely home again. I will bandage the injured and strengthen the weak"* (Ezek. 34:16 NLT). He is speaking of you. He is about to return to end all the sorrow, loneliness, and pain on this planet. Will you "give Him a shot" as I did? I have never regretted it! He longs for you to return to Him. I hear His voice in the words of the old hymn, "Come home... come home..." Will you?

"I will arise and go to my father, and will say unto him, Father, I have sinned against heaven, and before thee, And am no more worthy to be called thy son: make me as one of thy hired servants. And... when he was yet a great way off, his father saw him, and had compassion, and ran, and fell on his neck, and kissed him. And the son said unto him, Father, I have sinned against heaven, and in thy sight, and am no more worthy to be called thy son. But the father said to his servants, Bring forth the best robe, and put it on him; and put a ring on his hand, and shoes on his feet: And bring hither the fatted calf, and kill it; and let us eat, and be merry: For this my son was dead, and is alive again; he was lost, and is found" (Luke 15:18-24).

An appeal to the "No Man's Landers"

*"...knowing the time, that now it is high time
to awake out of sleep: for now is our salvation
nearer than when we believed"*
Romans 13:11

So lastly, how about us in the camp of the "No Man's Landers?" What liberation does the truth about this inheritance of perfection give us? When we examined those of us in this group, we saw that our lives contain a constant struggle between trusting partly to ourselves and partly to Christ for salvation. This modern day idolatry is a great curse to God's people. The underlying problem lies in this realization: We know that to be in God's presence, we must be without sin. Not having a scriptural understanding of how this is to come about, we have held onto our works- many times in a subconscious way. We have, being thus crippled, limped back and forth between the salvation offered by two gospels, a true and a false.

Between a salvation by faith alone, and a false gospel of faith and works. We know that it is the sacrifice provided by God that saves us, but like the pagan priests of Baal, we think that our salvation requires more. In order to bring down the fire and rain, we try to augment our spiritual offering with our own "attained righteousness" or "sanctification". Elijah asked Israel an all important question, and it needs asking again,*"How long halt* [limp] *ye between two opinions?"* (1 Kings 18:21)

My prayer is that now that we understand where our actual moral perfection will come from, we can break from this snare of double-mindedness and really, wholeheartedly embrace righteousness by faith alone. There does not need to be any doubt regarding our ultimate salvation. We may now kneel in simple faith as Elijah did at the foot of God's altar. We may/must stop looking partly to God and partly to ourselves. We may/must look up to the bleeding victim upon a hill of stone. We may see Him bound upon the wooden tree and trust fully in His sacrifice. That Sacrifice needs no augmentation, no additions of our own works. If we will kneel there in self distrusting faith, the fire and rain will come down! [95]

It was the simple admission by Israel that *"The Lord, He is God"* (1 Kings 18:39) that brought the rain upon them. We are like the children of Israel, who after their refusal to trust God to bring them into the promised land have wandered in the wilderness for forty years (remember 1888). We seem to have been under the frown of God's displeasure. There is a beautiful promise found in Hosea. It is a call to know God, and in it is a wonderful promise as well: *"Come, let us return to the LORD: He has injured us; now He will bandage up our wounds. In just a short time He will restore us*[96] *so we can live in His presence. Oh that we might know the Lord! Let us press on to know Him! Then He will respond to us as surely as the arrival of dawn or the coming of rains in early spring"* (Hosea 6:1-3 NLT 1996). The King James renders the last part of this promise: *"and He shall come unto us as the rain, as the latter and former rain unto the earth."* It is God who has rejected our idolatrous offerings of "faith

---

95 Latter rain:"In the light of the king's countenance *is* life; and his favor *is* as a cloud of the latter rain." (Prov. 16:15)

96 As a companion verses see Acts 3:19,20

and works." He is the one who has promised to *"...save them to the uttermost that come unto God by Him"* (Heb. 7:25). So now, with a true understanding of where our fitness for heaven has/will come from, we may discard our misapprehensions regarding perfection. We can abandon forever this partial trust in our works/choices and place our trust wholly in Christ alone! It is my most fervent prayer that we all, by the grace of God, will do just that!

Benediction

"Now unto Him that is able to keep you from falling,
and to present you faultless before the presence of His glory
with exceeding joy...
Jude 1:24

Dearest Brothers and Sisters, the time for repentance is short. Jesus is soon to come again. One last time, I appeal to you as Paul did when he wrote in the book of Hebrews, *"... dear brothers and sisters, listen carefully to what I have said in this brief letter"* (Heb. 13:22 NLT 1996).

The "covenant" promise is sure. If we trust His promise, we are secure in Christ. This promise cannot fail. *"I will make an everlasting covenant with them, that I will not turn away from them, to do them good; but I will put my fear in their hearts, that they shall not depart from me."* (Jer. 32:40) Very soon, this promise will become a reality forever!

"Now we live with great expectation,
and we have a priceless inheritance—an inheritance that is
kept in heaven for you, pure and undefiled, beyond the reach
of change and decay. And through your faith,
God is protecting you by His power until
you receive this salvation, which is ready to be
revealed on the last day for all to see."
1 Peter 1:3-5 NLT

May God Bless You.

How This Book Came To Be...

I have had many personal encounters with perfection over the last 30 years as an elder and preacher in our church. Over and over again I have been confronted by this problem and its very destructive influence. I have openly related some of these experiences in this book. I have also encountered the very real problems of perfection on a ministerial level. It has been exhibited in the attitudes of legalism, liberalism, rebellion, and most frustratingly, the lukewarm condition of us as a people.

For many years, I would not/could not confront this perfection issue in any meaningful way. I simply tried to get by and live with this elephant in the room. Then God brought perfection into glaring focus in my life again. God says that if any man wishes to know of the doctrine, it will be revealed to him if he asks God. So I threw this problem back in His teeth and told Him plainly that if He wished to trouble me with this problem, then He had better show me the solution. He did just that. He did it by way of this simple and yet profound Bible study.

I began to share this Bible study over a number of years until one day, over a year ago, Dennis Davis, my brother in Christ, said, "Troy, you need to write this in a book." I am not a writer, and what's more, I have an objection to people spending too much time in other books, robbing themselves of meaningful Bible study. I resisted his appeals, but he, being a kindly and persistent chap, kept at me. Finally, to get him off my back, I told Him I would pray about it… I did pray, but not enthusiastically. I told God that if He wanted me to write a then He should tell me plainly to do so, and that by the way, I didn't have time to write much as I had a company to run and many ministerial duties to attend to… God has said, *"If you need wisdom-if you want to know what God wants you to do-ask and He will gladly tell you"* (James 1:5 NLT). Well I did ask, and He made things crystal clear in a hurry!

Here I must give a brief personal back history; I have had a small business for the last 27 years. Most of that time we were located in the far north of British Colombia Canada. Up there the population is very low. More than that, for most of the time I have been in business, we were in an area with an unemployment rate, above 90%! (government figures, not mine). All those years God was faithful to us, providing work in an economic desert. My boast when trying to inspire others with faith in God had been that, for 25 years, He had never left me one single day without work in the shop! It was incredible, and I was very proud of Him for His faithfulness!

Then, as I mentioned above, I "prayed about it." Work stopped cold! I, not being the dimmest bulb on the tree as they say, recognized the answer to my prayer. I began to write every day… for 5 ½ months! Now I don't know how much it costs others to live per month and carry the overhead of a small business, but I know how much it costs us! We did not go into this financial desert with anything left of our savings. No credit cards or lines of credit to rely on. We had just completed a move from Canada to the United States. We had put almost all we had into the building of a new house and shop. Somehow God provided the money for us to live while I wrote this book. By big/little blessings and miracles here and there He managed the "Mana." The only work I had during this almost 6 month famine, was two small wood trophy bases. The disruption these tiny projects caused in the book writing process, showed me why God had cut off work so completely (I'm no good at doing two things at once). Then one day, suddenly it seemed, I had finished the rough draft of the main body of this book. Literally fifteen minutes after I wrote the last sentence, a man walked into my shop and handed me a check for the down payment on a kitchen which he needed right away. I have been drowning in work ever since! I have no doubt that God not only gave me the answers to my prayer for understanding, but that He also wants these answers to be shared with others.

Troy Wright

A Note From Shawna

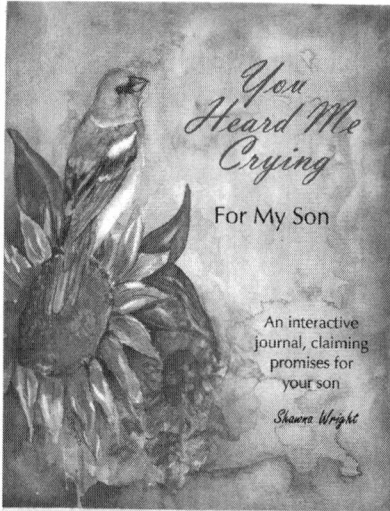

When God reveled this truth, we were excited! Immediately we began to share this Bible study with our church family and friends. After one particular Bible study, while we were headed to the door, the man of the house made a comment that struck my heart strings. "I'm now excited for Jesus to come, this gives me so much peace..." but as quickly as the smile of peace flashed across his face, so did the furrowing lines of sorrow. "What about our children," he asked?

I understood his sentiments. Burdened for our own children, I had recently taken a fresh new journal and filled it with Bible promises that I had personalized by replacing pronouns with our children's names. Doing this gave me much comfort. It had also produced results, there is power in claiming God's promises!

I went home with a burden on my heart. What should I do, photocopy my journal and share it with him? I went to bed with a heavy heart. When I awoke the next morning the words from Isaiah were ringing in my ears. *"Comfort, comfort ye my people"* Almost simultaneously, the inspiration to create an interactive journal for parents to personally claim Bible promises for their children was spread out before my mind. Within two days of that Bible study, work began on what is now a series of interactive journals. "You Heard Me Crying

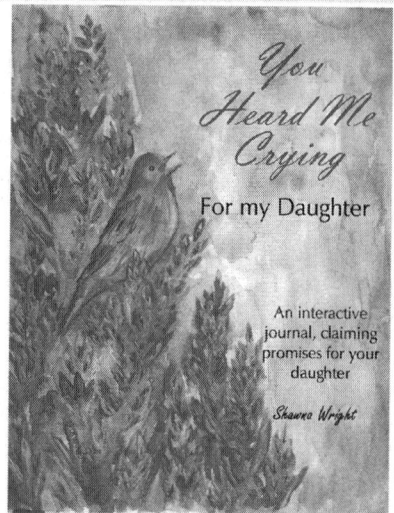

For My Son" and "You Heard me Crying for My Daughter."

Jesus is coming very soon, there is little doubt in our minds about that. The evidence is all around us. Along with that knowledge is the sad realization that many of our loved ones have been chased away, or are wondering around with no firm footing.

It is our prayer that these journals will be both a resource and comfort to you, as you pray for your children.

Blessings,

Shawna

Cast all your worries and anxiety on God, because He cares about _____
- I Peter 5:7

... You heard me crying! Yes you came and told me "Do not fear."
Lamentations 3:57

...You have wonderful plans for _____,
far more than I could list...
- Psalm 40:5

I will direct _____ and teach her the way which she should go. I will guide her and watch over her.
- Psalm 32:8

Original Art By:

Shawna Wright

Calendars
Interactive Journals
Prints & Cards

Be sure to visit:
shawnawrightart.com

and sign up for the weekly blog/devotional
focusing on Bible Promises

He will cover you with His feathers
He will shelter you with His wings,
His faithful promises are
your armor and protection
Psalm 91:4 NLT